WHITMAN COLLEGE LIBRARY

D0359422

The State
of the States

WHITMAN COLLEGE LIBRARY

The State
of the States

Edited by

Carl E. Van Horn
Rutgers University

PRESS

A Division of Congressional Quarterly Inc.
1414 22nd Street N.W., Washington, D.C. 20037

JK
2408
.S825
1989

PENROSE MEMORIAL LIBRARY
WHITMAN COLLEGE
WALLA WALLA. WASHINGTON 99362

Copyright © 1989 Congressional Quarterly Inc.

All rights reserved. No part of this publication may be reproduced or transmitted in any form or by any means, electronic or mechanical, including photocopy, recording, or any information storage and retrieval system, without permission in writing from the publisher.

Printed in the United States of America

Library of Congress Cataloging-in-Publication Data

The State of the States.

    Includes index.
    1. State governments—United States. I. Van Horn, Carl E.
JK2408.S825 1989   353.9   88-34217
ISBN 0-87187-503-9

PENROSE MEMORIAL LIBRARY
RECEIVED

JUN 15 1989
S. D.
ACQUISITIONS DEP'T
OCT 2 4 1989

To
Christy

CONTENTS

PREFACE

During the 1980s state governments moved to the center of American domestic politics. This change came about through the combined interaction of independent reforms, the federally mandated reapportionment of state legislatures, and the enactment of national civil rights laws. As the states assumed new roles, they also developed more professional staffs, elected better qualified officials, and produced more revenues, all of which strengthened their ability to address a wide variety of problems. In an era when the federal government is saddled with huge budget deficits and preoccupied with the politics of subtraction, states are increasingly carrying out the public's business and providing political and policy leadership for the nation.

But greater activism has strained state political institutions and placed new burdens on those who participate in state politics. Moreover, the new high-stake politics of state government can produce competitive policy agendas in an atmosphere of fragmented power and blurred lines of responsibility.

Unfortunately, state government and politics have not received much attention; indeed, political scientists have only recently begun to focus on the "state of the states." This book brings together many of the leading observers of state politics and government to describe and assess the performance of their political institutions and processes. Chapters on federalism, governors, legislatures, courts, bureaucracies, political parties, and campaigns and elections highlight the profound changes that state governments have undergone during the last thirty years.

This collection of essays is part of a larger enterprise called the State of the States Project. Funded by a major bequest from the estate of Charles and Inez Howell to the Eagleton Institute of Politics at Rutgers University, the project is designed to help scholars, students, and the state government communities assess institutional and procedural problems and performance. Toward that end, the Eagleton Institute sponsors an annual symposium on state government institutions and politics and commissioned the essays in this book.

Cosponsors of the State of the States Project include the National Governors' Association, the National Conference of State Legislatures, the Council of State Governments, the National Center for State Courts, and the Advisory Commission on Intergovernmental Relations.

I appreciate the support of the members of the State of the States Advisory Committee: Geoff Callas, National Center for State Courts; Barry Van Lare, National Governors' Association; Neal Peirce, *National Journal;* William Pound, National Conference of State Legislatures; Larry Sabato, University of Virginia; Raymond Scheppach, National Governors' Association; Carl Stenberg, Council of State Governments; and Carl Tubbesing, National Conference of State Legislatures.

Lawrence Baum wishes to thank John Kilwein for research assistance on his chapter. Barbara and Stephen Salmore are grateful to Ronald Hrebenar and Clyve Thomas for making available papers on interest groups.

I would like to thank several people for their advice and assistance. Alan Rosenthal generously shared his knowledge of state government with me. My research assistant, Kristin Phillips, made significant contributions to the preparation of the manuscript. Joanne Pfeiffer, my secretary, handled her duties with dispatch and good cheer. It was also a pleasure to work with Joanne Daniels, director of CQ Press, and Colleen McGuiness, project editor.

The State
of the States

1. THE QUIET REVOLUTION

Carl E. Van Horn

For more than forty years, state governments languished in relative obscurity—overshadowed by a burgeoning national government responding to the crises of depression, war, and internal strife. The stewardship of peace and prosperity was firmly in the hands of the federal government. Americans turned to Washington, D.C., for leadership and for their share of a growing federal pie.

Sweeping national and international events and a generation of political leaders shifted governmental activism to the federal level. State governments were bypassed as the federal government was aggrandized beyond anything contemplated by the framers of the Constitution. State governments were scorned by countless opinion leaders, with some validity, as being racist, incompetent, unwilling to change, and politically and economically emasculated.[1] For thirty years the Democratic and Republican parties, with few exceptions, chose presidential standard bearers from the U.S. Senate instead of from the statehouse.

How profoundly state governments have changed. They now are arguably the most responsive, innovative, and effective level of government in the American federal system.[2] State governments have reformed and strengthened their political and economic houses. Taxes have been increased and made more progressive.

States are more capable and willing to tackle the tough problems facing their citizens. The states' governors, legislators, judges, and bureaucrats are setting national agendas. Innovative economic development, education, and human service programs have laid the foundations for federal statutes. States are handling some of the country's most vexing problems, from homelessness and acquired immune deficiency syndrome (AIDS) to fostering competitive industries and disposing of toxic wastes. Increasingly, federal policy makers are asking state government officials to assume greater responsibilities. States have increased their commitment to subsidize and manage local government services, from law enforcement to education.

A sign of the increased political strength of states is that several strong and effective governors have risen to national prominence. Lamar Alexander, former governor of Tennessee, helped galvanize a nationwide education reform movement. Bruce Babbitt, former governor of Arizona and contender for the 1988 Democratic presidential nomination, and Neil Goldschmidt, governor of Oregon, have advanced pathbreaking policies on behalf of children and families. Since 1977, the White House has been occupied by former governors—Jimmy Carter, of Georgia, and Ronald Reagan, of California. The 1988 Democratic presidential nominee was Massachusetts governor Michael S. Dukakis.

The coming decades may be remembered as an era of state government leadership—the consequence of a quiet revolution in American politics. As state governments become more important, more will be expected of them. By and large they are well positioned to assume central roles in the federal system. However, problems already experienced by state institutions and those responsible for governing raise a cautionary flag. The transformation of state governments and politics has not been a smooth one. Greater pressure for state activism will undoubtedly create stresses and strains for the nation's statehouses.

A Tidal Wave of Reform

Powerful and effective state governments did not emerge overnight. A series of reforms in the structure and process of state government—some carefully planned, others accidental—have occurred over the last three decades. The cumulative effects of these independent reforms have been stronger, more capable state governmental institutions and a desire on the part of state government officials to expand the scope of their responsibility even further.

State government reform was not entirely the work of enlightened state politicians. Two national policy mandates—the reapportionment of state legislatures and the enactment of national civil rights laws—provoked much of the upheaval in state capitals. Initially, these decisions were considered slaps in the face of state governments. Ultimately, they helped transform state politics and substantially strengthened state governments.

In 1962, in a sweeping decision, the U.S. Supreme Court mandated in *Baker v. Carr* that state legislatures should be reapportioned so that political representation would be based on the principle of one person, one vote.[3] Up until that time, many state legislatures were dominated by rural and suburban lawmakers, intent on preserving the status quo of local government control, low taxes, and conservative public policy. Over time, legislatures evolved from weak and ineffectual organizations to powerful and effective political institutions, more accurately reflecting the broad range of interests and needs in their states.[4] It did not take long for reformed legislatures to expand the reach of government in accordance with the wishes of the voters.

The enactment and implementation of landmark civil rights legislation—the Civil Rights Act of 1964, the Voting Rights Act of 1965, and other laws—extended the influence of federal law throughout the federal system. Overt discrimination in education, employment, business, and government has declined dramatically.[5] Gradually, the composition of the electorate and the membership of legislatures began to more accurately reflect the citizenry of each state.

Prior to the civil rights statutes, federal lawmakers often argued persuasively that state governments could not be trusted with the stewardship of the disadvantaged and minorities.[6] Within less than a decade, the critical argument against giving state governments more power, and in favor of greater federal control, has essentially evaporated from political discourse. Twenty years ago, Gov. Lester Maddox of Mississippi became a symbol of southern state government intransigence when he barred the door of the state university to a black student. Today, Mississippi's governor, Ray Maybus, symbolizes progressive southern governors whose coalitions include prominent representation from blacks and other minorities.

The urge for modern and effective political and governmental institutions also came from within the states. Since the 1960s, nearly forty states ratified new constitutions or significantly amended existing ones.[7] The office of governor has been enhanced with better qualified individuals, an allowance for longer terms of office, and increased opportunities for succession.[8] Statewide elections for many governmental positions, such as secretary of state, attorney general, and chief state school officer, have been reduced. As a result, the governor's visibility as well as power—by having the ability to appoint and remove important administration officials—has increased. Chief executives have consolidated their power over the budget process, expanded planning and personal staffs, and strengthened the National Governors' Association to advocate for the collective interests of the states.

Legislatures also prepared themselves to play a larger role in governing the state. For decades, state legislatures were ridiculed as "inefficient and corrupt." [9] During the 1960s and 1970s, "legislatures undertook to rebuild themselves practically from scratch," according to political scientist Alan Rosenthal.[10] They devoted more time to lawmaking, streamlined rules and procedures, and tightened rules governing campaign finance and conflicts of interest. Turnover of legislators declined as more able people began to make a career in the institution.

Most important, legislatures hired professional staff to prepare legislation, review state budgets, and oversee program administration. It was estimated that in 1988 nearly twenty thousand people worked for legislatures on a full-time basis—an increase of more than 200 percent since the mid-1960s.[11]

State courts and state bureaucracies have also increased their ability to carry out the public's business. State courts have been strengthened through statewide unification and increases in administrative capacity.[12] State bureaucracies have grown in size and professionalism. Personnel are now much more likely to be recruited on a merit system. State employees are better trained and educated than ever before. The structure of state government has also changed in nearly all the states.[13] Almost two dozen states have experienced comprehensive reorganizations since 1965, and the rest have been partially reorganized.[14]

Growing State Treasuries

In the 1950s and 1960s, state governments were the fiscal stepchildren of the federal system. They depended heavily on the sales tax and user fees. With few exceptions, states were required to balance their budgets—a constitutional restriction that was then regarded as a distinct liability. In contrast, the federal government enjoyed the powerful and progressive income tax, which tapped into the rapid income growth of the post-World War II era. When revenues slumped during downturns in the business cycle, the federal government could pull itself out by borrowing money.

Today, state budgets have grown fat. The amount of money spent for public purposes has increased dramatically. In 1964, for example, state governments spent $24 billion; by 1986, they were handing out $228 billion—nearly a tenfold increase. During this period, state spending increased at a slightly faster rate than federal government spending and considerably faster than local government spending.[15]

Federal aid to the states jumped sharply during the 1970s, but it has been declining, as a percentage of total state spending, for more than a decade. While the casual observer might assume that President Reagan initiated the decline in federal financial support for the states, this trend actually started during Carter's presidency and accelerated during the 1980s. In 1975, four out of every ten dollars spent by the states were from the U.S. Treasury. But by 1983, states obtained only three of every ten dollars in their budgets from the national government.[16] Recently, federal aid has inched up again, but it is nowhere near the levels reached in the mid-1970s.[17]

When federal officials reversed course and called a halt to the rapid increase in federal aid for states and localities, state governments moved in to pick up some of the slack. This action reflected the Reagan philosophy: "Federalism means that the central government speaks to the states and lets the states speak to the cities," according to John Shannon, former executive director of the Advisory Commission on Intergovernmental Relations.[18] From 1980 to 1986, for example, total state spending for local government grew by 57 percent, from $83 billion to $130 billion. (Inflation over the same period was 32 percent.) Most state aid goes to public elementary and secondary schools—five of every eight dollars. The balance is allocated for public welfare, highways, public transit, housing, corrections, and general government support.[19]

States have moved aggressively into the capital market to borrow funds for the construction of highways, sewer and water treatment plants, prisons, schools, and mass transit systems. In 1977, states borrowed $71 billion. In anticipation of federal tax reform legislation, states went on a borrowing binge in 1985—issuing nearly $250 billion in tax-exempt bonds. Although this fell to $121 billion in 1987, states are still remarkably active investors in the nation's infrastructure.[20]

The revenue-raising power of states has been enhanced. Individual and corporate income taxes are now far more important than sales taxes and other fees. In 1967, only 22 percent of state government revenue was derived from the income tax. By 1984, income taxes provided nearly 40 percent of state revenues.[21] States have also found significant new sources of revenue in state lotteries, which have been created in twenty-two states—an opportunity that the federal government has thus far foresworn.[22]

State fiscal policy has experienced four fairly distinct phases since the early 1960s.[23] From 1960 to 1977, state governments added new taxes and increased existing taxes. These policy changes were necessary to underwrite real expenditure growth and to satisfy constituent demands for new and expanded services in such areas as health, education, environmental protection, and transportation.

During the late 1970s, many states experienced a modern tax revolt. Spurred by California's Proposition 13, which reduced property tax revenues by 57 percent and limited future increases to no more than 2 percent annually, citizens and legislators clamped down on the rapid growth in state spending. Between 1978 and 1984, only three of the nine states that voted on Proposition-13 type initiatives approved them. But voters in eleven states approved moderate tax and spending limitation measures.[24] Legislatures in dozens of other states heeded the message from the nation's most populous state. No new taxes were added from 1978 to 1980, and taxes declined in dozens of states.[25]

Between 1981 and 1983, states were forced to impose substantial tax increases to cope with the twin crises of the worst economic recession since World War II and the deepest reductions in federal aid in more than thirty years. Unlike the federal government, the states are required to raise sufficient revenues to pay the bills of operating state programs each year. States responded by jacking up the sales tax, increasing income tax rates, adding a penny or two to the gasoline tax, extending the concept of user fees for services, and creating state-sponsored lotteries.

In the late 1980s, many states have reaped a fiscal bonanza.[26] The income and sales tax increases levied to stave off financial disaster in the early 1980s became the driving force behind expansionary government spending programs. As the nation recovered from the recession, the states were well positioned to capture the dividends generated by sustained economic growth. Not much of this unanticipated windfall government profit has been returned to taxpayers, however. And a few states, such as Texas and Louisiana, in the energy producing regions of the country and states heavily dependent on single revenue sources or weak industries, such as Oregon, have yet to experience a surge in financial horsepower.

Just as state budgets began to soar, the federal government began to run up huge deficits. Between 1981 and 1988, the total national debt doubled to more than $2.3 trillion. Annual budget deficits rose from $25 billion in 1968, when the budget was $178 billion, to $200 billion in 1983, when the budget was $800 billion. After concerted efforts to reduce spending, the 1988 deficit still exceeded $145 billion.[27]

Bloated federal deficits created two strong ripple effects for state governments. To pay for substantial increases in defense and entitlement programs, federal lawmakers sharply cut aid to state and local governments. Thus states received less money from the national government and more pleas for help from local governments.[28] Second, the federal government became unable to launch large domestic program initiatives or significantly expand existing ones. The demand for new government spending shifted to state capitals, as interest groups came for money, regulations, and programs. State governments were forced to cope with new societal problems, such as homelessness and AIDS.

With strong support from state officials, the president and members of Congress began to rethink the nature of American federalism and the role of the states. During the 1960s, the typical approach to domestic policy was to create a categorical aid program. The assistance often bypassed state governments and went directly to localities or particular groups. The federal government specified the what, when, and how of program administration and tried to monitor program compliance closely. All this was consistent with the underlying distrust of state government capacity and intentions.[29]

Deregulation and devolution of federal control have been the key governmental concepts of the 1980s. Although the bulk of federal aid still flows through narrow-purpose categorical grants, the restrictions on those grants have declined and the autonomy of state governments has grown.[30] The expansion of state control over federal aid was inspired by Reagan's desire to lessen the role of the federal government in domestic policy. But it also reflected a widespread understanding that the federal government had become a paper tiger in the eyes of state government. Federal officials were unable to enforce mandates on autonomous and newly capable state governments. Washington lawmakers came to realize that state-managed programs made more sense.

Policy Innovation

From Franklin D. Roosevelt's New Deal to Jimmy Carter's Urban Policy, the national government created progressive public policies. By the late 1980s, however, state governments were the driving force in domestic policy innovation. Important new policy initiatives have come from the states in a broad range of policy areas—natural resource and energy policy, human services and health care, economic development and education, and business and insurance regulation. State governments are deeply engaged in issues that affect state residents on a daily basis—the quality of schools, the supply of water, and the condition of roads and waterways, for example. States are also tackling some of the nation's most difficult problems—surrogate motherhood, the care and treatment of the medically indigent, drug abuse in the public schools, teenage pregnancy, pay equity, the liability insurance crisis, and the right to die.

State policy leadership is perhaps best illustrated by recent developments in four policy domains—economic development, education, welfare, and environmental protection. In each instance, the states, not the federal government, have initiated successful policy experiments that have eventually been copied or endorsed by the national government. And in each case, state governments are providing the lion's share of funds to carry out new public strategies.

Economic development has always been an important responsibility of state governments. States fund bridge and highway construction; maintain ports, rivers, airline terminals, and mass transit systems; and support the education and training of the workforce. During the 1980s, the states reconceived and expanded their economic development strategies. Facing double-digit unemployment and massive disruptions in communities, states initiated programs and policies to make themselves economically competitive and to inoculate their economies from the ravages of future recessions. States invested heavily in the development of new technologies, in the retraining of workers, in the growth of small business opportunities, and in the expansion of export markets. As journalist David Osborne noted: "While the national government debated whether it should develop a new industrial policy, the states were already implementing one." [31]

Education reform was another recurrent theme of state policy innovation in the 1980s. Governors and legislators led an ambitious attempt to increase the academic rigor of schools, upgrade the quality of teachers, and increase the achievements of students. What is remarkable about the education reforms of the 1980s is that nearly every state participated in reviewing and improving their educational systems. For example, forty-five states modified requirements for high school graduation, usually by increasing math and science requirements; and forty-six states created new techniques for assessing the quality of classroom teachers. [32] The national government was not the central player, for nearly all of the changes were undertaken without federal mandates or appropriations.

Welfare reform has also been a high priority in state governments. For twenty-five years, federal lawmakers, administrators, and policy experts bemoaned the nation's ineffective welfare programs but failed to achieve significant improvements. In the 1980s, state governments seized the initiative and restructured public assistance programs. Led by such diverse governors as liberal Democrat Michael S. Dukakis of Massachusetts and conservative Republican George Deukmejian of California, the states forged a new consensus: welfare had to be changed from an entitlement program that fosters dependency to an education, training, and work program that fosters economic independence. The National Governors' Association, under the leadership of Gov. Bill Clinton of Arkansas, focused on welfare reform and advocated changes in federal legislation. By the end of the decade, more than thirty states had revised their welfare systems, and the federal government adopted legislation to implement approaches already undertaken in the states. [33]

Landmark environmental statutes mandating action to clean up the air, water, and land were enacted by the federal government in the 1960s and 1970s. In the late 1980s, state governments were at the cutting edge of environmental policy. The states are now primarily responsible for the implementation of basic environmental statutes. Recent federal laws have put the states in charge of some very tough environmental problems. Thus, decisions about where to dispose of toxic and low-level radioactive waste will be made by the states.[34]

Environmental policy innovations came from traditional sources—legislatures and governors—and from the voters, too. For example, Arizona governor Bruce Babbitt was able to break a forty-year deadlock over water conservation policy in his state with effective public and private leadership. The New Jersey legislature passed sweeping legislation that requires industries to inform employees about the potential health effects of chemicals in the workplace. And California voters supported an initiative in 1986 that requires the state government and industries to identify and stop the release of toxic chemicals into the groundwater.

Power and Conflict

Observers of American federalism no longer dismiss state governments as politically irrelevant and incompetent. Several underlying forces affected the ability, willingness, and, indeed, necessity of enlarging the role of the states in the nation's governance and politics. Reformed, modernized, and more capable governmental institutions have entered a void left by a deficit-ridden and politically conservative federal government. Six years of sustained economic growth throughout much of the nation have invigorated state treasuries.

What effects have this quiet revolution in the states had on state political institutions and processes? How are the states coping with their new power and authority? In the chapters that follow, some of the nation's leading students of state government and politics train their skillful eyes on important trends in state political institutions and political processes. They provide perspective on the impact of major changes that have occurred in the last thirty years, characterize the status of state politics and government today, and identify the challenges facing state political leaders in the late 1980s.

In Chapter 2, "The Role of the States in American Federalism," Richard P. Nathan describes the paradox of devolution during the Reagan administration. Contrary to the conservative dream of reducing government, Reagan's policies fostered governmental activism at the state level. According to Nathan, there is a cyclical pattern in the role of state governments. During liberal periods, the 1930s through the 1970s, for example, those who favored increased governmental activity concentrated their energies on the national government in Washington, D.C. During conservative periods, those seeking governmental action turned to the states. State governments have played a pivotal role in bringing changes and improvements in domestic affairs in conservative times.

In Chapter 3, "From Governor to Governors," Thad L. Beyle traces the strengthened role of governors and their growing significance on the national policy scene. As governors exercised more power in their respective states, they came in conflict with courts, legislatures, and other members of the executive branch. Nonetheless, they have usually gotten their way, especially on major policy initiatives. As the importance of being governor has grown, more able people work harder and spend more to get the job. Governors have joined together to advocate such major national policy initiatives as economic competitiveness, welfare reform, and more effective public education. Governors are now active participants in national policy debates.

Chapter 4, "The Legislative Institution: Transformed and at Risk" by Alan Rosenthal, documents the progress of the legislative institution from the rural-dominated political backwaters of the 1950s to the modern, more representative institutions of the 1980s. New-generation legislators are unwilling to take a back seat to the governors, the courts, and the bureaucracy. Instead, they are exercising greater influence on the allocation of money and the direction of state policy. Rosenthal argues, however, that careerism among state legislatures, increased politicization of legislatures, and greater fragmentation of decision making are subtly undermining the recent positive developments in the legislative institution.

Chapter 5, "State Supreme Courts: Activism and Accountability" by Lawrence Baum, examines the institutions that are often called upon to referee conflicts between governors and legislatures, or governors and other executive branch agencies. But the state courts are much more than referees in the power struggles of other institutions. They make policy and thus generate conflict with other governmental actors. State courts have made policy for decades, but in recent years they have become more liberal. In tort law, state courts have expanded the rights of people who have suffered personal injuries or property damage. In civil liberties, the courts have relied upon provisions in state constitutions to expand individual rights. But this increased activism has not gone unchallenged. State legislatures have tried to overturn or modify court decisions. Initiatives and referendums have been used to overturn court decisions, especially those that expanded the rights of criminal defendants. Voters removed liberal justices from office in several states. Incumbent judges are rarely defeated, but they now are more vulnerable and must be more accountable for their actions.

In Chapter 6, "Custody Battles in State Administration," William T. Gormley, Jr., summarizes the proliferation of controls intended to curb the power of state bureaucracies to make policy and carry it out. As state governments, and hence state administrative agencies, took on greater responsibility for the implementation of public policy, other politicians, judges, and citizens began to demand more accountability from state agencies. States have responded by increasing legislative oversight and executive management techniques and by involving citizens in a greater range of bureaucratic decisions. At the same time, federal agencies and federal and state judges have increased their control over the functions of state bureaucracies. As the competition for control grew fiercer, various state political institutions were pitted against one another. The role of judges—and especially federal judges—as ultimate arbiters expanded significantly. As a result, courts, wielding considerable power in deciding how state bureaucracies are to behave, no longer function as disinterested parties.

Chapter 7, "The Persistance of State Parties" by Samuel C. Patterson, argues that despite claims to the contrary, political parties remain important participants in the states. Instead of becoming obsolete, state political parties are adapting to the new politics of the 1980s, which involves media consultants, public relations firms, and political action committees. State parties vary enormously across the nation, but on balance, they have profound influence over who runs for state office, who is elected, and what the nature of political participation is in American politics.

In Chapter 8, "The Transformation of State Electoral Politics," Barbara and Stephen Salmore describe the rise of candidate-centered campaigns, in which personal qualities and issues communicated directly to voters compete with party labels and organizations as the principal voting cues in state elections. The larger role state governments have come to play as policy makers has raised the stakes in state-level elections. Greater interest is generated in their outcomes; more resources are devoted to campaign efforts. The trend toward candidate-centered campaigns is most pronounced in gubernatorial elections because of the rise in split-ticket and cross-party voting, the use of direct primaries, the effective use of incumbency, the decoupling of federal and state elections, and the increase in spending on elections. These same trends have made legislative races—especially in the larger states—more like races for the U.S. Congress.

In Chapter 9, "Challenges for the States," I summarize *The State of the States*. I consider some of the major problems facing state political institutions in the 1990s and how states are coping with the strains created by their new responsibility as central players in the federal system.

The quiet revolution in state governments has touched every state political institution and political actor. The stakes are higher than ever before. Competition for the exercise of power—a permanent feature of politics—has grown more intense. Conflict over questions of governance and political leadership has spread within and across political institutions. How well state political institutions and leaders handle these difficult challenges will determine how the nation is to be governed and how its citizens are to be served in the coming decades.

Notes

1. Terry Sanford, *Storm over the States* (New York: McGraw-Hill, 1967).
2. Ann O'M. Bowman and Richard C. Kearney, *The Resurgence of the States* (Englewood Cliffs, N.J.: Prentice-Hall, 1986).
3. Timothy O'Rourke, *The Impact of Reapportionment* (New Brunswick, N.J.: Transaction Books, 1980).
4. Alan Rosenthal, *Legislative Life* (New York: Harper and Row, 1981).
5. Charles S. Bullock III and Charles M. Lamb, eds. *Implementation of Civil Rights Policy* (Monterey, Calif.: Brooks/Cole, 1984).
6. Carl E. Van Horn, *Policy Implementation in the Federal System* (Lexington, Mass.: D.C. Heath and Co., 1979), 155-161.
7. Albert L. Sturm and Janice C. May, "State Constitutions and Constitutional Revisions: 1980-81 and the Past 50 Years," in Council of State Governments, *The Book of the States, 1982-83* (Lexington, Ky.: The Council of State Governments, 1982), 115-133.
8. Larry Sabato, *Goodbye to Goodtime Charlie: The American Governor Transformed*, 2d ed. (Washington, D.C.: CQ Press, 1983).
9. Sanford, *Storm over the States*, 39.
10. Rosenthal, *Legislative Life*, 3.
11. National Conference of State Legislatures, unpublished data.
12. Robert A. Kagan, Bloos Cartwright, Lawrence M. Friedman, and Stanton Wheeled, "The Evolution of State Supreme Courts," *Michigan Law Review* 76 (1978): 961-1005.
13. Deil S. Wright, *Understanding Intergovernmental Relations*, 2d ed. (Monterey, Calif.: Brooks/Cole), 1982.
14. The Council of State Governments, *The Book of the States, 1982-83*, 145-147; *The Book of the States, 1984-85* (1984), 44-45; *The Book of the States, 1986-87* (1986), 45-47; and *The Book of the States, 1988-89* (1988), 47-48.
15. Advisory Commission on Intergovernmental Relations, *Significant Features of Fiscal Federalism, 1988* (Washington, D.C.: Advisory Commission on Intergovernmental Relations, 1987), 2.
16. Advisory Commission on Intergovernmental Relations, *Significant Features of Fiscal Federalism, 1984* (Washington, D.C: Advisory Commission on Intergovernmental Relations, 1984), 62.
17. "Measuring Federal Aid: Whose Straw is Shortest?" *Governing*, prototype, 1987, 48.
18. "Measuring Federal Aid," *Governing*, 49.
19. "More State Dollars for the Localities," *Governing*, May 1988, 60-61.

20. "The Zigzag History of Tax-Exempt Borrowing," *Governing,* March 1988, 58.
21. Advisory Commission on Intergovernmental Relations, *Significant Features of Fiscal Federalism, 1984,* 51.
22. Steven D. Gold, Brenda Erikson, and Michelle Kissell, *Earmarking State Taxes* (Denver: National Conference of States Legislatures, 1987), 6.
23. Advisory Commission on Intergovernmental Relations, *Significant Features of Fiscal Federalism, 1984,* 71.
24. Patrick B. McGuigan, *The Politics of Direct Democracy in the 1980s* (Washington, D.C.: Free Congress Research and Education Foundation, 1985), 52, 54, 55.
25. Advisory Commission on Intergovernmental Relations, *Significant Features of Fiscal Federalism, 1984,* 71.
26. Steve D. Gold, ed., *Reforming State Tax Systems* (Denver: National Conference of State Legislatures, 1986).
27. U.S. Congress, Joint Economic Committee, *The 1985 Joint Economic Report* (Washington, D.C.: U.S. Government Printing Office, 1985), 47; and Executive Office of the President, *Budget of the United States for Fiscal Year 1987* (Washington, D.C.: U.S. Government Printing Office, 1986).
28. Richard P. Nathan and Fred C. Doolittle, *Reagan and the States* (Princeton, N.J.: Princeton University Press, 1987).
29. James L. Sundquist, *Making Federalism Work* (Washington, D.C.: The Brookings Institution, 1969).
30. Nathan and Doolittle, *Reagan and the States.*
31. David Osborne, *Laboratories of Democracy* (Cambridge, Mass.: Harvard Business School Press, 1988).
32. Susan Fuhrman, "State Politics and Education Reform," New Brunswick, N.J., Center for Policy Research in Education, Rutgers University, unpublished manuscript.
33. National Governors' Association, *Making America Work: Productive People, Productive Policies* (Washington, D.C.: National Governors' Association, 1987).
34. National Conference of State Legislatures, *State Issues 1987* (Denver: National Conference of State Legislatures, 1987), Chapter 2.

2. THE ROLE OF THE STATES IN AMERICAN FEDERALISM

Richard P. Nathan

Political scientists revel in identifying the unanticipated effects of politicians' actions, often with the subtle, though undeserved, implication that they knew what was going to happen in advance. The experience of state governments during the Reagan administration featured such an unanticipated effect. The success of Reagan's brand of "New Federalism," which highlighted the role of the states, helped to activate state governments in a manner that undermined the Reagan administration's own superordinate objective of reducing the size and scope of the role of the public sector in domestic affairs. One can think of this as the paradox of devolution under the Reagan administration.

All modern presidents have had ideas about U.S. federalism. This is reflected in Roosevelt's New Deal, Truman's Fair Deal, Eisenhower's decentralization policies, Kennedy's New Frontier, Johnson's Great Society, and Nixon's New Federalism. Ronald Reagan is no exception. As governor of California and as president of the United States, he held to a strong and clear conception of American federalism. He consistently emphasized the idea that greater reliance should be placed on state governments. Because of Reagan's emphasis on the states, the current period is a good time to consider their role in American federalism. This chapter discusses the paradox of devolution under Reagan and assesses recent trends against a backdrop of the theory and history of American federalism.

Theories of Federalism

British political scientist Kenneth C. Wheare's seminal work on federal government, first published in 1946, began by stating that the modern idea of federalism was determined by the United States.[1] Before 1787 the term "federal" was used to refer to a league in which the constituent states were members of a general polity, like a club. In the United States, by contrast, both the general government and the regional governments operate directly upon the people; "each citizen is subject to *two governments*." [2] Wheare said the general and regional governments are "co-ordinate in a federal system." Furthermore, according to Wheare, both types of governments—national and regional—must have "exclusive control" in some areas of activity.[3] In a similar vein, American political scientist Arthur W. Macmahon said, "The matters entrusted to the constituent governments in a federal system (whether their powers are residual or delegated) must be substantial and not trivial." [4] This is the formal or traditional theory of federalism found in the writings of political scientists.

There is a newer theory that rejects Wheare's notions of exclusivity and Macmahon's idea of substantial powers entrusted to the regional governments. Instead, it stresses the idea of shared powers or cooperative federalism. This view is associated with University of Chicago political scientist Morton Grodzins's famous essay on "marble cake" federalism.

> The American form of government is often, but erroneously, symbolized by a three-layer cake. A far more accurate image is the rainbow or marble cake, characterized by an inseparable mingling of differently colored ingredients, the colors appearing in vertical and diagonal strands and unexpected whirls. As colors are mixed in the marble cake, so functions are mixed in the American federal system.[5]

Edward S. Corwin, another political theorist, came to a similar conclusion from an opposite point of view. He did not like the role of the states being downgraded. In an article published in 1950, Corwin said the passing of dual federalism was the result of the U.S. Constitution having "been overwhelmed and submerged" by events.[6] He was referring to decisions by the U.S. Supreme Court that increased the powers of the national government at the expense of the states.

In another essay, Grodzins embellished his theory: "All areas of American government are involved in all functions. . . . There has never been a time when federal, state and local functions were separate and distinct." [7] Much of the contemporary scholarship reflects Grodzins's view of modern federalism. Many experts on federalism, writing on the subject after Grodzins, have agreed with his dynamic/sharing model featuring the "inseparable mingling" of functions in federalism and, as a result, the inability to tightly define "federalism." British political scientist M. J. C. Vile, for example, described "a gradual slide away from what was felt to be the excessive legalism and rigidity of Wheare's definition to the point where the definitions that are offered are almost totally vacuous." [8] Likewise, G. F. Sawer in *Modern Federalism* said attempts now to define federalism are "futile," [9] and Michael D. Reagan and John G. Sanzone refer to "the bankrupt quality of federalism as an operational concept." [10] In a study of American federalism published in 1970, Richard H. Leach concluded: "Precisely what 'federalism' means is now and never has been clear." [11]

This chapter advances a contrary position from the dominant theme of Grodzins's theory. It is true that the relationships between the federal and state governments in American federalism are complex and fluid and that over the long haul the federal government has become more powerful. But there is a geographical division of power between the central and regional governments in the American federal system and in other federal systems that makes them different from countries with nonfederal systems. The essence of modern federalism is that it is a political form in which regional governments have a major role in the political system and process. [12] Previous studies of federalism focused too heavily on legal powers and intergovernmental relationships. Not enough attention has been given to empirical, behavioral studies of the role of different types of governments, particularly state governments. [13]

A further important attribute of the role of state governments exists that helps to understand the American federal system. In the United States, there has been a *cyclicality* in the relative role of state governments, with the swing variable in this cyclical pattern being *political ideology*. [14] In conservative periods, the role of state governments has been enhanced, whereas in liberal or progovernment periods, the role of the national government has grown. This cyclical pattern has an almost mathematical character. In liberal periods, those who favor increased governmental activity often find that it is efficient to lobby for their interests at one place, the center. In conservative periods, the proponents of increased governmental activity have fewer opportunities; they have to try to get changes adopted wherever they can. It is not surprising, therefore, that progovernment lobbying activities are focused on those subgovernments, particularly states, in which there is support for a stronger role for the public sector. States—not all states, but many of them—have been the centers of activism and innovation in domestic affairs in conservative periods in U.S. history.

In the early years of the twentieth century, the states were the source of such progressive policy initiatives as workers' compensation, unemployment insurance, and public assistance. Twenty-one states enacted workers' compensation laws prior to 1913. [15] Other states followed suit. The same is true of public welfare programs. According to Michael B. Katz, "Between 1917 and 1920, state legislatures passed 400 new public welfare laws; by 1931, mothers' pensions in all states except Georgia and South Carolina supported 200,000 children; and in constant dollars, public welfare expenses, fueled especially by mothers' pensions, increased 168 percent between 1903 and 1928." [16] In a similar vein, James T. Patterson noted that the states "preceded the federal government in regulating large corporations, establishing minimum labor standards, and stimulating economic development," although he added, "the most remarkable development in state government in the 1920's was the increase in spending." [17] In this period when the United States was "Keeping Cool with Coolidge," it was state policy initiatives that planted the seeds of Franklin Roosevelt's New Deal. State initiatives formed the basis for many of the major national government programs adopted under Roosevelt.

A similar spurt of state initiatives in domestic affairs characterized the conservative period in the latter part of the nineteenth century: "The first great battles of the reform movement were fought out in the states." [18] Examples of state innovations adopted during that time are compulsory school attendance laws and the creation of state boards of education, reforms of political processes, a growing role for state boards of charity, child labor laws, and state regulatory policies in licensing and zoning.

The Rising Role of the States

One hundred years later, in the 1980s, the pendulum of U.S. domestic policy has again swung to a conservative position: the states again are on the move. Five factors have contributed to the rising role for the states. One is the conservative, devolutionary domestic policies adopted by the Reagan administration. Reagan's policies to cut federal grants and rely more heavily on the states have made their mark. A second and longer-run factor underlying the recent state activism is "the modernization movement in state government," which has occurred over the past twenty years. The phrase refers to reforms adopted by states to increase their managerial and technical capacity to take on new and expanded functions. In a 1985 report, the U.S. Advisory Commission on Intergovernmental Relations concluded that "state governments have been transformed in almost every facet of their structure and operations." [19] A third factor has been the effects of the U.S. Supreme Court decision in *Baker v. Carr* (1962). This decision reduced the rural-urban political imbalance of state legislatures and increased general public support for an increased role for state governments. A fourth and related factor is "the end of southern exceptionalism." Martha Derthick believes that integration in the South has created a situation in which "the case for the states can at last begin to be discussed on its merits." [20]

Finally, the strong recovery of the U.S. economy from the 1981-1982 recession contributed to the resurgence of the states in the 1980s. This factor interacted in an important way with Reagan's devolutionary policies to highlight the state role. Typically, state governments overreact to national recessions, battening down their fiscal hatches by cutting spending and raising taxes to balance their budget. The strong recovery from the 1981-1982 recession beginning late in 1982 meant that state coffers were filling up just as Reagan's federal aid retrenchment policies were beginning to be felt. This high volatility of state finances put state governments in a position after 1982 to spend more and do more in those functional areas in which the federal government under Reagan was pulling back or signaling its intention to do so.

The coming together of all these trends produced a resurgence of the state role in American federalism. Evidence of this change can be seen not only in the response to Reagan's domestic budget cuts, his creation of new block grants, and other changes in federal grant-in-aid programs, but also in efforts being undertaken in many states to reform major functions of state government, for example, in the fields of education, health, and welfare.

In the field of education, initiatives have been launched by many governors and state legislatures to do things such as mandate early childhood education, strengthen instruction in basic disciplines, and upgrade the performance of teachers through merit pay. According to Denis P. Doyle and Terry W. Hartle, writing in 1985, "The last two years have witnessed the greatest and most concentrated surge of educational reform in the nation's history. . . . Indeed, the most surprising aspect of the 'tidal wave of reform' is that it came from state governments." [21] Reforms by state governments are also being undertaken in the health programs, especially to overhaul Medicaid, by revising and focusing benefits and attempting to control costs.

Important state policy shifts are occurring in public welfare programs, too. Two-thirds of the states have developed new-style workfare programs. These programs require welfare family heads to participate in activities linked to the labor market and the reduction of dependency, such as job search, remedial education, job training, and community work experience. The aim is to convert welfare payment programs for able-bodied, working-age recipients into service systems that emphasize jobs and job preparation.[22] In addition, many state governments are assuming a stronger leadership role in planning for growth management and in providing infrastructure to promote economic development.

Data from the U.S. Bureau of the Census show in the aggregate that state governments increased their role during the Reagan years. From 1983 to 1986, as the Reagan retrenchment and federalism policies took effect, state aid to localities increased by an average of 5.6 percent a year in real terms, that is, adjusted for inflation. Total state spending rose by nearly the same percentage. Prior to that, from the mid-1970s to 1983, both state aid to localities and total state spending had been level in real terms. Considerable variation does exist, however, in all of these program areas reflecting U.S. Supreme Court justice Louis Brandeis's famous characterization in 1931 of state governments as laboratories that can "try novel social and economic experiments without risk to the rest of the country." [23]

There are no ready calipers for measuring the activism of individual states. Studies by political scientists Jack L. Walker and Virginia Gray indicate that over time it has been the larger, older, and ideologically most liberal or progovernment states that have tended to be most innovative.[24] Contemporary research suggests a broader distribution of state innovation. Newer states, and those that are changing ideologically toward a more liberal stance on the role of government, are also enhancing the role of state government.

The argument that the role of American state governments changes on a cyclical basis differs from much of the writing on American federalism. The dominant theory has highlighted the idea of a steady centralizing trend in federalism, whereby, gradually and over time, federal governmental systems become more integrated and uni-fied. Part of the reason that this view has been dominant is that the United States recently experienced a liberal period in which the role of the national government expanded. The United States has always been a country in a hurry that lives in the present. In the long period of growth in the role of the national government, from Franklin D. Roosevelt's New Deal through the late 1970s, some observers forgot that in conservative periods, states were the engines of innovation in domestic affairs. State initiatives in the 1920s were the models for New Deal programs. This cyclical pattern of state leadership and innovation reflects the normal equilibrating tendency of the American political system for states to move into areas of public policy when the national government is moving out, or at least not taking the initiative.

Public choice economists depict federalism as a governmental system that creates competition among the states, which in turn has the effect of holding down governmental taxing and spending. The opportunity of citizens to move freely among political jurisdictions produces pressures that hold back increases in the level of public service. Geoffrey Brennan and James M. Buchanan characterize federalism as "an indirect means of imposing constraints on the potential fiscal exploitation of Leviathan," referring to "the monopoly-state model of government." [25]

Another way to interpret the role of states in American federalism is grounded in the cyclical nature of the role of state governments.

Federalism can be seen as a growth force underlying government spending whereby the activism of state governments in conservative periods causes a *ratchetting-up* effect over time. State initiatives undertaken in conservative periods become the basis for national policy actions in liberal periods, such as many of the New Deal reforms.

Two main types of national government action have influenced the roles of the national and state governments in American federalism: grants-in-aid and judicial decisions. Increased activity by the national government has undercut the role of the states. Decreases in national government activism—cuts in grants as under Reagan and pro-state court decisions—have contributed to the rising role of the states.

Grants-in-Aid

Michael D. Reagan and John G. Sanzone state that the "sharing of functions [in American federalism] is most clearly and dramatically seen in the explosive growth of federal grants-in-aid." [26] This was the case particularly in the post-World War II period, although grants as a form of government interaction have much deeper roots. For example, land grants to the states predate the American Constitution.[27] Federal spending under grant programs tripled as a percentage of federal outlays from 1950 to 1978, which was the peak year for federal aid in real terms.

According to Morton Grodzins's dynamic/sharing theory of federalism, the expanded fiscal role for the national government in intergovernmental affairs involves not only the federal-state relationship but also the federal-local relationship. Beginning under Truman and continuing into the Nixon-Ford period, direct federal grants-in-aid to local governments increased dramatically. This direct relationship between the national government and local governments, described as "the expanded partnership" by Roscoe Martin,[28] goes against the traditional theory of federalism that highlights "Dillon's rule." John F. Dillon, an expert on municipal finances in the late nineteenth century and an Iowa state Supreme Court justice, argued that local governments are creatures of the state and stressed a two-level (national-state) view of federalism. Dillon said the state legislature gives local governments "the breath of life without which they cannot exist." [29]

Federal grants-in-aid have had a major effect on American federalism. Still, the tendency to assign a major role to this type of intergovernmental relationship frequently leads observers to overstate their importance. Research by political scientists reveals that federal grants, despite their heralded goals and requirements, often end up simply reinforcing state and local programs already in place. State and local officials are not above bending the goals and conditions of federal grant-in-aid programs to fit their purposes. The result is that grants often have much less effect on state programs and activities than is assumed.

In sum, federal grants-in-aid are a barometer of American federalism. They have grown in liberal periods. They have become more intrusive in these periods, especially when the national government bypassed the states and provided grants directly to local governments. But all grants are not the same. The revenue sharing and block grants that Republicans tend to favor are not as far reaching as "categorical" grants generally favored by Democrats and targeted on narrower purposes. Moreover, the government does not always exercise the authority it has to influence state governments. Indeed, the Reagan period marked a decline in the size and influence of grants-in-aid from the national government to states and localities. Reagan's policies, in particular, have downplayed direct federal-local grants.

Judicial Decisions

The other federal level action that influenced the role of state governments in American federalism is the activity of federal courts. It can be argued that court decisions, more than legislative actions, have shaped federalism in the United States. In the country's early history, the courts were a centralizing force. In the nineteenth century, they shifted to a pro-state position. However, since the mid-1930s, the courts, especially the U.S. Supreme Court, have emerged as an aggressive nationalizing force.[30]

This current phase, in which the courts tend to favor the federal government, is still very much with us. Most recently, in *Garcia v. San Antonio Metropolitan Transit Authority* (1985), the Supreme Court held to a centralizing theory, saying, in effect, that there are no intrinsic and immutable divisions of power and responsibility in American federalism. Writing for the majority in *Garcia,* Justice Harry A. Blackmun said efforts by the courts to impose limits on the power of Congress in relation to the states ultimately fall short because of "the elusiveness of objective criteria for 'fundamental' elements of state sovereignty."[31] Dissenting, Justice Lewis F. Powell, Jr., said the Court's decision in *Garcia* "reduces the Tenth Amendment to meaningless rhetoric when Congress acts pursuant to the Commerce Clause."[32] It is the Tenth Amendment of the Bill of Rights that "reserves" to the states and to the people powers not enumerated as powers of the national government in Article I of the U.S. Constitution.

In an unusual dissenting opinion in *Garcia,* Justice William H. Rehnquist, now chief justice, joined with Powell, predicting a reversal of this decision: "I do not think it incumbent on those of us in the dissent to spell out further the fine points of a principle that will, I am confident, in time again command the support of a majority of this court." [33] Despite Rehnquist's assertions, one would be hard put to predict such a reversal. If President Reagan had had one more appointment to the U.S. Supreme Court, Rehnquist's prediction could have come true.

It is instructive to consider the types of actions the federal courts have taken on U.S. federalism. The role of the courts in expanding the authority of the national government has occurred in some areas, but not others. The expansion of the federal role has been greatest, for example, in matters involving individual rights, civil rights, voting rights, and legislative apportionment. It has not been as extensive in programmatic areas that affect state and local finances more directly, such as welfare and education. The courts, particularly the U.S. Supreme Court, have tended to stay out of the fiscal thicket. They have been reluctant to take responsibility for causing the national government or the states to change policies that would create appreciable new fiscal burdens. This is less true of lower federal courts and appeals and district courts than of the Supreme Court. U.S. district courts, especially, have asserted the rights of prisoners and patients in state mental institutions in a way that caused major increases in state spending by setting specific standards for these facilities. The prison systems of more than forty states are currently operating under some form of federal court order.

The Sorting-Out Theory

The story of American federalism can be seen as one in which two theories—the widespread-sharing position and the traditional federalism theory—have competed for attention. In both the legislative and judicial arenas, liberals have tended to act in a way that reflects the dynamic federalism theory, while conservatives have tended toward the traditional theory and dual federalism.

A more recent position—the "sorting-out" theory of federalism—emerged in the latter part of the 1960s. Its rise was in large part a reaction to the growth of the national government's role under Lyndon Johnson's Great Society programs.[34] This theory, as the name implies, argues that it is important to sort out functions in American federalism, so that each function is clearly assigned and the responsible governments can be more easily held accountable for their actions. In effect, this effort moves back from the Grodzins position and toward the traditional view.

Proponents of the sorting-out theory have been particularly interested in federal grants-in-aid. They criticize the proliferation of federal grants, which they see as undermining accountability in U.S. domestic affairs and causing political resentment, confusion, and inefficiency. The U.S. Advisory Commission on Intergovernmental Relations has been a leading proponent of rationalizing functions and finances in American federalism. The Commission is a hybrid agency; it is federally chartered and funded, but state and local government officials constitute a majority of its members. President Nixon's New Federalism program, which included welfare reform, revenue sharing, and block grants, reflected this middle sorting-out position on federalism. President Reagan's position reflected the older state-oriented dual federalism theory.

As the idea of sorting out functions in U.S. federalism gathered steam in the 1970s, economists came to play an increasingly larger role in shaping this and other theories about federalism. Economic concepts of public goods, spillovers, and externalities were brought to bear to devise criteria for selecting those functions that should be assigned to the national government because their benefits extend beyond state or local political boundaries. Such analyses were used as the basis for designating functions such as air and water pollution control and income maintenance as appropriate for national governmental action. Other functions such as police and fire protection, mass transit, and elementary and secondary education were considered areas in which the national government should have a limited role.

Much of the economic literature on federalism concentrates on fiscal equalization. The focus is on disparities in wealth and industrial capacity among regions and the ways in which central governments in federal nations, not just the United States, do or do not deal with these conditions. Surely, this subject is important. However, the question of how to achieve horizontal equity among regions is not exclusive to federal systems of government. Equalization schemes are found both in federal political systems and those defined as "unitary."

Reagan's Brand of 'New Federalism'

Reagan's domestic policies have had a significant effect on the role of state governments in American federalism. Although Reagan did not use Nixon's term "New Federalism," the press often described his domestic program as his brand of a "New Federalism." Going beyond Nixon's sorting-out theory, which assigned some functions to local governments as well as to the states, Reagan's theory of federalism was much more sweeping in the way it emphasized the states and the Tenth Amendment. One of Reagan's major goals throughout his public career was the devolution of powers and functions from the national government to the states. As governor of California, he argued strongly for such a shift. When he was running for the Republican presidential nomination he continued to do so. In 1976, when he challenged incumbent president Gerald Ford for the Republican nomination, Reagan delivered a memorable speech calling for wholesale transfer of authority and resources to the states:

> Federal authority has clearly failed to do the job. Indeed, it has created more problems in welfare, education, housing, food stamps, Medicaid, community and regional development, and revenue sharing to name a few. The sums involved and the potential savings to the taxpayer are large. Transfer of authority in whole or in part, in all of these areas would reduce the outlay of the federal government by more than $90 billion, using the spending levels of fiscal 1975. With such a saving it would be possible to balance the federal budget, make an initial $5 billion payment on the national debt and cut the federal personal income tax burden of every American an average of 23 percent.[35]

At the time, Reagan's proposal was considered quite controversial and it caused a firestorm of criticism, especially from governors. Some political analysts saw it as the most important factor in the failure of Reagan's bid for the Republican nomination in 1976. Nevertheless, Reagan's federalism theory had not changed four years later when he was elected president. In his inaugural address in 1981, he promised to curb the power of the national government and to "demand recognition of the distinction" between national government powers and "those reserved to the states"—a phrase found in the Tenth Amendment.

During his first year in office, Reagan successfully pressed for changes in domestic policy reflecting this point of view. He won substantial cuts in federal grant-in-aid programs as a way to reduce both federal spending and the national government's role in domestic affairs. Also in 1981, Reagan proposed the establishment of nine federal block grants, seven of them new programs, the purpose of which was to reduce federal requirements and increase the discretion available to state governments. Unlike the block grants enacted under his Republican predecessors, Nixon and Ford, no funds provided under Reagan's block grants were paid directly to local governments; they went to the states instead.

Reagan stepped up his efforts to devolve federal programs to the states in 1982 when he devoted the bulk of his State of the Union message to an elaborate swap and turn-back plan to rearrange the responsibilities for $47 billion in federal grant-in-aid funds, roughly half of the amount spent on federal grants at the time. This plan, for example, would have assigned the family welfare program and the food stamp program to the states, while the federal government would have taken over the Medicaid program, which provides health and medical care services for the poor.[36]

Although Reagan was not successful, either in 1976 in his primary campaign against Gerald Ford or later in 1982, in achieving such a sweeping turn-back and realignment of governmental responsibilities, his federalism policies did have a major impact. They have strengthened state governments. And, they undercut the superordinate retrenchment goal of the Reagan administration in the domestic public sector.

Reagan's biggest cuts came in 1981. The 1981 Omnibus Budget Reconciliation Act reduced federal aid payments to states and localities by 7 percent, the first such cut in actual dollar terms in twenty-five years.[37] Research on the effects of these reductions and changes in federal grants-in-aid revealed that state governments took on a larger role in areas in which the federal government under Reagan was decreasing its aid or threatening to do so. Princeton University conducted a study on the effects of Reagan's federal aid policies on fourteen states and forty local governments within these states. (The sample sites were chosen as representative on the basis of their size, location, and economic and social characteristics.) Florida, Massachusetts, New Jersey, New York, and Oklahoma were classified as having made the "most pronounced" response to the Reagan cuts and changes in federal grants-in-aid. These states replaced actual or threatened federal aid cuts out of state funds. They also took steps to play a stronger policy-making and administrative role in the functional areas of the Reagan federal aid cuts and block grants. New block grants were enacted under Reagan in his first term in the areas of public health, education, community development, social services, and employment and training.

Eight states in the study were classified in "intermediate-response" groups. Three of these states—Mississippi, Ohio, and Texas—replaced some, although not appreciable, amounts of federal aid cuts out of state funds and also adopted a stronger policy-making and administrative role in the areas affected by the Reagan federal aid cuts and block grants. One state, Washington, voted to replace federal aid cuts but then was hard hit by the 1981-1982 recession and rescinded these restorations. Washington state, however, did take advantage of the block grants created by the Reagan administration. The remaining four states in the intermediate-response group—Arizona, Illinois, Missouri, and South Dakota—did not replace any federal aid out of their own funds but took steps to exercise a stronger policy-making and administrative role in the functional areas in which the devolutionary policies of the Reagan administration were most pronounced.

California was classified as having made a minimal response to the Reagan changes. According to the field researchers, the enactment of referendums affecting state finances, and the debates about others, overwhelmed the effects of the Reagan federal aid policy shifts.

Prior studies suggest that innovative policies by the states tend to be adopted by the larger, older states with generally more liberal or progressive state governments. The Princeton University study provides support for these findings. The most pronounced response to the Reagan changes usually, although not always, came in states that fit this definition. These states were most willing to commit new or additional revenues from their own sources to replace actual or anticipated federal aid cuts. But, evidence also existed of a broader response to the Reagan policy changes involving relatively newer and traditionally less progressive states where the political ideology was shifting during the period of this study from a conservative or moderate to a more liberal stance.

Although state governments took on a larger role in the Reagan period, this shift in the long run is likely to disappoint conservatives. According to one analysis of the Reagan record, "Conservatives who gleefully assumed that shifting the responsibility for social programs to the states would mean the end of the programs have discovered that state governments were not as conservative as they thought." [38]

The rising role of state governments in the 1980s can be seen in U.S. Bureau of the Census data on state taxation. Thirty-eight states increased taxes in 1983. Overall, the tax revenues of state governments rose by 14.8 percent from 1983 to 1984. Steven D. Gold, of the National Conference of State Legislatures, also noted that "real state general fund spending rose at a significant rate in 1984, 1985, and 1986." [39]

Summary

The activities of government have three dimensions—policy making, financing, and administration. Governmental functions in a federal system can be analyzed in terms of the level of government that has the principal responsibility for one or several of these dimensions for any given function or program. Grants-in-aid affect policy and financing in important ways. A federal grant may set rules for a program involving an increase in the policy and fiscal role of the national government, though a Washington-based view of federal grant programs often overstate these effects. The third dimension of governmental activities, administration, is likely to be unaffected, or much less affected. Under federally aided programs, the administration of the benefits or services provided by the national government is carried out by the recipient government. Even though the national government has come to play a larger policy and financial role in the affected functional areas, state and local governments—because they also play a policy and funding role and because they administer the aided benefits or services—retain more control than they are often credited with by those who highlight the intrusiveness of the national government in domestic affairs.

The one who pays the piper does not always call the tune. Under federal grants-in-aid, the recipient governments retain substantial power. In this sense, the Grodzins theory of federalism goes overboard. The widespread-sharing view of American federalism, looking from the top down, does not give enough attention to the behavior of state and local governments. For many functions, the state role is substantial and definitive on all three dimensions of governmental activity. Grodzins's point about the sharing of functions in American federalism need not be rejected, but it should be recognized as overstated in interpretations that do not dig deeply enough into the actual functioning of modern government. Federalism in its traditional formulation is not a relic of earlier days to be preserved under glass or only in nostalgia, the rhetoric of conservative politicians and unsophisticated introductory American government textbooks.

It is important to sharpen the focus. In the area of higher education, for example, the federal government provides student aid and is instrumental in setting the research agendas of many public and private universities. But the predominate role in chartering, structuring, locating, paying for, and administering public institutions of higher education lies with the states. The three-dimensional state role—in policy, finances, and administration—is much less marbleized in the real world than in the academic literature. Much the same can be said for elementary and secondary education; the federal role has always been chary and limited. States now pay for well over half of public elementary and secondary education. They charter and regulate local school districts and set standards on a wide range of matters affecting teachers' certification, salaries, and school curriculum. Public elementary and secondary education are often regarded as local functions, but an updated theory might argue that state governments have the predominate role in this area. In any event, the federal government certainly does not. Likewise, the state role in regard to highways, except for interstate highways, is a critical one. The same applies to natural resources and recreational and environmental programs.

Similar observations can be made about regulatory activities. The regulation of public utilities, insurance, marriages, adoptions, foster care, divorces, as well as the licensing of drivers, animals, and child-care centers, are all areas in which federal involvement is very limited or nonexistent.

In much the same vein, new areas at the cutting edge of social policy tend to be a primary or at least heavy responsibility of state governments. For example, laws and regulations relating to AIDS patients and treatment, surrogate parenthood, death with dignity, and the rights of homosexuals are all dealt with at the state level. States predominate in these areas in a way that is not out of line with the Wheare and Macmahon ideas about federalism. Neither Congress nor the courts have regarded all areas of domestic affairs as shared governmental responsibilities. State governments have a substantial role, and the clearly dominant role, in many areas of U.S. domestic government.

Public policies involve both signals and substance. The signal given by Reagan's devolutionary policies was that the states should do more and they did. The result was that Reagan's devolutionary policies reinforced the traditional theory of federalism and undercut what many observers believed to be the much more important fiscal retrenchment goal of his administration in domestic affairs.

What are the political lessons of this experience? In a liberal period, conservative politicians may be well advised to press for devolutionary measures as they did in the period from the New Deal through the 1970s. But in conservative periods, they perhaps should employ the opposite strategy. In conservative periods, states are likely to be the sources of activism and innovation. The concept and goal of decentralization in these periods may actually stimulate the states to action instead of serving, as they do in liberal periods, as a cover for budget and program reductions.

The role of the states as the broker of American federalism shifts as conditions change. In liberal periods, the relative role of state governments diminishes as the federal government's role in domestic affairs increases. However, the opposite is true in conservative periods. Then the American governmental system tends, as was the case in the Reagan era, to more strongly reflect the traditional state-focused model of American federalism. Neither the marble cake nor the traditional federalism theory fully serves our needs. American federalism can be thought of as involving a continuum between the two positions, with the crucial broker role of state governments greatly influenced by ideological changes in the society.

Notes

1. K. C. Wheare, *Federal Government,* 4th ed. (New York: Oxford University Press, 1963; reprint, 1987), 1.

2. Wheare, *Federal Government*, 1.
3. Wheare, *Federal Government*, 4-5.
4. Arthur W. Macmahon, "The Problem of Federalism: Survey," in *Federalism Mature and Emergent*, ed. Arthur W. Macmahon (New York: Doubleday, 1955), 4.
5. Morton Grodzins, "The Federal System," in *Goals for Americans: The Report of the President's Commission on National Goals* (New York: Columbia University Press, 1960), 265.
6. Edward S. Corwin, "The Passing of Dual Federalism," *Virginia Law Review* 36 (February 1950): 1-24.
7. Morton Grodzins, "Centralization and Decentralization in the American Federal System," in *A Nation of States*, ed. Robert A. Goldwin (Chicago: Rand McNally, 1961), 3, 7.
8. M. J. C. Vile, "Federal Theory and the 'New Federalism,'" in *The Politics of "New Federalism,"* ed. D. Jaensch (Adelaide, Australia: Australian Political Studies Association, 1977), 1.
9. G. F. Sawer, *Modern Federalism* (London: C. A. Watts & Co. Ltd., 1969), 2.
10. Michael D. Reagan and John G. Sanzone, *The New Federalism* (New York: Oxford University Press, 1981), 19.
    William Anderson was also wary of precise definitions of federalism, preferring to regard it as less a formal structure than "a concept of mind." See William Anderson, *Intergovernmental Relations in Review* (Minneapolis: University of Minnesota Press, 1960), 17.
11. Richard H. Leach, *American Federalism* (New York: W. W. Norton and Co., 1970), 9.
12. Regional governments are called states in the United States, India, and Australia; provinces in Canada; cantons in Switzerland; landers in West Germany; and Republics in Yugoslavia.
13. Richard P. Nathan and Margarita M. Balmaceda, *Comparing Federal Systems of Government* (Oxford, England: Oxford University Press, forthcoming).
14. This point is suggested by Albert O. Hirschman in *Shifting Involvements: Private Interest and Public Action* (Princeton, N.J.: Princeton University Press, 1982).
15. Edwin Amenta, Elisabeth Clemens, Jefren Olsen, Sunion Parikh, and Theda Scocpol, "The Political Origins of Unemployment Insurance in Five American States," Center for the Study of Industrial Societies, The University of Chicago, unpublished manuscript, 10.
16. Michael B. Katz, *In the Shadow of the Poorhouse* (New York: Basic Books, 1986), 208.
17. James T. Patterson, *The New Deal and the States: Federalism in Transition* (Princeton, N.J.: Princeton University Press, 1969), 4, 7.
18. Allan Nevins and Henry Steele Commager, *A Pocket History of the United States* (New York: Washington Square Press, 1981), 346.
19. Advisory Commission on Intergovernmental Relations, *The Question of State Government Capability* (Washington, D.C.: Advisory Commission

on Intergovernmental Relations, January 1985).

20. Martha Derthick, "American Federalism: Madison's 'Middle Ground' in the 1980s," *Public Administration Review* 47 (January/February 1987): 72.

21. Denis P. Doyle and Terry W. Hartle, *Excellence in Education: The States Take Charge* (Washington, D.C.: American Enterprise Institute for Public Policy Research, 1985), 1.

    Governors have taken a leadership role in the field of public education. Please see National Governors' Association, *Time for Results: The Governors' 1991 Report on Education* (Washington, D.C.: National Governors' Association, August 1986), 7. Governor of Tennessee Lamar Alexander, at the time chairman of the National Governors' Association, said, "The Governors are ready to provide the leadership needed to get results on the hard issues that confront the better schools movement. We are ready to lead the second wave of reform of American public education."

22. U.S. General Accounting Office, Report to the Chairman, *Work and Welfare: Current AFDC Work Programs and Implications for Federal Policy* (Washington, D.C.: Government Printing Office, January 1987).

23. *New State Ice Co. v. Ernest A. Liebmann* (285 U.S. 262-311), *United States Supreme Court Reports* 76 L. Ed., (1931), 771.

24. Jack L. Walker, "The Diffusion of Innovation among the American States," *American Political Science Review* 63 (1969): 880-899. Walker's analysis is for the period 1870-1969.

    See also: Virginia Gray, "Innovation in the States: A Diffusion Study," *American Political Science Review* 67 (1973): 1174-1185.

25. Geoffrey Brennan and James M. Buchanan, *The Power to Tax Analytical Foundations of a Fiscal Constitution* (Cambridge, England: Cambridge University, 1980), 16, 174.

26. Reagan and Sanzone, *The New Federalism*, 75.

27. Richard P. Nathan and Fred C. Doolittle, *Reagan and the States* (Princeton, N.J.: Princeton University Press, 1987), Chapter 2.

28. Roscoe C. Martin, *The Cities and the Federal System* (New York: Atherton Press, 1955), 171.

29. *City of Clinton v. Cedar Rapids and Missouri RR Co.*, 24 Iowa 475 (1868) as quoted in James A. Maxwell and J. Richard Aronson, *Financing State and Local Governments* (Washington, D.C.: The Brookings Institution, 1977), 11.

30. Martha Derthick, "Preserving Federalism: Congress, the States, and the Supreme Court," *The Brookings Review* (Winter/Spring 1986).

31. *United States Supreme Court Reports* 89 L. Ed. 2d., no. 9, March 22, 1985, 1032.

32. *United States Supreme Court Reports*, 1040.

33. *United States Supreme Court Reports*, 1052-1053.

34. For a discussion of this position, see David B. Walker, *Towards a Functioning Federalism* (Cambridge, Mass.: Winthrop Publishers, 1981).

35. This speech was delivered to the Executive Club of Chicago on September 26, 1975. For a discussion of the speech and the controversy it engendered,

see Lou Cannon, *Reagan* (New York: G. P. Putnam and Sons, 1982), 201-209. The quotation is from Cannon, 203.

36. Richard S. Williamson, "Reagan Federalism: Goals and Achievements," in *Administering the New Federalism,* ed. Lewis G. Bender and James A. Stever (Boulder, Colo.: Westview Press, 1986), 41-73.
37. Nathan and Doolittle, *Reagan and the States.*
38. Jerry Hagstrom, "Liberal and Minority Coalitions Pleading Their Cases in State Capitals," *National Journal,* February 23, 1985, 426.
39. Steven D. Gold, "Developments in State Finances, 1983 to 1986," *Public Budgeting and Finance* 7 (Spring 1987): 15.

3. FROM GOVERNOR TO GOVERNORS

Thad L. Beyle

Since the 1960s, state government and politics have been in a constant state of change. Reform has been most apparent in the governorships of the fifty states. Individually, governors have been strengthened; as a group, they have solidified their position as a leader within the federal system.

This change in the governorships has had ramifications in other areas of the states' political and governmental policy systems. Conflicts have grown between the governors and certain actors in the executive branches, as well as stronger state legislatures. The state supreme courts have become a part of the political process, often serving as the umpires in many of these conflicts.

Making the governorship stronger has made it a more attractive position. So, the type of politics used in seeking these offices has changed, as have the types of people who run for them. Dollar and consultant politics have replaced party leader and factional politics in many of the states.

Interestingly, with these political changes in the governorship came a change in the presidential recruitment process. In the last four presidential elections, at least one of the major party candidates for president had served as governor. In the past twelve years, two former governors became president.

The governors have also sought to play a more significant role in national policy debates by joining together for common objectives. Governors have moved from the defensive to the aggressive mode in recent years. Recent trends in the federal system have placed the states in key positions to act on many domestic policy concerns. As policy activism moves away from the federal level, the governors jointly stand ready to assist each other and the nation.

Before analyzing the modern governorship, two basic cycles that have a considerable impact on the states in the federal system, and on the governors within their states and in the federal system, need to be understood. The first is the cycle of values undergirding the development of American government—representativeness, neutral competence, and executive leadership. The second is the cycle of leadership, which oscillates between the state and national levels—the shifting locus of activism with the federal system to provide government services.

Tensions between the values of representativeness, neutral competence, and executive leadership affect governors within their own state governmental systems. Shifting policy activism affects the governors within the federal system as responsibilities for various governmental services are transferred, in subtle and not so subtle ways, from the states to the national government and, more recently, back to the states. These two cycles provide the setting in which states and their governors function.

Governors as Chief Executive Officers

The office of governor has developed significantly since the establishment of colonial governments in America. After an initial period of imposed executive dominance, the new state constitutions promoted the value of representation. Legislatures reigned supreme, with governors often serving as mere figureheads. By 1800, the situation began to change as the power and prestige of governors gradually increased. However, the direct election of a number of state administrative officers was an important legacy of the pursuit of representativeness.

Following the Civil War, and in reaction to the excesses of the pursuit of representativeness, the value of neutral competence gained in stature. The goal was to remove favoritism and patronage from government, substituting neutrality or the concept of "not who you know, but what you know." This movement fostered the establishment of independent boards and commissions that diluted gubernatorial power. During this period, the drive for a civil service or merit system was launched. Thus, the goal of attaining neutral competence in government was added to the goal of ensuring representativeness. Thousands of state merit service employees were insulated from the winds of politics, but also from management by the governor.

In the twentieth century, the need for strong executive leadership emerged. New Jersey governor Woodrow Wilson championed the cause, along with several other strong governors early in the century—Charles Evans Hughes in New York, Robert La Follette in Wisconsin, Hiram Johnson in California, and Frank Lowden in Illinois.

The stature of governors has increased greatly across the states and in the federal system over the last few decades. This is due to historical reforms, the type of individuals holding office, the actions taken under their direction, and an increased capacity in the office. Governors are now compared with private-sector corporate leaders—public-sector, state-level chief executive officers (CEOs). Expectations for gubernatorial performance have increased, perhaps beyond realistic levels.

Enhanced Capacity

Governors are responsible for running large enterprises that are similar in scope to Fortune 500 companies. For example, when the general revenues of the states are compared with the sales of the nation's largest companies, sixteen states rank with the top fifty corporations. Thirty states have revenues equal to or greater than the sales of the top one hundred companies in the Fortune 500 listing.[1]

The magnitude of the dollar decisions made by California and New York governors and legislators is comparable to those made by executives at Mobil Oil and General Electric, the fifth and sixth largest companies; those by Texas and Pennsylvania governmental leaders are comparable to management at Amoco and United Technologies, the fourteenth and fifteenth largest companies; those by New Jersey elected leaders are comparable to executives in BNP America and USX, the twenty-second and twenty-third largest companies; and those by Minnesota, Georgia, and Washington governors are comparable to the management at Hewlett-Packard and Johnson & Johnson, the forty-ninth and fiftieth largest companies.

Do the governors have adequate executive tools to manage such large enterprises? Are they as prepared to be the CEOs of their states as their private-sector counterparts are? Do the offices of the governors have the necessary capacity to assist the governors in managing their enterprises in state government?[2] Certainly, progress has been made. Over the past twenty-five years, there has been no shortage of reforms throughout the states. The agenda for these reforms was drawn from changes seen at the national level on behalf of the presidency and a series of reports calling for reform in state governments.[3]

The general goals of government reforms have been to enhance gubernatorial and legislative abilities to lead the states in more progressive directions. In 1967, former governor Terry Sanford of North Carolina called upon the states "to make the chief executive of the state the chief executive in fact"; and a decade later political scientist Larry Sabato declared that executive branch reforms had made governors "truly the masters" of state government.[4]

One common reform is longer terms of office. Since 1955, the number of governors eligible for four-year instead of two-year terms has increased from twenty-nine to forty-seven. This change allows governors to spend more time on policy and administrative concerns and less on reelection campaigns.[5] Only New Hampshire, Rhode Island, and Vermont still restrict their governors to a two-year term.

Another reform increased opportunities for succession. Since 1955 the number of governors precluded from succeeding themselves for a second term has declined from seventeen to three—Kentucky, New Mexico, and Virginia. Meanwhile, those states allowing a governor to serve two consecutive terms has increased from six to twenty-four. In 1988, twenty-two states had no constitutional limits on the number of terms a governor could serve. These changes potentially allow a governor a longer time to spend on policy and administrative concerns, if the voters decide to return the governor to office for another term. They also allow the voters to retain a governor who is doing a good job.[6]

Yet another reform shortens the ballot. In 1956 there were 709 separately elected state level officials, beside the governor, heading 385 state agencies. In 1988, there were 514 separately elected officials, other than the governor, heading 293 state agencies. This change gave the governor a broader policy and administrative reach, and it gave the citizens what they thought they were voting for: a governor who is more in charge of the executive branch of state government. However, the numbers indicate more modifications are needed in the states to reduce the still large number of separately elected officials.

Finally, there is the veto. Between 1956 and 1988 the number of governors who could veto all legislation rose from forty-seven to forty-nine. Only the governor of North Carolina lacks the veto power, but that may be changed soon. The number of governors with an item veto rose from thirty-nine to forty-three; and ten governors now have the power to cut individual appropriations items.[7]

Governors' offices have expanded rapidly over the past decades. In 1956, Coleman Ransone reported governors' offices averaging 11 staff members, with a range from 3 to 43 among the states.[8] In 1976, the National Governors' Association (NGA) found an average of 29 staff members, with a much broader range from 7 to 245.[9] The most recent survey in 1988 indicated there were slightly more than 48 staff members per governor's office, with a range from 8 in Wyoming to 178 in Texas and 216 in New York.[10] Thus, over this thirty-two year period, the average number of gubernatorial staff members grew fourfold. More staff means more flexibility and support for the governor in the many roles to be fulfilled. Growth also creates more patronage positions and a greater chance for confusion.

The configurations of gubernatorial staffs can be classified from the very personal to the very institutional. Their makeup correlates

closely with the size of the state. Larger states have larger and more institutionalized offices and processes, with adequate and specialized staff
resources to assist the governor. Smaller states have smaller and more
personalized offices, often lacking the breadth and depth possessed by
the larger offices. In these smaller offices, the governor must rely on the
same people to cover the necessary responsibilities—and more. In
between are the growing midsize states, in which the governors may
feel the need for an institutionalized office but often have only small,
personalized staffing structures and processes.[11]

The budget process is critical; it is an expression of gubernatorial
authority. A chief executive must be able to control the development
and execution of the organization's budget. Only the governors of South
Carolina and Texas lack the power to develop an executive budget for
submission to the legislature; they must share that responsibility with a
joint legislative-administrative committee.[12] Mississippi's governor obtained this power through legislation passed in 1984; North Carolina's
governor achieved this responsibility via a 1982 state supreme court
decision based on the separation-of-powers clause in the state constitution.

Governors have consolidated their power over the budget process
by placing state budget offices under their direct control. With that, the
budgetary process has often changed from an earlier preoccupation
"with the custodial functions of auditing and accounting to undertaking
new and conceptually rich systems of management decision making." [13]
The budget and the budgetary process are still methods of financial
control used by the governors. But, as the budget process is opened up
to include planning and policy analysis approaches, the management
capability of governors is greatly enhanced, and the budget can more
nearly approximate being "the ultimate statement of any government's
(and governor's) policy choices." [14]

The policy-planning process is also critical. Initially seen as part
of the economic development function of state government and located
in those departments, state planning agencies have been migrating
closer to the governor. In 1960, only three of the thirty-seven state
planning agencies were located in the governor's office and two others
were housed in departments of administration or finance. By 1971, all
fifty states had state planning agencies. Twenty-nine were in the
governor's office and seven were in departments of administration or
finance.[15]

Since the 1970s, many of these planning offices have become
policy-planning offices and took on a broader set of activities and
responsibilities. All but five states now have such offices to assist the
governor. In forty of the states, these offices are located either in the

governor's office or with the budget office in the department of administration or finance. The stronger the governorship, the more likely the policy-planning agency is to stand free of the budget agency and process. This suggests that these agencies are closely tied to the governor and the governor's position within the state governmental system.[16]

What do these offices accomplish? A 1985 Council of State Planning Agencies survey indicates they have two major responsibilities that vary in emphasis from state to state. The first is policy development: policy analysis and new initiatives (thirty-four states), briefing the governor on policy concerns (twenty-eight states), assisting on major gubernatorial initiatives (fifteen states), and impact analysis (seven states). The second is administrative: coordinating and providing service to the governor's cabinet and subcabinet councils (seventeen states) and to interagency commissions, task forces, and working groups (twenty-four states), and programmatic responsibilities in specific functional areas (sixteen states) and in the regulatory areas of state government (ten states). Policy-planning offices increase the possibility that factors other than protective agency perspectives and purely budgetary or political concerns will be brought to bear in the policy process.

The ability to reorganize government is important to the governor. In the 1960s, many reformers argued that the residue of past trends and decisions had left state governments unmanageable and unresponsive to gubernatorial direction. However, since 1965 the executive branches of nearly two dozen state governments have undergone comprehensive reorganization, and nearly all states have engaged in partial reorganizations. In comprehensive reorganizations, the executive branch is consolidated to varying degrees under the control of the governor. Most partial reorganizations consolidate many specific programs and agencies working in the same functional area under one departmental roof. Such reforms have been most prevalent in environmental protection, transportation, and human services.[17]

In 1956, governors in only two states had the power to initiate state government reorganization by executive order subject to legislative confirmation; by 1988, twenty-four governors had this power. Reorganization enables a governor to reshape the executive branch for a variety of reasons, which include providing a clearer focus on particular problems and delivering governmental services efficiently.

Clearly, additional steps can be taken to allow governors to make state government more focused and responsive. Several states still need comprehensive reorganization, fewer separately elected officials, and governors able to initiate reorganization subject to confirmation by the legislature.

Table 3-1 Selection Methods for Selected State Administrative
          Officials, 1986

	Separately elected		Appointed by governor		Appointed, not by governor	
	Number	Percent	Number	Percent	Number	Percent
Average	6	14.5	18.5	44.5	17	41
High	11 (North Dakota)	29.7 (North Dakota)	32 (Virginia)	82.1 (New York)	28 (Oregon)	65 (South Carolina)
Low	1 (Maine, New Hampshire, and New Jersey)	2.4 (New Jersey)	5 (South Carolina)	12.5 (South Carolina)	1 (New York)	3.6 (New York)

SOURCE: Washington Research Council, *The Power to Govern: The Reorganization of Washington State Government* (Olympia: Washington Research Council, February 1987), 5.
NOTE: All fifty states were included in the study.

Appointing and Removing Personnel

Chief executive officers, whether in the private or public sector, must be free to chose those who will serve in their administration. The power of appointment is a dual power, for it also includes the power to remove.

Many governors are constrained by the number and types of positions to which they can make appointments, as indicated in Table 3-1. The table excludes one set of positions that governors have little or no appointment powers over—statewide elected boards and commissions. It, however, does include between twenty-eight and forty-seven of the major offices in the states as contained in *The Book of the States, 1986-87.*[18] The number of offices among the states varies because some offices fulfill several different functions.

First, as already noted, the governors cannot appoint any of the 203 members of the forty-three separately elected boards and commissions in twenty-eight states. These boards are charged with responsibilities in public education (twelve states), public utilities (nine states), higher education (five states), and various regulatory activities.

Second, governors cannot appoint separately elected officials to another office, unless they fill a vacancy created by death or resignation.

These officials have their own constitutional base of authority and their own constituency of supporters. On average, there are six statewide elected officials per state that are elected separately, including the governor, or an average of 14 percent of statewide offices involved. The range is from only one statewide elected official—the governor in Maine, New Hampshire, and New Jersey—to ten in Mississippi and North Carolina, and eleven in North Dakota.

Third, governors cannot appoint officials who by the constitution are to be appointed by some other officer or by the legislature. On average, seventeen such appointments are made per state, or 41 percent of the offices involved. The range is from a low of one in New York to a high of twenty-eight in Oregon.

Some argue that this constraint is less than it seems, as the officials making the appointments are the governor's own appointees. Thus, there is a two-step appointment process. This may be true in some states, but in Texas, for example, boards and commissions in effect run most of state government. The governor appoints members of Texas's boards and commissions. But, because of the staggered terms of the members, a governor may be well into a second term before gaining some control, and then only indirectly through the newly appointed members.[19]

The data presented in Table 3-1 thus indicate that the governors may appoint between eighteen and nineteen state administrative officials on average, or 45 percent of the offices involved. South Carolina's governor has the fewest to appoint with five, Virginia's the most with thirty-two.

There are also practical, political restrictions on the governors appointment powers:[20]

The sheer number of appointments governors must make can be so overwhelming that governors fail to focus sufficiently on the key appointments. Replacing too many people angers those being replaced and can draw the governor's presence too deeply into the bureaucracy for any policy or administrative benefits.

Patronage appointments serve as rewards, but many individuals and groups feel they should be rewarded. They evaluate appointments with a very jealous eye, and jealousy is not a positive basis on which to build a working relationship.

The governor and those interested in a position often have conflicting expectations that can lead to struggles within the governor's coalition.

Table 3-2   A Comparative Index of Governors' Appointment Power,
1960-1986

	1960	1968	1980	1986
Appointment power[a]				
Very strong	17	11	19	18
Strong	9	6	6	9
Moderate	7	9	10	9
Weak	6	7	6	6
Very weak	11	17	9	8
Average power[b]	45.2	41.8	46.0	46.9

SOURCES: Data developed from The Council of State Governments, *The Book of the States* for the years involved; Joseph A. Schlesinger, "The Politics of the Executives," in *Politics in the American States,* ed. Herbert Jacob and Kenneth N. Vines (Boston: Little, Brown, 1971), 210-237; and Thad L. Beyle, "Governors," in *Politics in the American States,* 4th ed., ed. Virginia Gray, Herbert Jacobs, and Kenneth N. Vines (Boston: Little, Brown, 1983), 201-203, 458-459.

NOTE: All fifty states were included in the study.

[a] Figures represent the number of states.

[b] Based on scores ranging from 0 to 75.

The governor's power of appointment did not change dramatically from 1960 to 1986 (see Table 3-2). In 1986 Carol Weissert issued an examination that was based on fifteen offices—those for which data are available from three other studies, two by Joseph A. Schlesinger in 1960 and 1968 and one by myself in 1980.[21] Those officials were administration and finance, agriculture, attorney general, auditor, budget, conservation, education, health, highways, insurance, labor, secretary of state, tax commissioner, treasurer, and welfare. As indicated in Table 3-2, the governors' average power of appointment increased slightly, from 45.2 to 46.9. The number of governors with strong or very strong appointment powers increased from twenty-six to only twenty-seven; those with weak or very weak powers decreased from seventeen to fourteen.

The opposite side of the power of appointment is the power of removal. When positions are filled, then some officeholders must be removed. If changes in policy are needed, people often must be replaced with those who will carry out the proposed reforms.

Only twenty-three state constitutions have provided their governors with the power to remove individuals from positions in the state executive branch, and all but six put varying degrees of restrictions on this power. The governor of Indiana has unrestricted power of removal under a state court decision, while the governor of Georgia is greatly restrained by a state court decision. This power is contained in the original constitutions of five states. Eleven of the fourteen states that revised their constitutions after 1945 included this power for the governor. Only the constitutions of Connecticut (1965), North Carolina (1971), and Georgia (1982) did not. As the original constitutions of the states are being revised, the power of removal is being built in. Other states provide statutory removal powers for their governors.

Governors do experience problems exercising this power. Thus, "even when a governor can remove an official, he is constrained by the wrangle which would result." [22] It is a power, therefore, that tends to be used only as a last resort. Moreover, a series of federal court decisions have placed potentially severe restrictions on the removal power. In a 1976 case, *Elrod v. Burns,* the U.S. Supreme Court decided (5 to 4) that patronage firing violates an individual's political liberties under the First Amendment. The decision points out that "political belief and association constitute the core of those activities protected by the First Amendment of the U.S. Constitution." [23]

This strict standard was relaxed in subsequent decisions. In a 1980 case, *Branti v. Finkel,* the Supreme Court reaffirmed its 1976 decision (6 to 3) but also ruled that "If the employee's private political beliefs would interfere with the discharge of his public duties, the First Amendment rights may be required to yield to the state's vital interest in maintaining governmental effectiveness and efficiency." The burden of proof would be on the employer.[24] In a 1983 case, *Connick v. Myers,* the Supreme Court decided (5 to 4) to add another restriction on the employee's right by holding "that the First Amendment does not protect from dismissal public employees who complain about their working conditions or their supervisor." [25] In these cases, the Court indicated a balance test between an individual's rights and the administration's needs. It was the Court's rule to weigh the needs.

None of the above U.S. Supreme Court cases involved governors, but they are aware of the problems these decisions may cause for them. At the 1982 "New Governors' Seminar" governors were cautioned:[26]

> Know the *Elrod v. Burns* case, the 1976, five-to-four Supreme Court decision regarding the firing of personnel. You cannot fire for a political reason, and you are personally liable. It even destroys the privacy privilege of counsel.

> The *Elrod v. Burns* decision requires an indemnification statute, and be sure that it covers the unpaid boards and commissions as well as the full-time state officials.

In late 1988, a case involving a governor, *Scott v. Martin,* was pending in the federal district court in Raleigh, N.C. It directly addresses the question of a governor's right to remove individuals from their positions during a gubernatorial transition and replace them with the governor's own appointees. The plaintiffs—three Democrats who were removed from state government positions by appointees of Republican governor James Martin—are citing the First Amendment precedents of the earlier cases as the basis of their suit. This case may be significant for all governors, at least it is so viewed by the presiding federal district court judge and the litigants. Politically, there is an ironic twist: the Republican governor being sued by the three ousted Democrats is being defended by the separately elected Democratic attorney general.

Gubernatorial Powers

Political scientists often have attempted to compare the powers of the fifty state governorships.[27] Research results are presented in a series of comparative indicies and analyses, which are in turn followed by critiques of the indicies and rejoinders to these critiques. The first such comparative gubernatorial power index was published by Joseph A. Schlesinger in 1965; it has served as the foundation of subsequent academic efforts.[28]

A question persists as to whether these academic pursuits and countersuits have any meaning in the real world of the governors. There may not be an answer to this question, but in 1987 the Office of State Services of the National Governors' Association issued a *State Management Note* in which the same questions pertaining to the comparative institutional powers of the governors were addressed.

NGA concluded that "the framework in which a Governor performs his or her job can be an important factor in a successful governorship." NGA noted the indices were used only as a suggestion of the framework and that some "governors have proven to be vital and strong leaders in many areas despite institutional shortcomings that may hamper their success," while other governors "have failed to provide strong leadership to their states even where formal provisions indicate an authoritative office." [29]

The NGA analysis included six items: the governor's tenure potential, appointive powers, budget-making power, veto power, political strength in the legislature, and the legislature's ability to change budgets. The first three indicies primarily concern the governor's power within the executive branch, while the second three concern the governor's power vis-à-vis the legislature.[30]

The powers of governors have grown over the past two decades (see Table 3-3). A considerable differential in the growth in these powers has occurred, although the overall growth was not great (.4

Table 3-3 The Institutionalized Powers of the Governorship, 1965-1985

Power	Range of scores possible	1965 average	1985 average	Change in scores	Percentage change in scores
Tenure potential	1-5	3.3	4.1	+.8	24
Appointment	0-7	3.6	4.0	+.4	11
Budget making	0-5	4.3	4.6	+.3	7
Legislative budget-changing authority	1-5	1.3	1.2	−.1	8
Veto	0-5	4.2	3.6	−.6	14
Party control	1-5	3.8	3.4	−.4	11
Overall scores	3-32	20.7	21.1	+.4	1.9

SOURCE: Office of State Services, "The Institutional Powers of the Governorship: 1965-1985," *State Management Notes* (Washington, D.C.: National Governors' Association, June 1987).

points or 1.9 percent). Those powers primarily aimed at gubernatorial performance in the executive branch have increased—tenure (24 percent), appointment (11 percent), and budget making (7 percent). However, those powers aimed at gubernatorial-legislative relations have decreased—veto (14 percent), party control (11 percent), and legislative budget-changing authority (8 percent).

These findings demonstrate what many have suggested: reforms have been made on both sides of the separation-of-powers relationship, and while governors may have more institutionalized powers at their disposal, state legislatures have powers that often are used at the expense of the executive.

How has the power of governors in individual states fared from 1965 to 1985? Fifteen states remained in the same power categories between the two years,[31] two states moved up three categories,[32] two others moved up two categories,[33] and fifteen advanced by one category.[34] Moving downward in power by two categories were four states,[35] while twelve states dropped one category.[36] Governorships in the midwest gained the most power (12 percent), followed by those states that had less than 40 percent of their population in metropolitan areas (11.7 percent). The Pacific West states lost the most power (13.6 percent). Other states gaining more than 10 percent above the average gain across all fifty states were those in which the per capita income was between $12,000 and $13,500, up 5.7 percent; New England states, up 5.1 percent; and states in which the Republican party is the majority party, up 5.1 percent.

The only variable that appears to be directly related to changes in institutional power is the percentage of the state's population living in metropolitan areas. The lower the percentage, the greater the change. However, those states with more people living in metropolitan areas already had provided their governors with more institutionalized powers by 1965, which indicates that the more rural states played catch-up over the period in making their governors more powerful.

Gubernatorial Conflict with Other State Government Actors

Political reforms do not always achieve their intended purposes. Some create unanticipated consequences that then generate additional reforms; others create conflict with previous reforms. And politics may render some reforms unworkable.

Conflicts within the Executive Branch

Governors often face their greatest conflicts within the executive branch. Several governors have had serious problems with their lieutenant governors concerning the extent of the lieutenant governor's power while the governor is out of state. Specific issues have arisen over calling special legislative sessions, appointments to administrative and judicial positions, pardons, the governor's salary, and control of the national guard. Other problems come about when the governor and lieutenant governor are of different parties or of different factions within the same party; or when the lieutenant governor has constitutional leadership responsibilities in the legislature that provide a separate power base.

Governors also have found themselves at odds with the state's attorney general when legal issues take on a political cast. An attorney general may challenge a gubernatorial action in court on constitutional grounds. Who is to serve as the governor's legal adviser in a legal battle when the attorney general is not on the governor's side? Who is to lead the prosecution of a governor for wrongdoing? This problem arose during Arizona's recent impeachment of Gov. Evan Mecham.

Finally, many governors must face other statewide elected officials who intend to seek the governorship, some even to challenge the incumbent for reelection. In such a milieu, conflict instead of cooperation is often the rule.

Conflicts with Other Branches of Government

With the concept of "separation of powers" built into most state constitutions and the American constitutional system, conflict between the executive and legislative branches is inevitable. Conflicts may occur over setting state government policy, raising and spending money, administering policy, appointing officials to executive and judicial positions, controlling the legislative process, and calling special sessions.

Clearly, gubernatorial-legislative tensions are greatest in most states at budget time, when the money and policy decisions must be made. It is the "governor's budget," but the legislature has to pass it; and it must be balanced. The governor then "executes" the budget, which leads to a second area of conflict—the legislative interest in how its actions are administered.

Legislatures have tried several ways to make sure "legislative intent" is followed. Governors often read these efforts as legislative intrusion into executive branch responsibilities. For example, some executive branch positions are appointments that must be confirmed by the legislature. This is clearly within constitutional bounds. However, in some states, legislatures have either constitutional or statutory authority to make appointments. In certain cases, they can even appoint legislators to boards, commissions, or councils in the executive branch. If these boards remain in an advisory role, problems may be reduced.

However, if they exercise management responsibilities, as twenty states allow, charges of "legislative intrusion" may be lodged and challenged in state courts as a violation of separation of powers.[37]

Another area of conflict concerns vetoes, both gubernatorial and legislative. In 1947, governors vetoed about 5 percent of the bills presented to them; the bills were overridden by a legislative vote in only 1.8 percent of the cases.[38] In 1977-1978, 5.2 percent of the legislation was vetoed by governors; 8.6 percent were overridden. While the frequency of gubernatorial vetoes remained roughly the same, legislative overrides jumped fivefold.[39] As the ability of governors to use the item and amendatory vetoes grows, conflicts between the two branches escalate. A governor can check special policy provisions in budget bills that have not run the full course of legislative review, thereby forcing the legislature to consider the issues in open debate.[40]

State legislatures have turned to the legislative veto—a procedure permitting them "to review proposed executive regulations or actions and to block or modify those with which they disagree." [41] The legislative veto became increasingly popular over the past decade, with forty-one states adopting it by mid-1982. However, both the federal and state courts have called it an unconstitutional violation of the separation of powers.[42] Voters in Alaska, New Jersey, and Michigan recently rejected giving this power to the legislature.

Gubernatorial-legislative tensions also are exacerbated by political facts of life. After the 1986 elections, twenty-nine states had a "power split"—one party controlling the governorship, the other controlling one or both houses of the legislature.[43]

Conflicts between the executive and legislative branches of state governments have caused the state courts to become more active as they are called upon in law suits to sort out which of the other two branches is correct. They usually decide in favor of the governor and the executive branch, citing the separation of powers clause in the state's constitution.[44] However, they sometimes rule against the executive when separation of powers is not at question, as in policy and civil rights issues.

Governors and judges often are at odds over specific decisions, such as the death penalty or the selection and appointment of judges. In 1986, there were three states with highly contested, negative, policy-related contests for the chief justiceship of the state's supreme court. In all of these races—California, North Carolina, and Ohio—the incumbent governors were actively involved in judicial politics.

As governors seek to carry out their responsibilities conflicts arise—conflicts that are built into the very charters of state government and exacerbated by political and policy differences.

Governors and Elections

Political reformers have long sought to separate the very intrusive presidential election campaigns from the contests for state level office. This has been especially important for those political actors, mainly Democrats of late, who see the fortunes of their state politics, state parties, and party candidates hurt by popular presidential candidates of the opposite party. A more substantial argument for separating national and state elections lies in the attempt to ensure that state level issues and candidates' positions on those issues do not have to compete with the noise and excitement of the national presidential campaign.

In 1960, twenty-six states held gubernatorial elections while U.S. senator John F. Kennedy defeated Vice President Richard Nixon for the presidency. Sixteen of these states restricted their governors to two-year terms. In 1988, only twelve states held their gubernatorial elections during the presidential year, and three of them—New Hampshire, Rhode Island, and Vermont—by limiting their governors to two-year terms, alternate between holding their elections in presidential and nonpresidential years. Five other states hold their elections in odd-numbered years—New Jersey and Virginia had gubernatorial races in 1985 and Kentucky, Louisiana, and Mississippi in 1987.

Since 1960, thirteen states have moved from a two-year to a four-year gubernatorial term. Of these states, only North Dakota opted to hold its elections in conjunction with presidential elections. Florida and Illinois shifted their four-year-term elections from the presidential year to an "off year," and others are considering a similar move. These changes have created a certain rhythm to American politics, with presidential elections dominating in one even-numbered year, and the gubernatorial elections, along with the congressional races, dominating in the next.

The Costs of Running

Campaign funding questions are occupying more of the governors' attention.[45] Those seeking the office of governor must address the expense of campaigning and how they will raise enough money. In most cases, the decision whether to run or not is directly tied to the potential candidate's ability to raise the necessary funds.

Given changes in campaign methods over the past two decades—including polling, the use of television and radio, campaign management consultants, and direct mail—politics in the states has been transformed from a contest between parties to a contest for money. How much change has there been in the cost of running for governor? Campaign finance reforms and disclosure provisions of the 1970s provide a clear picture of the cost of elections. (All figures presented in this section are expressed in constant 1987 dollars to adjust for inflation.[46]) The cost of campaigns in Virginia were up 731 percent between the 1965 and 1985 elections; Oregon, up 708 percent between the 1966 and 1986 elections; Ohio, up 356 percent between the 1974 and 1982 elections; Massachusetts, up 311 percent between the 1966 and 1982 elections; California, up 268 percent between the 1958 and 1982 elections; New Jersey, up 224 percent between the 1965 and 1985 elections; and New York, up 147 percent between the 1966 and 1982 elections.

Considerable sums of money are involved in electing governors. As is indicated in Table 3-4, the average gubernatorial contest cost $6.3 million between 1977 and 1987. As officially reported, in 1977-1987 nearly $775 million actual dollars and $941 million normalized 1987 dollars were spent in 149 separate contests.

There is a major caveat, however. "As officially reported" figures are an unknown percentage of the actual monies raised and spent on behalf of the candidates. These are figures that "must be reported" by law. Not accountable are contributions of free telephones and the use of corporate and labor quarters and supplies, which are donations that can hardly be traced but certainly represent important campaign resources.

In addition, the figures are skewed upward because of sixteen very expensive gubernatorial races that cost more than $15 million each (see Table 3-5). Eleven of these races were for open seats, two led to the defeat of an incumbent governor, and three saw an incumbent governor reelected. These sixteen elections alone accounted for $346.6 million or 36.8 percent of the officially reported monies spent for all 149 gubernatorial races from 1977 to 1987. Removing these sixteen races from the totals leaves the remaining 133 gubernatorial elections averaging $4.5 million each; the top sixteen averaged $21.7 million.

California consistently has expensive elections. The last three elections averaged $24.7 million, with the successful 1986 reelection bid of George Deukmejian being the least expensive. The Texas story is of rapidly escalating costs; the 1982 governor's race was 35.4 percent greater than in 1978, and the 1986 race was 30 percent greater than the 1982 race—a growth of 81 percent over the eight-year period.

Two other southern states have moved into the high dollar stakes of gubernatorial politics. Kentucky's two most recent elections for the one-term governorship are among the most expensive. In Tennessee, Lamar Alexander won a $11.5 million race in 1978. After his two terms, the 1986 race to succeed him cost 33 percent more than the 1978 race.

Table 3-4   Total Cost of Gubernatorial Elections, 1977-1987

Year	Number of races	Total campaign costs in actual dollars (in thousands)	Total campaign costs in constant 1987 dollars[a] (in thousands)	Average cost per election in constant 1987 dollars[a] (in thousands)
1977	2	9,118	16,458	8,474
1978	36	99,733	169,903	4,720
1979	3	32,744	49,239	16,413
1980	13	35,551	47,528	3,656
1981	2	19,996	24,535	12,267
1982	36	181,743	214,826	5,967
1983	3	39,954	45,506	15,169
1984	13	46,830	51,349	3,950
1985	2	18,142	19,157	9,579
1986	36	254,136	265,278	7,369
1987	3	37,194	37,194	12,398
Total	149	775,141	941,463	5,202/6,319[b]

SOURCES: The Council of State Governments, *The Book of the States, 1986-87* (Lexington, Ky.: Council of State Governments, 1986), 25, and *The Book of the States, 1988-89* (1988), 25; Rhodes Cook and Stacy West, "1978 Gubernatorial Contests: Incumbents, Winners Hold Money Advantage," *Congressional Quarterly Weekly Report,* August 25, 1979, 1757-1758; Thad L. Beyle, "The Cost of Becoming Governor," *State Government* 56 (1983): 74-84; Public Affairs Research Council of Louisiana, "Financing the 1983 Gubernatorial Campaign in Louisiana," *PAR Analysis* No. 171 (March 1984), and "Campaign Finances in the 1987 Governor's Race," *PAR Analysis* No. 284 (May 1988); and Malcolm E. Jewell of the University of Kentucky.

[a] The constant 1987 dollar figures were ascertained by dividing the actual dollar expenditures for the election year by the percent value that year's dollar was of the December 1987 dollar. The normalizing divisors by year were: 1987, 100; 1986, .958; 1985, .947; 1984, .912; 1983, .878; and 1982, .846. These divisors were derived from the Bureau of Labor Statistics, *Consumer Price Index, Detailed Report* (Washington, D.C.: Government Printing Office, February 1988), 9.

[b] First number is based on actual dollars; second is based on constant 1987 dollars.

On the reverse side are the states that still have relatively inexpensive races. For example, the 1982 elections in South Carolina, South Dakota, and Wyoming each cost less than a million dollars—but in each case an incumbent successfully won reelection, a situation generally associated with a less expensive race. In 1986, the same was true for the reelection of the governors of Georgia and Vermont.

The experience in two other states dramatically demonstrates the effect of incumbency on election costs. In New York, Gov. Mario Cuomo was reelected in 1986 in a race costing only $7.6 million compared with the 1982 race for an open seat costing $27.9 million.

Table 3-5   The Sixteen Most Expensive Gubernatorial Races,
1977-1987

Year	State	Amount spent (in millions)	Seat
1978	California	$23.0	open
	New York	19.2	incumbent reelected
	Texas	19.1	open
1979	Louisiana	31.0	open
1980	West Virginia	17.0	incumbent reelected
1982	California	27.7	open
	New York	27.8	open
	Texas	26.5	incumbent defeated
1983	Kentucky	18.8	open
1984	North Carolina	15.1	open
1986	California	23.5	incumbent reelected
	Florida	25.1	open
	Pennsylvania	16.9	open
	Tennessee	15.3	open
	Texas	34.6	incumbent defeated
1987	Kentucky	15.4	open

NOTE: Figures are in constant 1987 dollars.

The 1978 Florida election for an open seat, which Bob Graham won, cost $10.2 million; the 1982 election in which Graham was reelected cost $4.8 million. But, the 1986 campaign to fill the seat Graham was vacating due to constitutional constraints cost a record $24 million. The eleven candidates who ran in the 1986 Florida party primaries spent an estimated $15.7 million for their party's nomination alone. Most of the funds spent were for TV advertising.[47]

Some perspective can be offered on how fast the costs of becoming governor have risen by pairing gubernatorial elections at four-year intervals, matching the costs of the gubernatorial campaigns in each of the four-year-term states and the costs of every other election in the two-year-term states (see Table 3-6). The costs of gubernatorial campaigns across the states rose rapidly between the 1977 and 1981 elections (45 percent) and the 1978 and 1982 elections (26 percent). However, beginning with the 1979-1983 elections, overall election costs stabilized, either decreasing as in the 1979-1983 elections (-8 percent) and the 1981-1985 elections (-21.9 percent) or increasing moderately as in the 1980-1984 elections (+8 percent). Costs again rose considerably between the 1982 and 1986 races, only to back off in the 1983-1987 and 1984-1988 elections. The stabilizing of election costs has been noted in campaigns for other offices, such as U.S. Senate and House

Table 3-6   Changes in the Costs of Gubernatorial Elections,
1977-1985

Election Years[a]	First election expenditures (in thousands)	Second election expenditures (in thousands)	Dollar difference (in thousands)	Percentage difference
1977, 1981	$ 16,948	24,535	+7,587	+44.8
1978, 1982	169,903	214,826	+44,923	+26.4
1979, 1983	49,239	45,506	−3,733	−7.6
1980, 1984	47,528	51,349	+3,821	+8.0
1981, 1985	24,535	19,157	−5,378	−21.9
1982, 1986	214,826	265,278	+50,452	+23.5
1983, 1987	45,506	37,194	−8,312	−18.3
1984, 1988	51,349	45,000[b]	−6,349	−12.4

SOURCES: The Council of State Governments, *The Book of the States, 1986-87* (Lexington, Ky.: Council of State Governments, 1986), 25, and *The Book of the States, 1988-89* (1988), 25; Rhodes Cook and Stacy West, "1978 Gubernatorial Contests: Incumbents, Winners Hold Money Advantage," *Congressional Quarterly Weekly Report,* August 25, 1979, 1757-1758; Thad L. Beyle, "The Cost of Becoming Governor," *State Government* 56 (1983): 74-84; Public Affairs Research Council of Louisiana, "Financing the 1983 Gubernatorial Campaign in Louisiana," *PAR Analysis* No. 171 (March 1984), and "Campaign Finances in the 1987 Governor's Race," *PAR Analysis* No. 284 (May 1988); and Malcolm F. Jewell of the University of Kentucky.

NOTE: Figures are in constant 1986 dollars.

[a] Two states held elections in 1977, 1981, and 1985: New Jersey and Virginia; thirty-six states held elections in 1978, 1982, and 1986: Alabama, Alaska, Arizona, Arkansas, California, Colorado, Connecticut, Florida, Georgia, Hawaii, Idaho, Illinois, Iowa, Kansas, Maine, Maryland, Massachusetts, Michigan, Minnesota, Nebraska, Nevada, New Hampshire, New Mexico, New York, Ohio, Oklahoma, Oregon, Pennsylvania, Rhode Island, South Carolina, South Dakota, Tennessee, Texas, Vermont, Wisconsin, and Wyoming; three states held elections in 1979, 1983, and 1987: Kentucky, Louisiana, and Mississippi; thirteen states held elections in 1980 and 1984: Arkansas, Delaware, Indiana, Missouri, Montana, New Hampshire, North Carolina, North Dakota, Rhode Island, Utah, Vermont, Washington, and West Virginia; and twelve states held elections in 1988: all states that held elections in 1980 and 1984 except Arkansas.
[b] Estimate. In 1988, one fewer election was held than in 1984; only three elections were for open seats; and only two candidates ran in North Carolina, the state with the most expensive race in 1984, which fielded eleven candidates.

races at the national level, and state legislative races in several states.[48]

Has the spending of campaign dollars in races for the governorship reached the point of diminishing returns, in which candidates are finding little additional electoral benefit to spending more money? [49] Were the larger increments of growth in spending in the late 1970s and early 1980s tied to rapid diffusion of new campaign technologies across the states? Now that these technologies are in place, will there be any significant increases in the costs of future gubernatorial races?

Studies of gubernatorial campaign expenditures have found that money alone is not the critical factor in an election. Not surprisingly, incumbency and party strength remain important, and the mix of these, along with the amount of money available, varies from election to election and state to state.[50] Elections seeking change, a partisan shift, unseating an incumbent, and hotly contested elections tend to cost more.[51] The weaker the political party in a state, as measured by the selection process for the nominee (a direct primary or the noninvolvement or ineffectual role of party leaders), the more expensive the race.[52] Evidently, the more Republican candidates spend, the greater their vote share can be; for Democratic candidates, however, the same may not be true.[53]

Who Can Run?

Gubernatorial nomination and election processes are so expensive fewer individuals can participate. Those with considerable money or access to it have the advantage. Spending great sums of money does not assure victory, however. Between 1977 and 1987, ten individuals spent more than $10 million on their campaigns; only three lost. But only four of the nine who spent between $7.5 million and $10 million and only four of the thirteen who spent between $5 million and $7.5 million won. In total, of the thirty-two candidates spending more than $5 million, fifteen won.[54]

Who are these candidates? Some are wealthy and willing to spend their own money on their campaigns, such as Jack Eckard (R-Fla., who ran in 1978 and lost), Lewis Lehrman (R-N.Y., who ran in 1982 and lost), John D. "Jay" Rockefeller IV (D-W.Va., who ran in 1982 and won), and Wallace Wilkinson (D-Ky., who ran in 1987 and won). Others are well known statewide as either incumbent governors, former governors, or current holders of statewide offices such as lieutenant governor or attorney general. They are known commodities and can attract financial support easier than the unknowns who must start from scratch out of the legislature, a local government position, or no office at all.

What the Money Buys

"Everyone knows that half the money spent in a political campaign is wasted. The trouble is that nobody knows which half."[55] Money buys the "best" media consultants, the "best" campaign strategies, the "best" pollsters, the "best" direct mail operations. For the not-so-well-known candidate in a party primary, "electronic advertising is the only way to gain visibility."[56] At least two questions need to be asked about how money is now spent in campaigning.

First, does the use of polls make the candidate a prisoner of the printout? Is the candidate discouraged from showing the qualities and direction of leadership a voter could expect when the candidate becomes governor? Polls can be very informative; the worry is when the results are followed slavishly.

Second, in hiring the range of campaign specialists now needed, are the candidates buying a package of what the specialists know from experience elsewhere, without an understanding of the unique aspects of a particular state's electorate, candidates, issues, and history? Do the hired guns bring into the state a realization of the heterogeneity of the states and their politics or do they bring in canned formulas that homogenize state politics?

The Shift of Activism in the Federal System

Campaigning is only the beginning of the governors' money concerns. Over the past decade, activism in the federal system has shifted from the national level to the state and local governments. The state and local governments have been "shocked" by what John Shannon, former director of the Advisory Commission on Intergovernmental Relations, calls the three *R*s: the *revolt* of the taxpayers, as seen in Proposition 13 in California and 2½ in Massachusetts; the *recession* or economic downturn of the early 1980s, which is still being felt in some sections of the country; and the *reduction* in federal grant-in-aid funds, which accelerated under the Reagan administration.[57]

States and local governments have taken steps to pick up part of the slack that these three "shocks" have created; that is, they have been raising additional funds to meet their responsibilities. For local governments, the decline in federal aid has been partially compensated by the increase in state aid, and more than compensated by their own money-raising efforts.

In 1987, for example, governors and legislators made some tough fiscal decisions—fifteen states raised gas taxes, ten states increased the cigarette tax, seven states upped sales tax rates, four states increased income taxes, and four states raised business tax rates. Thirteen were forced to lay off state employees even after raising taxes. Only seven states were able to reduce tax rates.[58] *Washington Post* reporter David Broder estimated that "40 states revamped their tax codes this year [1987] and even more revised their spending priorities to adapt to changing conditions." [59] The 1987 tax increases followed closely upon earlier tax increases. Between 1981 and 1983, twenty-eight states increased personal income taxes and thirty states increased sales taxes. Between 1984 and 1985, nineteen states increased either their income or sales taxes, but thirty-two reduced theirs.[60]

The fiscal trauma in Florida during 1987 illustrates the dilemma facing governors and legislatures. Taxes must be raised, but will a new sales tax on professional services be imposed (as first advocated by Gov. Bob Martinez and adopted by the legislature) or will the general sales tax be increased (as later advocated by Martinez after feeling the heat of aggrieved interest groups)? The governor's proposals for general sales tax increases angered legislators who were loath to enter another tax debate, especially after being led into adopting the controversial professional services tax.

Increasing taxes, even to provide popular and needed services, carries substantial political risk. Several studies have concluded there is a negative electoral effect for the party and, especially, the governor when tax increases are adopted.[61] A recent study of the 407 gubernatorial elections held between 1954 and 1985 indicated that tax increases had a marginal, negative effect on the vote at the next election. Making changes in existing programs has a greater impact than starting new programs. Raising sales taxes has the greatest negative impact, but governors who decrease taxes do not appear to be rewarded.[62]

Regardless of whether voter retribution over tax increases can be proved statistically, most politicians fear it and act accordingly. Fiscal policy making was not difficult in 1988, at least prior to the impact of the drought in the midwest. By March, eleven states had cut back their budgets, fourteen were considering tax increases, and six were thinking of tax reform. Spending was being kept under control and tax revenues were growing because of economic growth and tax decisions made in previous years. As the executive director of the National Governors' Association, Ray Scheppach, indicated, when "the economic climate is uncertain, states are reluctant to initiate major departures from current policy." [63]

Auctioning Federal Projects

The changes are not all in taxes, budgets, and program priorities. An interesting process is now being developed in the federal system regarding how decisions are made on the location of major federal facilities. Instead of seeking the best location for a facility in both policy and political terms, an auction system for locating projects has emerged. The most spectacular example of this new system is the process undertaken to locate a multibillion-dollar supercollider facility. Like an old-fashioned auction, each interested state must put in a bid for the facility and include those "sweeteners" that could affect the federal decision. Of course, governors and states are used to playing this bidding game with industry as they vie to obtain major new plants.

The allocation of federal projects by auction forces states to raise a portion of the total project's cost. As a result of the bidding process, states and their governors must compete for major federal projects. Presumably, the state willing to provide the most sweeteners and absorb the greater portion of the project's cost will win. Studies of industrial location decisions suggest, however, that private-sector policy makers are often wary of such sweeteners when making their decisions. It is not clear whether public-sector decision makers will be as wary. Questions may arise over the ultimate policy rationale of an auction bought location, let alone the process itself. However, this process certainly fits with what John Shannon has called the return to "fend-for-yourself federalism." [64]

Governors in Association

Governors have taken significant steps to revitalize and redirect multistate organizations during the last decade. Foremost among these organizations is the National Governors' Association. The NGA originated in a call by President Theodore Roosevelt in 1908 for the governors to meet with him to discuss conservation issues.

Getting Organized

For many years, governors met regularly to discuss a broad agenda with the Council of State Governments (CSG) serving as secretary. During the mid-1960s, as federal grant-in-aid programs proliferated and the federal presence intruded further into the states, the governors felt the need for a more permanent organization. They set up an office in Washington, D.C., to press their views, interests, and needs upon the federal government. The trigger for this movement was the governors' concern over the rapid expansion of federal goals and demands upon the states as a result of President Lyndon Johnson's Great Society programs.

In Washington, an original staff of four was increased in size, capability, and versatility. The Governors' Conference began working with the National Conference of State Legislatures (NCSL) and the five other members of the "Big Seven"—CSG, the National Association of Counties, the National League of Cities, the U.S. Conference of Mayors, and the International City Managers Association—in serving as lobbyists for state and local governments.

The strong showing of governors' and legislators' organizations, individual governors, and state offices in Washington, D.C., is a significant development, because each state already has two U.S. senators and at least one U.S. representative working on behalf of its interests. States do not believe that members of Congress necessarily represent their concerns and needs. State leaders felt that a strong and independent state presence in Washington was one of several steps that had to be taken for adequate representation in the national policy process.[65]

Growth of the National Governors' Association

Under the leadership of a series of strong governors,[66] the Governors' Conference began to broaden its agenda and approach. In 1966, it changed its name to the National Governors' Conference "to distinguish it clearly from the regional conferences which had sprung up."[67] In 1967, it switched from an ad hoc committee structure to a system of eleven standing committees. The group began advocating a body of policy positions that were agreed to at annual meetings.[68] In 1977, the National Governors' Conference became the National Governors' Association "to signify the broad scope and ongoing nature of the organization."[69]

During the 1970s, NGA began a series of activities to enhance the performance of governors within their own states. "The New Governors' Seminar" was established and held within two weeks after the general election in even-numbered years, with incumbent governors serving as the faculty. The subjects were of direct concern to the newly elected governors: organizing the governor's office; press and public relations; management of the executive branch; executive-legislative relations; intergovernmental relations; the governorship as a partnership involving one's spouse; and the transition period.[70] In addition, printed materials and guidebooks were prepared for governors to take back to their home states,[71] and transition assistance was made available.

There was a growing emphasis on the states and governors as innovators in a series of surveys and publications.[72] These surveys and reports were seen as a way to help disseminate ideas on problems and programs across the states via the governors. Two national organizations of gubernatorial staff—the Council of State Planning Agencies (CSPA) and the National Association of State Budget Officers (NASBO)—became NGA affiliates, thereby providing NGA with needed policy and budget-planning capabilities.[73]

In 1976, NGA moved its Washington headquarters to Capitol Hill and into the Hall of the States, "a long-held dream of Washington Governor Daniel Evans."[74] Joining NGA were many of the other state organizations in Washington, including NCSL, CSG, CSPA, and NASBO, and as of 1988, twenty-seven state governors' Washington offices.[75]

By 1983, Carol Weissert concluded that NGA "has gone from serving primarily as a social event to providing information, technical assistance and research needed for responsible state leadership; from shying away from taking issue stands to assuming leadership in charting a national policy course; and from having no Washington presence to spearheading a strong Washington lobbying effort." [76] Larry Sabato argued that the governors have used NGA as a vehicle to assert themselves at the "national level in an unprecedented and surprisingly effective manner ... revolutionized from the hollow shell of yore to a bustling, professional lobby that can achieve results (and overcome the serious handicaps to effectiveness inherent in a high-powered constituency such as the governors)." [77]

Regional governors' associations—the Midwestern, Northeastern, Southern, Western—have became more active in policy concerns. Some of these policy interests flowed naturally from the regions, for example, energy and natural resources in the West, agriculture in the Midwest, race and economic development in the South, while some stemmed from the allocation of federal grant-in-aid funds. The most notable example was the conflict that arose over the formula for distributing federal funds, which was to the advantage of the Sun Belt states and to the disadvantage of the Snow Belt states.[78] Other examples are those instances in which states of a region band together to provide better services, as in higher education, or to seek a particular federal "pork barrel" project.

Although the results of these activities vary, the governors of the fifty states, by joining together, have become more a part of the national policy-making process. They have undertaken new and innovative steps to provide their states with representation that the members of Congress have failed to provide.

National Policy Leadership

Beginning with the NGA chairmanship of Gov. Lamar Alexander of Tennessee (1985-1986), the association and the governors took another significant step to further their impact on public policy. Discontinuing the series of "show and tell" reports on particular state innovations, and under the guidance and prodding of Governor Alexander, the governors conducted a fifty-state assessment of the status of American education. Seven separate gubernatorially directed subcommittees were established to assess the components of educational policy: readiness; parental involvement and public school choice; teaching; school facilities; college quality; technology; and leadership and management. At the 1986 NGA annual meeting, a report was presented, *Time for Results: The Governors' 1991 Report on Education*,[79] that set an agenda for each governor and state to follow in education. Through 1991, the governors are to give an account at their annual meeting of the specific steps they are taking in their individual states to achieve educational reform. This kind of exercise is considerably more focused and directed than past efforts have been.

During the chairmanship of Gov. Bill Clinton of Arkansas (1986-1987), the governors concentrated on economic development and job creation. The NGA "devoted virtually its entire annual midwinter meeting to the issue" of welfare reform. The association adopted a welfare reform concept, with only one dissenting vote, calling for "a mandatory education and training program for able-bodied welfare recipients," which would make "work more attractive than welfare." The dean of the fifty governors, fourth termer James Thompson of Illinois, said, "I have never seen such unity on the end to be achieved." [80]

The 1987 NGA report, *Making America Work: Productive People, Productive Policies,* which was based on the work of six task forces, focused on two separate components, "Jobs, Growth and Competitiveness" and "Bringing Down the Barriers." [81] In addition, the first of the annual reports on educational reform was heard.

The third yearlong study, 1987-1988, focused on the changing balance in the federal system. Three parallel efforts were undertaken by the governors: the identification of changes in federal rules that would enable state governments to operate more effectively; an examination of existing federal laws affecting states; and an NGA Task Force on Federalism to "develop a broad, direct, overall approach to restoring the balance of power." [82] The study, under the direction of NGA chairman John Sununu, of New Hampshire, culminated in the report *Restoring the Balance: State Leadership for America's Future,* which was issued at the NGA annual meeting in August 1988. [83] During the 1988-1989 tenure of Chairman Gerald Baliles, of Virginia, the focus was on the states and the international economy, with particular attention being paid to competitiveness and education.

To some governors, especially those newly elected, the process and the reports produced provide a road map of ideas. To other governors, it is a way to measure progress in their state. To certain other governors, such as Alexander, Clinton, Sununu, and Baliles, it can be a way to provide leadership to all the states and their governors in critical policy areas.

Sustaining an Activist Role

The growing activism among governors, via their national and regional organizations, has added a new dimension to setting national, state, and local policy agendas. States are aggressively asserting their role in the federal system with the leadership of governors and other state officials. But to the outside observer some concerns are apparent.

First, the most critical element in NGA's rise in stature and capability to become involved in the policy debates at all levels is the caliber of leadership the NGA chairperson provides. With high quality leadership, directions can be charted and tasks achieved. During the past two decades, however, there have been chairmen of NGA who have not provided solid leadership and who have damaged the organization and its newly established position. In one case, the chairman saw NGA as another organization into which he could make patronage appointments. That year was one of "hunkering down" by those on the NGA staff, with little forward movement by the organization.

Can the governors guard against such a situation in the future? The choice of chairperson rotates annually by party affiliation, so the question really is: Can the Democratic governors and the Republican governors each guard against a poor leader when it is their turn to make the selection? As former governor Scott Matheson of Utah, who served as NGA chair in 1982-1983, observed: "Poor leadership can only result in the paralysis and eventual demise of [this] organization." [84]

A second and related concern is the agenda the governors adopt each year. Is there a well-thought-out three- or five-year plan on the subjects to be addressed or does each year's agenda depend on what the incoming chairperson is interested in pursuing—perhaps for personal or political reasons? A multiyear plan need not be set in concrete. It can be open to new issues demanding gubernatorial input and thinking, but it would still serve as an overall route for NGA's efforts. In the mid-1970s, one chairman wanted NGA to address the question of state responsibility to local government. Other governors felt such a question had been addressed already, at least in their states, and was not worthy of major NGA attention. In fact, with the energy crisis in process and a recession at hand, one governor was able to break the regular agenda of NGA by demanding and getting an ad hoc session focused on the energy crisis. This session was conducted without any preparation, leading the governors in no specific direction. It left many embarrassed over their performance.

Third, much of what the NGA has achieved has been in reaction to events and trends occurring in the federal system. Have the governors, individually in their states and in concert through such organizations as NGA, so institutionalized their position and role that they must be part of whatever changes occur? Are the governors here to stay as part of the national policy-making process? The governors may indeed become that "house of governors" that William George Stewart advocated in 1907, which "should in time become an inherent part of the American idea of self-government and a powerful factor for good in the nation." [85]

Summary

Over the past two decades a host of state government reforms have strengthened governorships most everywhere. Governors now are better able to achieve their goals. Their terms of office are longer; most are allowed to succeed themselves for another term; their budgetary authority has been consolidated and enhanced; and most state government organization structures have been simplified.

However, some important tools of the trade are still missing in some states or are limited in others. A large number of officials, boards, and commissions are still separately elected, and some governors lack full veto power. Some governors have outdated and unresponsive administrative organizations, lack the ability to reorganize portions of state government by executive order, and must function with antiquated constitutions.

Although the analogy between a governor and a private-sector chief executive officer is apt, governors have a distance to go before possessing comparable power of appointment and removal. Governors need more flexibility in hiring and firing personnel. Even more important, their ability to remove officials when necessary is greatly constrained, first by the strong value of neutral competence and second by the protection afforded appointees by several U.S. Supreme Court decisions.

Conflicts between governors and legislatures have escalated in recent years. Tensions are exacerbated when the governor's office and the legislature are controlled by different political parties. Legislatures have intruded into traditional gubernatorial prerogatives by appointing legislators to state boards and commissions, by enacting legislative vetoes of administrative rules and regulations, and by exercising oversight of administrative agencies. State courts often side with governors in disputes with legislatures when separation-of-powers issues are involved.

The road to the governorship is changing in significant ways, primarily because of changes in the political system of nominations and elections. The importance of service in the party—working one's way up a state's political ladder—and service in state government are being replaced by the importance of the dollar. The new politics requires statewide polls, campaign strategists, media consultants and thirty-second TV ad producers, media buys, and, above all, money to pay for them.

The amount of money needed varies by state and electoral

situation, but generally more money is required to mount an effective campaign for governor. This need affects those who can seek and win the governorship. Those with wealth or access to it are the likely candidates, if not the winners.

The governors' own organization, the National Governors' Association, has developed into a vehicle by which the governors can help each other with problems, and through which all governors can address issues of national concern. NGA has joined with other similar organizations of public officials to become active participants in policy and administrative decisions made at the federal level by Congress, by the president or executive agencies, and by the federal courts.

An organization is only as good as the leadership that provides its guidance and charts its future directions. In the mid-1980s, NGA prospered in the national policy milieu under the leadership of several outstanding governors who brought their vision, competence, and national and state agendas to the organization. Such leadership must be assured for the future. The selection process has not always resulted in the strongest leadership; it should be made to serve the long-term goals of the governors and NGA.

Recently, NGA has adopted a new approach of focusing on particular issues of concern. For example, a yearlong study was conducted on education policy. The results proved to be a great help to the governors, their states, and NGA. Topics for study should be selected to allow NGA to build on previous actions instead of depending on the interests of the person selected chair for the year.

The movement of governmental policy activism has been swinging back to the states and their local communities. A declining federal presence has forced governors and other state leaders to make hard decisions on dollars, policies, and responsibilities. Governors appear ready to assume a major leadership role in this new federal system.

Notes

1. Jack Brizius and Sue Foster, "State Government General Revenues," *State Policy Data Book* (Alexandria, Va.: State Policy Research, 1988), Table C-10; and "Special Report: The New 'Fortune 500,' " *USA Today,* April 7, 1988, 5B.
2. Regina Brough, "Powers of the Gubernatorial CEOs: Variations among the States," *Journal of State Government* 59 (1986): 58-63.
3. Among these were: Advisory Commission on Intergovernmental Relations, various reports; Committee for Economic Development, *Moderniz-*

ing State Government (New York: Committee for Economic Development, 1967); Terry Sanford, *Storm over the States* (New York: McGraw-Hill, 1967); National Municipal League, *Model State Constitution*, rev. ed. (New York: National Municipal League, 1968); and Citizens Conference on State Legislatures, various publications between 1967 and 1971.

4. Sanford, *Storm over the States*, 188; and Larry Sabato, *Goodbye to Goodtime Charlie: The American Governor Transformed, 1950-1975* (Lexington, Mass.: Lexington Books, 1978), 63.

5. Advisory Commission on Intergovernmental Relations, *The Question of State Government Capability* (Washington, D.C.: Advisory Commission on Intergovernmental Relations, 1985), 129.

6. The Council of State Governments, *The Book of the States, 1988-89,* (Lexington, Ky.: Council of State Governments, 1988), 35-36.

7. Advisory Commission on Intergovernmental Relations, *The Question of State Government Capability*, 129; The Council of State Governments, *The Book of the States, 1988-89*, 113-114; and Ronald C. More, *Prospects for the Item Veto at the Federal Level: Lessons from the States* (Washington, D.C.: National Academy of Public Administration, 1988), 3-50.

8. Coleman B. Ransone, Jr., *The Office of the Governor in the United States* (University: University of Alabama Press, 1956), 44.

9. Center for Policy Research, National Governors' Association, unpublished data from a 1976 survey of thirty-eight governors' offices. The adjusted averages exclude the one or two largest states as their size would skew the overall averages.

10. The Council of State Governments, *The Book of the States, 1988-89*, 38.

11. Thad L. Beyle, "Governors' Views on Being Governor," *State Government* 52 (Summer 1979): 108-110.

12. The Council of State Governments, *The Book of the States 1988-89*, 38-39.

13. Lynn Muchmore, "Planning and Budgeting Offices: On Their Relevance to Gubernatorial Decisions," in *Being Governor: The View from the Office*, ed. Thad L. Beyle and Lynn Muchmore (Durham, N.C.: Duke University Press, 1983), 174.

14. Carl W. Stenberg, "States under the Spotlight: An Intergovernmental View," *Public Administration Review* 45 (March/April 1985): 321.

15. Thad L. Beyle and Deil S. Wright, "The Governor, Planning, and Governmental Activity," in *The American Governor in Behavioral Perspective*, ed. Thad L. Beyle and J. Oliver Williams (New York: Harper and Row, 1972), 194-195.

16. Thad L. Beyle, "The Governor as Innovator in the Federal System," *Publius* 18 (Summer 1988): 133-154.

17. The Council of State Governments, *The Book of the States, 1982-83* (1982), 145-147; *The Book of the States, 1984-85* (1984), 44-45; *The Book of the States, 1986-87* (1986), 45-47; and *The Book of the States, 1988-89*, 47-48.

18. Washington Research Council, *The Reorganization of Washington State*

Government (Olympia, Wash.: Washington Research Council, 1987), 5. Data for table from the Council of State Governments, *The Book of the States, 1986-87,* 51-57.

19. Jack Brizius, Brizius and Foster, Management Consultants, telephone conversation with author, September 11, 1987.

20. Dianne Kincaid Blair, "The Gubernatorial Appointment Power: Too Much of a Good Thing?" in *Being Governor: The View from the Office,* 118-121.

21. Joseph A. Schlesinger, "The Politics of the Executive," in *Politics in the American States,* ed. Herbert Jacob and Kenneth N. Vines (Boston: Little, Brown, 1965), 217-232; Joseph A. Schlesinger, "The Politics of the Executive," in *Politics in the American States,* 2d ed., ed. Herbert Jacob and Kenneth N. Vines (Boston: Little, Brown, 1971), 210-237; and Thad L. Beyle, "Governors," in *Politics in the American States,* 4th ed., ed. Virginia Gray, Herbert Jacob, and Kenneth Vines (Boston: Little, Brown, 1983), 203, 458-459.

22. Schlesinger, "The Politics of the Executive," 225.

23. Elder Witt, "Patronage Firings," *Congressional Quarterly Weekly Report,* July 3, 1976, 1726.

24. Elder Witt, "Supreme Court Deals Blow to Public Employee Firings for Solely Political Reasons," *Congressional Quarterly Weekly Report,* April 5, 1980, 889-890.

25. Elder Witt, "Employee Rights," *Congressional Quarterly Weekly Report,* April 6, 1983, 791-792.

26. Thad L. Beyle and Robert Huefner, "Evaluation of the 1982 Seminar for New Governors," report submitted to the National Governors' Association, February 23, 1983.

27. This section is adapted from Thad L. Beyle, "The Institutionalized Powers of the Governorship, 1965-1985," *Comparative State Politics Newsletter* 9 (February 1988): 23-29.

28. Schlesinger, "The Politics of the Executive," 217-232.

29. Office of State Services, *The Institutionalized Powers of the Governorship, 1965-1985* (Washington, D.C.: National Governors' Association, 1987).

30. There are some differences between the National Governors' Association index and previous ones: (1) The NGA indicies are called institutional and not formal, which allows a broader interpretation of what can be brought into the presentation and analysis; (2) Added are the legislative budget-changing ability and the governor's political strength in the legislature, which probably reflects a real-world view of the constraints on governors not captured in previous efforts. Including the governor's political strength in the legislature can lead to more varied results as each election can change this score, especially as so many states are now experiencing a political party power-split between the governor and the legislature; (3) Only six offices are used to develop the appointment power index—and the range of potential appointment power is greater (up to seven) than for the other indicators (up to five) reflecting the importance of this one indice for governors and where it can pinch the most; and (4)

There is a twenty-year comparison of these indicies that shows just how far the American governorship has come during the most recent era of state government reform.

31. Alabama, Colorado, Delaware, Hawaii, Illinois, Kansas, Maryland, Missouri, New York, Pennsylvania, Rhode Island, South Carolina, Utah, Vermont, and Wyoming.

32. North Dakota and West Virginia.

33. Indiana and Iowa.

34. Arizona, Arkansas, Connecticut, Florida, Louisiana, Massachusetts, Michigan, Minnesota, Mississippi, Nebraska, New Hampshire, New Jersey, Oklahoma, South Dakota, and Wisconsin.

35. California, Maine, Texas, and Virginia.

36. Alaska, Georgia, Idaho, Kentucky, Montana, Nevada, New Mexico, North Carolina, Ohio, Oregon, Tennessee, and Washington.

37. National Conference of State Legislatures, "Legislators Serving on Boards and Commissions," in *State Legislative Report* (Denver: National Conference of State Legislatures, 1983), 4-5; and North Carolina Center for Public Policy Research, *Boards, Commissions and Councils in the Executive Branch of North Carolina State Government* (Raleigh: North Carolina Center for Public Policy Research, 1984).

38. Charles W. Wiggins, "Executive Vetoes and Legislative Overrides in the American States," *Journal of Politics* 42 (1980): 1112-1113.

39. The Council of State Governments, *The Book of the States, 1980-81*, 110-111.

40. Ran Coble, *Special Provisions in Budget Bills: A Pandora's Box for North Carolina Citizens, A Special Report* (Raleigh: North Carolina Center for Public Policy Research, 1986), 9-12.

41. Walter J. Oleszek, *Congressional Procedures and the Policy Process*, 3d ed. (Washington, D.C.: CQ Press, 1988), 297.

42. *Immigration and Naturalization Services v. Jagdish Rai Chada* 462 U.S. 919 (1983).

43. Sharon Sherman, "Powersplit: When Legislatures and Governors Are of Opposing Parties," *State Legislatures* 10 (May-June 1984): 9-12; Thad L. Beyle, "Gubernatorial-Legislative Powersplits, 1968-1987: Adding to Separation of Powers Problems," *Comparative State Politics Newsletter* 7 (June 1986): 21-22; and Thad L. Beyle, "Adding to Separation of Powers Problems: An Update," *Comparative State Politics Newsletter* 7 (December 1986): 13-14.

44. Jody George and Lacy Maddox, "Separation of Powers Provisions in State Constitutions," in *Boards, Commissions and Councils in the Executive Branch of North Carolina State Government* (Raleigh: North Carolina Center for Public Policy Research, 1984), 51.

45. This section is adapted from Thad L. Beyle, "Gubernatorial Campaigns: Incumbency and Money," *Election Politics* 5 (Fall 1988): 18-23.

46. These normalized dollar figures are derived as indicated in Table 3-4, note a.

47. Richard Benedetto, "Florida Voters Uninspired by Costly Primaries,"

USA Today, August 29, 1986, 3A.

48. Associated Press, "Growth of Campaign Costs Slowed in '84," *Raleigh News and Observer,* December 8, 1985, C1; W. P. Welch, "The Effectiveness of Expenditures in State Legislative Races," *American Politics Quarterly* 4 (July 1976): 352; and Philip L. Dubois, "Penny for Your Thoughts?: Spending in California Trial Court Elections, 1976-1982," *Western Political Quarterly* 39 (June 1986): 265-284.

49. Philip L. Dubois, "Penny for Your Thoughts?", 272.

50. Samuel C. Patterson, "Campaign Spending in Contests for Governor," *Western Political Quarterly* 35 (December 1982): 476.

51. Thad L. Beyle, "The Cost of Becoming Governor," *Journal of State Government* 59 (October 1986): 98.

52. Sarah M. Morehouse, "Money versus Party Effort: Nominating for Governor" (Paper delivered at the annual meeting of the American Political Science Association, Chicago, September 3-6, 1987), 23.

53. Samuel C. Patterson, "Campaign Spending in Contests for Governor," 475.

54. Thad L. Beyle, "Governor's Chair Now Costs $7 Million," *State Government News* 29 (October 1986): 23. State Reports for the 1986 and 1987 elections.

55. North Carolina Center for Public Policy Research, *Campaign Finance in North Carolina* (Raleigh: North Carolina Center for Public Policy Research, forthcoming).

56. Sarah M. Morehouse, "Money versus Party Effort," 17.

57. John Shannon, "The Return to Fend-for-Yourself Federalism: The Reagan Mark," *Intergovernmental Perspective* 13 (Summer/Fall 1987): 35.

58. National Association of Budget Officers, reported in *USA Today,* September 29, 1987, 5A.

59. David Broder, "States Make Hard Decisions as Reagan Fantasies Wane," *Raleigh News and Observer,* August 5, 1987, 17A.

60. Jane Roberts, Jerry Fensterman, and Donald Lief, "States, Localities Continue to Adopt Strategic Policies," *Intergovernmental Perspective* 12 (Winter 1985): 20.

61. Gerald Pomper, *Elections in America* (New York: Dodd, Mead, 1968); Stephen Turett, "The Vulnerability of American Governors, 1900-1969," *Midwest Journal of Political Science* 15 (February 1971): 108-132; Theodore J. Eismeier, "Votes and Taxes: The Political Economy of the American Governorship," *Polity* 15 (Spring 1983): 368-379; and Susan L. Kone and Richard F. Winters, "Taxes and Voting: Electoral Retribution in the American States" (Paper delivered at the annual meeting of the American Political Science Association, Chicago, September 3-6, 1987).

62. Kone and Winters, "Taxes and Voting," 20.

63. "Tightened Belts, and Balanced Budgets," *Governors' Weekly Bulletin,* March 25, 1988, 1.

64. Shannon, "The Return to Fend-for-Yourself Federalism," 35.

65. Jacqueline Calmes, "444 North Capitol Street: Where State Lobbyists

Are Learning Coalition Politics," *Governing,* February 1988, 17-18, 20-21.

66. Among these governors were: John Volpe (R-Mass., 1965-1969); Marvin Mandell (D-Md., 1969-1977); Daniel Evans (R-Wash., 1965-1977); Calvin Rampton (D-Utah, 1965-1977); Robert Ray (R-Iowa, 1969-1983); Scott Matheson (D-Utah, 1977-1985); and Lamar Alexander (R-Tenn., 1979-1987).

67. Carol Weissert, "The National Governors' Association: 1908-1983," *State Government* 56 (1983): 49.

68. Weissert, "The National Governors' Association," 50.

69. Weissert, "The National Governors' Association," 49.

70. Thad L. Beyle, "Gubernatorial Transitions: Lessons from the 1982-1983 Experience," *Publius* 14 (Summer 1984): 13.

71. National Governors' Association, *The Critical Hundred Days: A Handbook for New Governors* (Washington, D.C.: National Governors' Association, 1975); National Governor's Association, *The Governor's Office* (Washington, D.C.: National Governors' Association, 1976); National Governors' Association, *Governing the American States: A Handbook for New Governors* (Washington, D.C.: National Governors' Association, 1978); National Governors' Association, *Transition and the New Governors: A Critical Overview* (Washington, D.C.: National Governors' Association, 1982); and National Governors' Association, Office of State Services, *The Transition: A View from Academia* (Washington, D.C.: National Governors' Association, 1986).

72. National Governors' Conference, *Innovations in State Government* (Washington, D.C.: National Governors' Association, 1974); and National Governors' Association, Center for Policy Research, *Governors' Policy Initiatives: Meeting the Challenges of the 1980s* (Washington, D.C.: National Governors' Association, 1980). The 1982 survey was conducted by the National Governors' Association, the Council of State Planning Agencies, and the Governors' Center at Duke University. The 1983 survey was conducted by the Council of State Planning Agencies.

73. Scott Matheson, *Out of Balance* (Salt Lake City, Utah: Peregrine Smith Books, 1986), 240.

74. Weissert, "The National Governors' Association," 50; and Calmes, "444 North Capitol Street," 20.

75. Calmes, "444 North Capitol Street," 17.

76. Weissert, "The National Governors' Association," 52.

77. Larry Sabato, *Goodbye to Goodtime Charlie: The American Governorship Transformed,* 2d ed. (Washington, D.C.: CQ Press, 1983), 180.

78. For a discussion of this conflict see Deil S. Wright, *Understanding Intergovernmental Relations,* 2d ed. (Monterey, Calif.: Brooks/Cole, 1982), 171-175.

79. National Governors' Association, *Time for Results: The Governors' 1991 Report on Education* (Washington, D.C.: National Governors' Association, 1986).

80. Julie Rovner, "Governors Jump-Start Welfare Reform Drive," *Congres-*

sional Quarterly Weekly Report, February 28, 1987, 376.

81. National Governors' Association, *Making America Work: Productive People, Productive Policies* (Washington, D.C.: National Governors' Association, 1987).

82. "Sununu Presents Agenda as New NGA Chairman," *Governors' Weekly Bulletin* 21 (August 7, 1987): 1-2.

83. National Governors' Association, *Restoring the Balance: State Leadership for America's Future* (Washington, D.C.: National Governors' Association, 1988).

84. Matheson, *Out of Balance,* 241.

85. Quoted in Glenn E. Brooks, *When Governors Convene: The Governors' Conference and National Politics* (Baltimore: Johns Hopkins Press, 1960), 9-10.

4. THE LEGISLATIVE INSTITUTION: TRANSFORMED AND AT RISK

Alan Rosenthal

Legislatures are probably the principal political institutions in the states—the guts of democracy. They have managed to survive, and on occasion even prosper, over the course of more than a two-hundred-year lifetime. But in contemporary times, their standing with the public has rarely been high.[1] Invective is heaped upon them, and little is said on their behalf. They deserve better. They have made considerable progress in a relatively brief period of time, and today they are performing remarkably well. Yet, there are indications that the legislature, as an institution, may be in jeopardy.

Prior to their revitalization, which began in the mid-1960s, legislatures deserved much of the criticism that was directed their way. They were unrepresentative, malapportioned, and dominated by rural areas of the states. The legislative process was, in many instances, a sham; power within the institution was narrowly held, and not democratically exercised. Major issues were sidestepped, and initiatives for state policy were left to the governor. The legislature's role in the most important business of government, that of allocating funds, was minimal. Whatever the positive outcomes and however well served the people of a state might be, relatively little could be attributed to the performance of the legislature.

The reapportionment revolution, precipitated by the Supreme Court decisions in *Baker v. Carr* (1962) and *Reynolds v. Sims* (1965), was the first stage in the transformation of American state legislatures. A new generation of members—led by a number of outstanding leaders and supported by allies drawn from the ranks of citizens, businesses, foundations, and universities—went to work to reshape legislative institutions. Within a decade legislatures had been rebuilt. They increased the time they spent on their tasks; they established or expanded their professional staffs; and they streamlined their procedures, enlarged their facilities, invigorated their processes, attended to their ethics, disclosed their finances, and reduced their conflicts of interest.

Thus, the decade from about 1965 to 1975 can appropriately be termed the period of "the rise of the legislative institution." Traditional assemblies became modern ones, and reformed legislatures emerged. They had developed the capacity to do their jobs, to perform the functions that they could be expected to perform. Some, such as California's, were ahead of their time, and others, such as Vermont's and Wyoming's, lagged behind as far as modernization was concerned. Each legislature adapted differently, depending upon its culture and politics, the people and personalities in office, and the circumstances of the time. Each put its newly developed capacity to work, and each continued to evolve in its own peculiar way.

One of the noteworthy results of the legislature's institutional development has been the strengthening of the legislative branch of state government. The new generations of postreapportionment legislators were not willing to settle for subordinate status. They believed that their branch should be independent of the executive, and they strove for coequality. With their newly acquired capacity—mainly professional staffs supplying their informational needs and feeding their self-confidence—legislators began to play a larger role in deciding on policy, allocating funds through the budget, and even controlling administration.[2] Legislators wanted to operate from greater strength in their relationship with governors. They had the wherewithal and, more important, the will to do so. As a consequence, governors no longer overpower legislatures, as used to be the case.

But the legislature that underwent reform and modernization in the 1960s and 1970s may be undergoing a more subtle transformation in the 1980s. Its capacity remains substantial and its power and assertiveness continue to be impressive. It continues to produce policies that are generally effective for the states. But the legislature's structure and institutional fabric are changing. This is attributable to several trends that are under way: first, the legislative career is becoming professionalized; second, legislative behavior and the legislative process are increasingly politicized; and third, the legislative institution is more fragmented. Not every state is being affected by each of these three trends, and not every one is feeling the trends equally. The larger states, with the most developed and modernized legislatures, are most affected. California, Illinois, Massachusetts, Michigan, New York, and Pennsylvania are in that category. But other states such as Colorado, Connecticut, Florida, Kansas, Minnesota, Missouri, Nebraska, Ohio, Washington, and Wisconsin are subject to these trends as well. Some, Indiana, for example, feel them but are resistant. Still others, such as

Montana, New Hampshire, Utah, and Wyoming, are being touched only lightly, if at all. Although these trends do not have universal application, in many states they are impacting significantly and are undermining the institutional development of the recent past.

Careerist Bodies

Along with reform and modernization came the professionalization of state legislatures. In the most commonly used sense professionalization refers to the improvement of legislative facilities, with the renovation of capitols and the construction of legislative office buildings, the increase in information available to the legislature, and, above all, the expansion of legislative staffs. Professionalization, however, applies not only to the capacity and conduct of the institution but also to the composition of its core personnel. Most significant in this respect is the growing number of career politicians among the membership of legislatures in many states. The careerist orientation of legislators is having an enormous impact on legislative life.[3] It is largely responsible for the increasing political nature of legislatures and partly responsible for their greater fragmentation as well.

Citizens and Professionals

Twenty years ago almost all members, except a few in California, failed to label themselves as legislators in their biographical sketches for the state directory. Instead, they identified themselves by their occupations outside the legislature—attorney, businessperson, insurance broker, farmer, rancher, or whatever. Not anymore. Now, significant proportions of members, in a number of states, acknowledge their occupation to be that of legislator. Even larger proportions are, in effect, full-time or virtually full-time legislators who have made politics their career. Nowadays "citizens" and "professionals" constitute the two principal breeds within the legislator species. The former, or old breed, generally have another occupation or substantial interests outside the legislature. The latter, or new breed, usually have no other significant occupation and little time or interest for anything other than politics. The new breed is on the rise, the old in decline.

The trend can be seen in Wisconsin. Of the 132 legislators who were serving in the 1983 session in Madison, 72 said they had no other occupation than that of legislator and were not retired. More than half were full time, or essentially full time. By contrast, in 1969 less than one-twentieth were full time, and in 1963 none were.[4] Today, about 70 percent of Wisconsin's members are professional legislators. It is primarily in the largest states, however, where the greatest proportions of members are committed to the legislature and political careers. At least two-thirds of the members in Michigan and Pennsylvania are career politicians, although a number of them practice law or have "something on the side" that provides additional income. Half or more of those in Illinois, Massachusetts, and New York are full time or practically so. Slightly fewer in Arizona, Iowa, Missouri, and Ohio are full timers, and about one quarter in Connecticut, Florida, and Minnesota are.[5] Only 15 percent are full time in Maryland.[6] And there are still legislatures at the other end of the spectrum, where nearly all the members, with the exceptions of homemakers and retirees, are part time. Indiana, Kentucky, Nevada, New Hampshire, North Dakota, Vermont, and Wyoming are examples. At present, about one-fifth of the nation's legislatures are mainly in the hands of professional legislators and one-fifth are moving gradually, but inexorably, toward the professional model. Another two-fifths probably will be up for grabs in the years ahead. The remaining fifth are not likely to be taken over; they will remain firmly in the hands of citizen legislators.

What Promotes Careerism

The professionalization of legislative careers is attributable to a number of factors. Among the most potent are the increasing demands on a member's time and the rising levels of legislative compensation.

The amount of time that legislatures are in session and that legislators are required to be at the state capital is two or three times greater today than in earlier years. It used to be that most legislatures met biennially; today all but seven meet annually.

Although most states constitutionally set limits on the length of legislative sessions, in about one-quarter there are no limitations. Thus, in Alaska, California, Illinois, Massachusetts, Michigan, New York, Ohio, Pennsylvania, South Carolina, and Wisconsin the number of days legislatures spend in session has risen markedly. Take California, for example. In 1966 the voters approved Proposition 1-A, which eliminated constitutional limits on session length (as well as on legislative pay). This measure allowed members to devote more time to the legislature, and they did. The length of sessions increased from 107 days in 1965 to 143 in 1967. In the 1983-1984 biennium the California legislature spent 282 days in session and in the 1985-1986 biennium, 251 days.[7] The legislature goes into session in January, and it adjourns in August during election years and in September when no elections for the legislature are being held.

Even where annual sessions are limited, as in Florida to 60 days or in Maryland to 90 days, the time legislators spend on their jobs has gone up dramatically.[8] In addition to regular and special sessions, legislators attend meetings of standing committees and special committees during the interim period when the senate and house are not convened. It is not only that the legislature as a whole meets for longer periods of time, but also that more individual legislators are involved in activity between sessions. In Maryland, for instance, relatively few members used to be named to interim committees; now everyone's time can be occupied between legislative sessions by virtue of membership on standing committees. In North Carolina, some legislators serve on as many as thirteen different commissions and councils during the interim period. Probably the greatest recent increase in time spent by members, however, is devoted to constituency affairs. In many states legislators now politick through their districts, appear before local groups and organizations, and deal with constituents in their legislative district offices practically year round.

Time commitments have been on the rise over past years; they have stabilized in a number of places by now. But in other places, there is still room for growth. Connecticut, for example, in 1988 provided offices for members in a new legislative office building. As a consequence, members can be expected in the years ahead to spend more of their time, when the legislature is not actually in session, working in their offices in Hartford. The push continues in Connecticut and elsewhere, too.

Whatever the time demands, it is unlikely that the professionalization of the legislative career would have hit with as much force without a marked rise in legislative salaries.[9] Higher salaries have made it possible for members to derive a substantial portion of their income from legislative service. Again, the case of Wisconsin is instructive. The salary of legislators went up from $8,900 in 1967 to $17,800 in 1976. Around 1970 the job paid enough to match teachers' salaries, and that was when more educators declared their candidacies for the legislature. Wisconsin now pays its legislators $30,000 (and some members can accrue another $5,000 in per diem). This amount is estimated to provide about three-quarters of the total income of the average member.[10]

Wisconsin's compensation is still modest; in other states the salaries are more attractive. California pays $37,105, plus $75 per diem; Illinois $35,152, plus $69 per diem; Michigan $39,881, plus vouchered expenses; Ohio $34,905; and Pennsylvania $35,000, plus $83 per diem. New York salaries are the highest at $57,500, plus $75 per diem. Beyond the base salary, legislators in many places receive supplements for holding leadership positions or in lieu of expenses.

In a number of states, by contrast, salaries lag far behind or are abysmally low. It is financially difficult for people to abandon outside occupations and income when legislative compensation is $15,000 or less a year, as in about half the states. Some do; they can afford it, are willing to make the sacrifice, or still have sufficient outside income to make do. Yet, it would not be easy for most people to spend a lot of their time on the legislature if the salary were $19,000 for the biennium, as it is in Kentucky. And it would be virtually impossible for most to serve for very long if the salary were $100 a year, with no per diem, as it is in New Hampshire.

But salaries are on their way up in the states, and thus the number of career politicians serving in legislatures keeps growing. States that value the citizen legislator, but also want to compensate members as fairly as practicable, are cross pressured. The Maryland General Assembly's Compensation Commission endorses a part-time legislature, but with a salary "high enough to enable [legislators] periodically to leave their professions, their businesses, or their homes to attend to legislative tasks, yet low enough so that members will not generally plan their personal finances solely around legislative compensation." Maryland's legislators received $23,000 in 1988. Connecticut's compensation commission also endorses the notion of the citizen legislator but notes that "service in the general assembly has come to demand a far greater proportion of a legislator's time than it did 10 years ago" and that "time devoted to the general assembly represents wages or salary lost from a legislator's private career." Connecticut's legislators are paid $15,200 a year.[11]

Holding salaries down has allowed states to preserve their citizen legislatures. In Florida, for instance, the salary had been kept at $12,000 a year since 1969 (when it was raised from $1,200), partly out of fear that more money would attract different types of people and the legislature would then lose its citizen status. In 1985, however, legislators voted themselves a pay raise to $18,000, also providing that their salaries would increase automatically every year by the same percentage that the average salary of state employees rose the preceding year. In view of the improved remuneration, as well as the increased time demands, chances are that in the years ahead the proportion of relatively full-time, professional members will grow in the Florida legislature.

As the Maryland and Connecticut compensation commissions suggest and as the Florida experience illustrates, the legislature itself has the choice of whether or not to become a place for careerist politicians. Democratic members are more inclined to professionalization than Republicans, because they are more positively oriented toward the role of government and more activist with respect to legislation. Democrats are in the business of government, while Republicans are in the business of business. That is one reason why the incidence of professionalization has been greatest in legislatures that have been controlled by the Democratic party.

In some places, however, the citizen legislature ethos is strongly held by members of both parties. Take Indiana, for example. Here, neither Democrats nor Republicans, on the whole, favor professionalization. Moreover, the leadership is especially dedicated to the avocational nature of the legislature. For leaders, and for the senate generally, the citizen legislature is gospel. Yet, there is a handful of members who want a full-time legislature; these individuals tend to be Democrats and teachers sponsored by the professional educational community. If educators increase in numbers and Democrats win a majority, it is possible that a new breed will attain power and the Indiana legislature will opt for professionalization.

In Vermont, the tradition of a citizen legislature may be eroding, albeit slowly. Vermont's legislative leaders are trying to devise responses to increasing pressure short of a full-time, professional legislature. There is some doubt, however, that the current system will survive. "I'm not optimistic that two decades from now," said one senate leader, "you're going to find a citizen legislature in Vermont." [12] The possibility may be remote, but it is certainly there.

A New Breed

With time demands and compensation increasing, the old breed of legislator is vanishing and a new breed emerging in many states. The numbers of businesspersons and practitioners of various private professions are diminishing. The decline in practicing attorneys is especially noticeable. Attorneys, and especially those in larger firms, cannot afford to spend the time required, and they refuse to jeopardize their practices by disclosing the names of clients, as required by regulations to reduce conflicts of interests. Nationally, the proportion of attorneys declined from 30 percent in 1960 to 20 percent in 1979, and was down to about 16 percent by 1986.[13] In states such as New York, attorneys still abound, but elsewhere precious few attorneys with substantial experience and law practices are left.

These old breeders, the mainstays of predecessor legislatures, are being replaced by career politicians who come from the ranks of unseasoned lawyers, teachers, preachers, spouses of professionals, single people who can live on a legislative salary, public organizers, legislative aides, and others of like ilk.[14] What distinguishes the new breed is that they have either more disposable time or little in the way of outside pursuits. In the first category are teachers in elementary and secondary schools, who can spend their fall semesters in the classroom and take leave during the spring to attend the legislative session. In recent years, teachers—frequently sponsored by local education associations—have been the largest growing occupational grouping in the legislature. In some states they account for almost one out of five members. Taking their cue from teachers, groups such as police officers and fire fighters, in a state such as Washington, are getting their members to run for the legislature and represent their interests. In addition, the number of women in state legislatures has increased substantially in the last twenty years, and percentagewise more women than men have no employment outside of legislative office.[15] They also tend to be full-time legislators. Then, there are the younger, newer members—men and women alike—who come out of college, graduate school, or law school and go directly into politics. No other significant occupational experience intervenes. More members are moving up through the political and governmental ranks and fewer by dint of having achieved successful careers in private life.

Thus far, only in a few states has recruitment been from the ranks of legislative staff, but staff may be a source of membership in the future. In California, one out of every four or five members has served previously as a personal aide to a member or as a consultant to a committee. In fact, a few California lawmakers are third-generation staffers. For example, Democrat assemblyman Charles Calderon served on the staff of Assemblyman Richard Alatorre, who had previously been on the staff of Assemblyman Walter Karabian.[16] In Wisconsin, one out of every six members served either as a congressional or legislative staffer before being elected. In Illinois, a number of former staffers are now in the General Assembly. And the floor leader of the Michigan senate was formerly a page and then the director of the Republican caucus staff.

Ambition for Public Office

What distinguishes the full-time, professional politicians from the part-time citizens is not only where they have come from but also where they are going to. Fewer of the old timers harbored career ambitions in politics. They intended to serve a while and return to private careers. Many of the new breed, by contrast, would like to spend their careers in government or politics. They find public office appealing, and the game of politics exhilarating. They take pleasure in their status, delight in the exercise of power, and have policies they want to advance.

These new breeders are professionals who want to stay in public office for the long haul. A number of them are content to remain in the house or senate for eight, ten, or twelve years. Some of them are very much like old breeders; they want to spend their last two or three years on the executive payroll, where a significantly higher salary will boost their overall pensions. A growing number are politically ambitious, interested in higher office. A veteran lobbyist in California described this species: "There is an overriding ambition to become something else." [17] Not only in California, but around the country, "something else" means U.S. representative or senator, state attorney general, secretary of state, lieutenant governor, or governor. It may even mean mayor or county commissioner, or, as in New York, judge. Normally, higher office means an expansion of one's electoral base and often an expansion of one's salary.

Not many contemporary legislators leave the legislature voluntarily. Some do leave when their pensions vest; a few become frustrated and decide not to run again. Some are frightened off by an unfavorable redistricting after a decennial reapportionment. Some exit for health reasons; and one or two, depending on the state, do not run again because they have been indicted. A few leave after bitter and extended legislative sessions. A number depart as soon as they have a shot—even a long shot—at higher office; others wait a while before making their attempt. Members of the house often run for the senate, and members of either body run for a congressional seat or for statewide office when and if the opportunity arises.

New Jersey, which still does not have a full-time legislature, illustrates the retaining power of the legislature. In 1983 all 120 seats were up. Of 119 eligible incumbents (one member had been convicted of a felony), 114 stood for reelection. Of the 5 who retired, one did so because he had his hands full as mayor of a small town, another had been elected mayor of Atlantic City and would certainly have his hands full, and a third left to run for clerk of Hudson County (which in Hudson County is higher office and pays substantially more in salary). Only two abandoned public office altogether. In 1985, with only the assembly up, 78 out of 80 incumbents sought reelection. Two years later, in 1987, every senator and all but 4 assemblymen (two of whom were ill and another under indictment) ran.

Political careers also have become attractive in a state such as Florida, despite the low salary paid legislators. In the Florida house from 1968 through 1988, of 120 members, the number of incumbents either running for reelection or for other office ranged from 103 to 117. The percentages ranged from 86.6 in 1972 to 97.5 in 1986 and has not fallen below 93.3 since 1978. In the Florida senate the pattern is similar. From 1974 through 1988, the percentages either running for reelection or for other office ranged from 80 to 100.

The same trend is evident elsewhere. One study, drawing on data from twenty-nine states for 1966 to 1976, found a decline in the proportion of voluntary withdrawals from office.[18] Another study, which focused on Indiana from 1958 to 1984, also found a smaller percentage of incumbents retiring voluntarily. During the first six years of this period, 20 percent of the members chose to leave. By the end of the period, only about 7 percent left of their own accord.[19]

The estimates are roughly the same for other states. California and Illinois lose only 5 percent or so of their members voluntarily at any single election. In Michigan and Wisconsin, the figure of voluntary retirees is roughly the same, and in Ohio it is only somewhat higher. In states such as Connecticut and Maryland, which still have predominantly citizen legislatures, about 10 percent of the members choose to return to private life at the conclusion of their terms. Even Kentucky and Tennessee, with their citizen legislatures, are moving along a similar path. Only 10 percent of Kentucky legislators depart voluntarily. In Tennessee, although legislators complain about the inadequacy of their pay ($12,500 a year) and working conditions, growing numbers want to return.[20] There are exceptions; New Hampshire is one. One out of every three members voluntarily leaves the legislature at term's end. Whatever the trend elsewhere, there appears to be no danger of a takeover by career politicians in New Hampshire.

An Electoral Machine

The legislature was always a political body; it has become increasingly so. Electoral considerations were always salient, especially to house members who had to run every two years; now they are even more so. This is because legislative office has become an appealing place—to ply one's political trade, to use as a springboard to higher office, or both. Members choose to run for reelection, with their decisions being made as a "result of assessments of the attractiveness of the legislature, the feasibility of getting reelected, and the availability of higher offices that are more attractive."[21]

State legislatures are becoming like the U.S. House of Representatives. Most members of the U.S. House view politics as a career and care a great deal about retaining their office. "As politics has become a profession, and service in the House a realistic and attractive career, job security has become as important for the professional representative as for any other professional—but more problematic."[22] As in the case of Congress, state legislative office also is prized, and thus, as in Congress, incumbents seek to solidify their hold on it.

Resources at Their Command

Not only is the reelectoral drive of legislators intense, but their opportunities to run successfully are excellent. Available to them are new technologies, ample finances, and in more and more places considerable legislative assistance.

The marvels of modern technology enable legislators to publicize their names, convey their images, and disseminate their messages to the electorate with more telling effect than in the past. Today's generation of politicians appreciates what new techniques can do for them. They have a better feel for public relations and a keen sense of how to enhance their prospects for reelection.

Radio is a popular medium for candidates because the rates are reasonable. Television may be expensive, and the costs keep going up; but TV has become a common feature of campaigning, especially in the larger and more competitive districts in the big states. In Illinois, for instance, senate Democrats hired a consultant who trained members in how to present themselves before television cameras. But even in a smaller state such as Kentucky, TV is used by candidates in urban areas and in some rural races as well. Public opinion polling, direct mail, and the targeting of voters are well-developed techniques. Not only is the technology more effective, but the corps of consultants and campaign staff also are more skillful. They are adept at marketing their wares, and legislators are willing to buy.

All that legislators need to purchase the fruits of technology for their reelection in campaigns are financial resources—the "mother's milk of politics," in the words of Jesse Unruh, long-time treasurer of California. The new technology is driving up the costs of politics tremendously, and the availability of campaign contributions is making it all possible. California no doubt leads the pack when it comes to levels of spending on legislative campaigns. Expenditures in the golden state totaled approximately $57 million in 1986, up 31 percent from the 1984 elections,[23] with the average campaign cost per seat 4,000 percent higher than the 1960 level of spending.[24] Competitive races in California commonly cost $500,000 and, on occasion, exceed $1 million. In a recent race, a special election for a senate seat in 1987, more than $2 million was spent. By contrast, senators in California whose seats are safe spend only about $250,000, still a huge sum in comparison with earlier times or other states.

Elsewhere both the totals and costs of single races are significantly lower than in California but are still relatively high. In Ohio a competitive election may cost $300,000, in Michigan $250,000, and in Wisconsin $100,000. Even in New Hampshire a contest for one of the twenty-four seats in the senate ran in the neighborhood of $100,000. In most states, as in Connecticut, competitive districts may go for $50,000, while safer districts cost half that—by no means exorbitant amounts by California standards. The cost of races in Indiana is lower still; with few exceptions they run several thousand dollars.

But the key fact is that everywhere the costs have risen from ten, or even five, years ago. New Jersey may be typical. In 1981 no assembly candidate spent more than $39,000 on a race, while two senate candidates contesting a seat spent in excess of $100,000. By 1983, however, eleven senate and two assembly candidates spent more than $100,000; two years later a total of nine assembly candidates hit the $100,000 mark. In the 1987 elections twenty-three senate and six assembly candidates spent more than that amount.[25]

In addition to what they can raise on their own, incumbents who wish to return find that the legislature itself provides considerable resources. First, and foremost, is staff. In the 1960s few legislatures had much staff other than those professionals located in central service agencies. By the 1970s, legislatures in competitive states began to staff their leadership, the party caucuses of the two houses, or both. In Wisconsin, for example, partisan staffing began in about 1967 with four or five people for each party in each chamber. Today these staffs have grown to ten to fifteen people each. In Illinois, over the last twenty years, the size of partisan staffs has tripled or quadrupled, so that today house Democrats and Republicans each have about eighty, while senate Democrats, in the majority, have sixty and senate Republicans, in the minority, somewhat fewer professionals on the payroll. Most of Michigan's nine hundred professionals are organized along partisan lines.

In Indiana, too, the principal growth has been in partisan staffing, while in Kentucky leadership staffing has made the greatest gains lately. Connecticut exemplifies one way in which partisan staff mushrooms. Until the early 1970s the Connecticut General Assembly had little in the way of professional staffing. Then, its nonpartisan central staff—research, fiscal, bill drafting, and program review— became firmly established. Somewhat later, the party caucuses added their own professionals. However, it was not until the Republicans took control of the legislature from the Democrats in 1984, the Democrats regained their majorities in 1986, and additional space was made available by a new legislative office building, that the staffing pattern in Connecticut changed dramatically. In 1987 another one hundred partisan staff positions were created, added to the fewer than three dozen already in existence, and divided up among the four legislative parties for allocation to their members.[26]

One of the primary purposes of expanding partisan staff is to improve the electoral prospects for the party's incumbents and even the party's challengers. Ten years ago, Connecticut's caucus staffs were oriented mainly toward legislation; now their orientation is toward constituencies and campaigns. The change has been noted by Connecticut's Auditors of Public Accounts, who recently uncovered questionable practices by partisan staff. They indicated that although they recognized "that it is difficult for partisan staff to be completely isolated from the election process . . . it appears to us that this activity has escalated to the point that the use of public funds for partisan political activity must be questioned." [27]

Indeed, wherever partisan staffs are of substantial size, their overriding objective today appears to be electoral rather than legislative. New York probably goes as far in this regard as any other place. It had become traditional practice for a number of so-called "no shows" and "seldom shows" to be carried on the legislative payroll, while their principal or even exclusive efforts were devoted to political campaigns. The practice was so blatant that in 1987 the Manhattan district attorney brought an indictment for grand larceny and conspiracy against the New York senate minority leader and one of his colleagues. The district attorney stated that: "In 1986, there was so much use of public funds for campaigns by the people involved here that it just cried out for prosecution." Apparently eight Democratic candidates, of whom six were challengers, were bolstered by workers on the senate minority's payroll.[28]

In California the politicization of staff has spread to standing committees. Earlier, committee staff was completely nonpartisan. Then the buildup of partisan staff began, so that today partisan professionals staff all the assembly committees as well as the senate fiscal committees. In the words of a long-time observer of the California scene, "The policy experts have been replaced by political hired guns whose main jobs is to get their bosses elected." [29]

Officially, partisan staff does not get involved in campaigns; unofficially, their principal job is to maintain their party's majority, help their party achieve a majority, or simply add to their numbers. As one professional, from a large partisan staff, described the task:

> We don't do anything *on* a campaign, but everything we do is *for* the campaign. The first year, we set them [members] up legislatively; the second year, we work their constituencies.

Actually, the legislative and constituency aspects of reelection intertwine. One's legislative accomplishments often are designed and nearly always are packaged for constituency consumption.

This is why the computerization of legislatures is such a boon to members who are seeking reelection. The primary interest legislators have in computers is not for lawmaking or simulation (those applications can be left to staff), but in compiling lists and targeting mail to folks back home. For example, in Wisconsin about $3 million is currently being spent on a computer system for direct mail, and in Connecticut mailing costs went up two-and-one-half times from 1984-1985 to 1985-1986. In matters of mail, legislative and political purposes are difficult to disentangle. Some states, such as Connecticut, have a cutoff date for mailings as the election approaches. Others try to specify what is more or less permissible by way of informing constituents. But, for the most part, anything that casts a member in a positive light accomplishes a political purpose.

The situation may take on an amusing cast, as when assembly Democrats, including the minority leader, in New Jersey filed suit in federal court charging six Republicans, including the speaker, with improper use of taxpayers' money to send mail with political, and not informational, messages. According to the Democrats, among Republican transgressions was the mailing of the Republican speaker's speech, which was "blatantly political and partisan, touting accomplishments of the Assembly under Republican control and attacking what used to happen in the Assembly when the Democrats were the majority party." The Democrats also charged that two Republicans sent a report to constituents about a bill to provide funds for the district, a mailing "clearly designed to enhance their political support by emphasizing their role in passage of the bill." As one might predict, the speaker responded that the object of the mailings was to "inform the public of actions taken in their state assembly." [30] Both sides had a point.

Probably of greatest help to members, as far as reelection is concerned, are the services they perform for constituents. Members of Congress recognized some time ago that constituency service is an important means by which they earn electoral support. State legislators are also aware of the benefits they derive from constituent service, and casework in particular. Although this is not a completely new realization, state legislators are now acquiring resources to engage in such endeavors. As resources increase, so does the amount of constituency service performed. [31] Indeed, one of the strongest tendencies among state legislatures today is that of providing members with personal staffing and district offices, both of which are used to reach out to constituents. As of 1985, eighteen state senates and eleven state houses provided personal aides for members, and ten legislatures had district office programs of one sort of another. In 1988 Michigan's senate was about to establish one. California's enterprise, which produces service of the highest quality, is in the forefront in this regard. In states where legislators have neither offices in their districts nor personal staff, they are helped in constituency service by caucus, committee, and central staffs.

Currently, legislators throughout the country are pressuring leaders for their own personal staffs—in small states such as Kentucky as well as larger ones such as Ohio and Illinois. It is only a question of time before personal staff is made available to the rank and file in more states. When available, the major function of personal staff will be that of delivering service to constituents and reelection to members, two very compatible tasks. That is where member priorities are being placed. In Michigan, for example, constituency service appears to have become the number-one priority of members, while legislating has become number two.

Constituency service by U.S. representatives and senators has been shown to help incumbents in their quest for reelection.[32] Although the precise electoral benefits at the state legislative level are not known, legislators—most of whom feel insecure electorally—believe that constituency service pays off. In any case, service is a fact of contemporary political life. In the smaller as well as larger states, the feeling is that if a legislator does not attend to constituent needs, constituents will find someone else who will.

Unbeatable Incumbents

Incumbency, or rather the resources that incumbents bring to bear to win reelection, conveys advantage. The success rate in recent elections of incumbents in the U.S. House is well over 90 percent. A number of state legislatures are approaching the congressional figure. In the professionalized legislatures of the large states—California, Illinois, Michigan, and New York—nine out of ten incumbents are returned. The same proportions are successful in Wisconsin, a somewhat smaller state with a professionalized legislature, and in Indiana, Maryland, Minnesota, New Jersey, and Ohio, where career professionalization has not gone as far. The advantages of incumbency can be seen in Florida. From 1968 through 1986, the success rate for incumbents running for the house ranged from 82 percent to 97 percent, and for the senate from 1974 through 1986 it ranged from 71 percent to 95 percent.

Even in legislatures such as those of Connecticut and Tennessee, which are still largely composed of amateur politicians, reelection rates have been high. Tennessee's rate is now about 90 percent. Of those incumbents defeated for renomination or reelection since 1970 in the Volunteer State, most suffered as a result of national tides.[33] The same pattern holds for Connecticut, where nine out of ten incumbents normally are returned to office. The elections of 1984 and 1986 were aberrations: President Reagan's coattails pulled in Republicans in the earlier year while Gov. William A. O'Neill's coattails pulled in

Democrats the later year. Even so, almost eight of ten incumbents won in these two elections. The staying power of Connecticut incumbents promises to increase in the future, since a recent constitutional amendment eliminates the party-line lever that had given voters the option of voting for the entire party slate on the basis of the appeal of the individual at the top of the ticket. No longer will a president, governor, or U.S. senator be able to aid challengers for the Connecticut state legislature to the same degree as in the past; incumbents will be better able to withstand negative coattail effects. Indeed, coattails are shorter just about everywhere. A recent study of state elections found that coattails were losing their pull, as state legislative elections were becoming insulated from outside influences and legislator resources were becoming more formidable.[34]

Not only are most districts relatively safe for incumbents, but most are also relatively safe for one party or the other. Decennial reapportionments in the states tend to draw district lines so that most incumbents will be reasonably secure. And as the proportion of competitive districts in a state declines, the likelihood of incumbents seeking and winning another term increases. Over time, the demography of districts may change and the partisan composition may shift. Thus, an incumbent's partisan advantage within specific districts may diminish. But one or the other party is still likely to maintain partisan advantage even a decade after redistricting and, in any case, the incumbent has had time to use the available resources to secure a "permanent" position.

Because the overall resources of incumbents are greater than those of potential challengers and because redistricting works in their favor, three to four out of every five districts are safe—by any objective standard. Yet, subjective standards are what count, for there is no such thing as a safe district for the professional legislator. Many incumbents may come to believe that they are entitled to their seats, but they still run scared. Perceptions of electoral insecurity are found not only among careerist members. They are found also among members who serve in part-time legislatures and who face little competition. A recent study in Alabama, for instance, reported that despite ample evidence of the safety of their districts, 93 percent of the members said their districts were electorally competitive.[35] Legislators everywhere realize that, however safe their district may appear, lightning can strike. Incumbents can be taken out by a national tide, a peculiar issue, or a scandal, especially if an opponent has a large enough war chest to exploit the situation. Therefore, they take no chances.

The more they have to lose, the harder they run. Professional legislators, committed to political careers, have the most to lose. Unlike citizen legislators, who can return full time to their law practices or other professions they have kept their hands in, the professionals have nowhere to return. For the most part, they have cut their ties if they had any to begin with.

It used to be that the goal of legislators who wanted to continue in office was to win their next race. Now their goal seems to be not only winning but also reducing uncertainty substantially—or even eliminating it entirely, if that were at all possible. If the districts of so many incumbents are considered safe, it is not merely by chance or by the design of reapportionment; it is in large part by virtue of the hard work of legislators who occupy the seats. They themselves feel unsafe whatever their earlier margins; so as soon as one race is over, they prepare themselves for the next.

Politicization of the Legislative Process

Politics and elections have become the principal concern of more and more legislators. "They start running the day they take their oath of office" is how one observer characterized their behavior in New Jersey. "Everything they do is geared toward the election" said another in Illinois. In California, where the stakes are high, campaigns and elections are seemingly constant, and the survival mentality has come to dominate legislative life. Even in New Hampshire, where the stakes are low, members appear to be paying more attention to their reelection.

Money and Politics

The most visible way in which legislators' preoccupation with reelection is manifested is through their efforts to raise funds. Just about everywhere—from California at one extreme to New Hampshire at the other—legislators are more involved than ever before in raising money for their campaigns. The number of fund-raisers held by individual members has increased sharply. In Ohio, for example, there used to be three fund-raisers a year; now there are three each week during the legislative session. Formerly, most fund-raisers were put on by Ohio's legislative party caucuses; now individuals, and particularly the chairpersons of key committees, hold them. Ten years ago only legislative leaders and senior members sponsored fund-raisers in Lansing. Today, just about every evening of the Michigan legislature's session, one member or another is holding a $100-a-seat fund-raiser in the capital. Even in Maryland, where legislators obtain funds from the gubernatorial or U.S. Senate candidate running at the top of the ticket, one out of four members holds a fund-raiser in Annapolis or Baltimore during the course of the session.

One consequence for the legislative process is that energies are being redirected from other tasks and toward that of raising funds. The enterprise is consuming, and sometimes it feeds on itself. Take the case of the Wisconsin legislator who complained about not having an opponent in a forthcoming election. Her problem was that without an opponent, it was difficult to raise money. That might seem bizarre, but if she could not raise money, then she might not be able to frighten off opponents in the future. Moreover, raising money is like milking a cow; one has to keep on milking the cow, or the milk will dry up. If the logic of the system is accepted, the rest follows.

Most unfortunate is the impact that the emphasis on money and some of the attendant solicitation methods are having on the political atmosphere. Occasionally a fund-raiser is held just before a vote on a controversial bill or while an appropriations bill is in its final stages. Usually a fund-raiser is held during the legislative session (although in some states, such as Kentucky, none is permitted until the session is over). The message that is communicated, lobbyists maintain, is blatant: "Contribute, or else." For lobbyists, interest groups, and political action committees, there seems to be no end to giving; they feel that they are being shaken down. The requests from legislators have doubled or tripled just in the last few years. One contract lobbyist in Sacramento, for example, indicated that in January and February of 1987 (an off-election year), he had received fifty solicitations for fund-raisers, at $500 each—a total of $25,000 that was expected of him. At that pace, the year would be a painfully expensive one; the biennium would be worse. If lobbyists used to prey on legislators, the tables have turned; now, legislators seem to be preying on lobbyists.

Leadership Politics

The impact of elections on the legislative process extends beyond the activities of individual members. It has made campaign management one of the essential tasks of legislative leadership. That task now absorbs much of their attention and energy.

Having been inaugurated by Jesse Unruh in California almost thirty years ago, the practice of leaders raising campaign funds for members has spread widely in the last few years. In those states where political parties compete vigorously in legislative elections, the main job of the leader has become that of winning or maintaining the majority of seats in the chamber. The difference between being a leader of the majority and that of the minority, as anyone who has been in both positions appreciates, is the difference between being at the center of the process and at its periphery. Even where the prospects for a change in party control appear slim, as in the New York senate, the Massachusetts senate, and the Ohio house, leaders such as Warren Anderson,

William Bulger, and Vernal Riffe leave little to chance.

Currently, leaders in more than half the states have taken on the job of raising funds and allocating money and other forms of support to members of their legislative parties. As the minority leader in the New York assembly commented, "Among the many things I do, I go out and raise money for my members, and that's heavy lifting." It is by no means unusual to see a speaker of the house or a president of the senate collaring a lobbyist in a capitol corridor and inquiring, "How is it that I don't have your check for tickets to my fundraiser yet?" Or confronting a lobbyist with, "Did you realize that you contributed $500 to the senate president's (or the house speaker's) fund and only $250 to mine?"

Willie Brown in California has set the pace. Not only does he raise millions for Democratic assembly candidates, but he intervenes in primary races as well. In 1986 Brown's candidates won in five of the six primaries in which the speaker played a significant role (while Minority Leader Pat Nolan's candidates lost in three out of five primaries). Brown justifies intraparty intervention, which most legislative leaders eschew, on the grounds that he has to get the candidates who will be strongest running in the general election. What he wants are people who will win, and thereby protect or enhance the Democratic majority. Failure to do so is a "good way to lose your job," he maintains.[36] In fact, Brown and David Roberti, the president pro tem of the senate, were both elected to their leadership positions on a platform that they would raise money and protect the seats of members. Raising money could be difficult for leaders to do in the future. In 1988 California's voters passed Proposition 73, which would prohibit the leaders from transferring funds they raise to candidates for the legislature. The question is whether California's legislative leaders can devise ways to get around the prohibition.

Leaders elsewhere are heavily involved in fund raising, too. Tom Loftus, speaker in Wisconsin, acknowledges that he has somewhat reluctantly become a "campaign manager." He chairs the Assembly Democratic Campaign Committee and in 1984 raised $150,000 for Democrats running in marginal districts. He helped recruit candidates, furnished them with schooling in campaign techniques, provided personnel and logistical support, and issued position papers on their behalf.[37] In New Hampshire, leadership also takes part in the election of members. The granite committee, for instance, is the organization of house Republicans. Chaired by the majority leader, it raises and doles money out to candidates in close races. The committee is a relative newcomer to the scene, having started only four years ago, but it is becoming an important part of the electoral environment. In Florida, the president of the senate and the speaker of the house each have leadership funds to help Democratic candidates. Speaker-designate Tom Gustafson planned to raise $1 million for the 1988 house elections, almost double the amount raised by his predecessor.

Just as in California and Wisconsin, in those states where political parties compete vigorously in legislative elections, one of the chief jobs of the leader has become that of winning or maintaining the majority of seats in the chamber. This is the situation in Connecticut, Illinois, Michigan, Minnesota, New York, Ohio, Pennsylvania, and Washington. For example, look at the experience of Chuck Hardwick, who had been minority leader in the New Jersey assembly. For a full year he spent part of every day working for the Republican's 1985 legislative campaign, holding the hand of each candidate with a chance of winning. His efforts (and Gov. Tom Kean's coattails) paid off; the Republicans won control, and Hardwick became speaker. In an address on his new role, enumerating twelve different tasks of the speaker, Hardwick put "preparing for the next campaign" first. The ordering was no accident, for if he neglected maintaining his majority, he would not have to concern himself with most of the other tasks. His work evidently paid off; the Republicans in 1987 kept control of the assembly, although by a smaller margin.

The primary focus of the legislative party and legislative party leadership used to be governing. Now, they are displacing party organizations at state and local levels, taking over the electoral function as well. Thus, a major shift in political power is occurring, at least in a number of states. Newly acquired power, however, can absorb much of the time of legislative leaders and distract them from their other responsibilities. Leaders, such as Tom Loftus of Wisconsin, see the benefits of the new system but acknowledge that it may go too far. According to Loftus:

> It's when it's overdone that I think it's of some concern. What happens is that the leaders then become expected to raise money for candidates, the system gets out of control, it isn't a unifying force. . . . And it may not bring a caucus together, it may not strengthen leadership, it may indeed give leadership an additional job and be a distraction.[38]

Furthermore, the electoral activities of leaders—and particularly their fund-raising efforts—becloud the atmosphere and raise questions regarding the ethics of the legislature. The issue of campaigning within the legislative context recently was posed most dramatically in New York by the indictment of the senate minority leader. "I don't know which side of the line those guys were on," the assembly minority leader commented, "because I'm not sure where the line is."[39]

Leadership takes care of the electoral needs of its party's incumbents in strictly legislative ways, too. Freshmen members from tough districts are helped by every means practicable. They may be given a vice chairmanship of a committee that can benefit them in their district or with a key group. They may be counseled on how to vote as safely as they can on a variety of issues, given the nature of their constituencies. Targeted members in competitive districts naturally receive special treatment, but all legislative party members are favored in ways that will benefit them and the party electorally.

Delivering Pork

A member's best chance of bringing home the bacon is to receive a coveted assignment to the appropriations committee. In some places projects for the district, known as "pork" or some equivalent, are tightly controlled. For example, in Illinois pork is doled out only sparingly by the governor and legislative leaders. In Maryland, the process is about the same; approximately $10 million out of a $230 million capital budget is dedicated to what are euphemistically known as "worthy legislative projects," not a lot and no larger a proportion than that of a decade ago. Kentucky cannot afford much fat, and there is precious little money for district projects available. Elsewhere legislators live somewhat higher off the hog. The substantial increase of pork in Wisconsin, for instance, relates to members' need to show their constituents that they can deliver. Speaker Tom Loftus describes pork in the budget process:

> . . . in the assembly, the majority party members would caucus and the leadership tried to gather 50 votes for the bill. Each member would state what changes or additions he or she wanted to the bill in return for their vote. An auction atmosphere would descend upon the room until the 50th and most expensive vote was obtained.[40]

One Wisconsin senator, who has earned a reputation for getting projects in the state budget, explained the appeal of pork:

> Maybe it's wrong. Maybe the whole process is wrong. But we get applauded more for what we bring home—the so-called pork. If the name of the game is to get reelected, pork greases the process along.[41]

In Florida, members spend what appears to be an inordinate amount of their time ensuring that one or several $50,000 to $100,000 projects for their district are included in the appropriations bill by the appropriations subcommittee, full committee, and conference committee.

The pork barrel process in North Carolina is illustrative; it works generally as follows.[42] After the state budget is approved and major legislation dealt with, legislative leaders estimate how much remains for "special entries." That money is divided equally between the senate and house. In 1985, $100,000 was made available to each senator and $50,000 to each representative. Although the totals are not large, the growth has been substantial. While state spending increased by 11 percent between 1981 and 1984, dollars in the pork barrel rose by 132 percent. One of the reasons for this is the growing Republican influence in North Carolina, which, among other things, has forced the Democratic leadership to make use of pork for exercising party control in the legislature.

Electoral Competition and Partisanship

Electoral concerns cannot fail to affect the legislative atmosphere and process. Members facing severe electoral challenges behave differently from how they would otherwise, because they are under severe stress.[43] Florida provides a good example.

The statewide candidacies of a number of legislators were especially disruptive of the Florida process during the 1986 session. Three of them, including the president of the senate, were running for governor. A former representative was also running for governor. Another representative was in the race for lieutenant governor, two senators and a representative were seeking the office of attorney general, and two representatives and one senator were vying for commissioner of education. Another senator was running for an open congressional seat, and two house members were competing to be mayor of Jacksonville. As might be expected, a number of house members were running for the senate. To complete the ticket, the Democratic governor was seeking to unseat the Republican U.S. senator. When asked before the session began whether politics would affect things, Speaker James Harold Thompson replied, "Has a cat got climbing gear?",[44] a country expression that was borne out in the months that followed.

Electoral considerations were pervasive throughout the legislative session. Photographers trailed candidates through the corridors; television crews wired them for sound and filmed them on the floor of the chamber; and several members left Tallahassee for campaign appearances around the state, even though important business was under way at the capitol. One candidate for attorney general attacked his opponent in radio and television advertisements, on the senate floor, and in committee. A contingent of house Republicans supported one of their own for governor; a contingent of house Democrats supported their former colleague (who ultimately won the Democratic nomination, but then lost the general election) for governor; and a contingent of senate Democrats favored the president of their chamber. Tension always exists between the house and senate, but that year it was sharper than usual.

Issues in the 1986 session of the Florida legislature were also influenced by electoral politics. Bills on drunken driving were introduced, not by chance but after polling and with the impending election very much in mind. The senate's reluctance to raise taxes for educational funding was in part a function of the president's candidacy and the tough reelection races facing several Democratic incumbents.

Electoral competition among individual members, as in Florida, weighs heavily upon the legislature. Competition between the parties weighs upon it even more. Thirty years ago, only a dozen or so states had competitive parties. Now half of the states have substantial competition at the legislative as well as the gubernatorial level, and in most other states competition has been increasing over the past decade. Partisanship, which is associated with party competition, is growing at the state level. A recent study found that roughly one-quarter of forty-four legislatures surveyed could be considered "very" partisan and another half "somewhat" partisan.[45]

Some legislatures, it should be noted, are not very partisan at all. This is the case in states where few Republicans hold seats. In Maryland, for example, only 6 members of the 47-member senate and 17 of the 141-member house in 1987 were Republicans. The last policy issue in Annapolis that saw a division by party arose more than ten years ago. The minority gives little thought to trying to embarrass the majority; nor does much sniping take place. In terms of partisanship, life in the Maryland General Assembly is calm; when conflict occurs it tends to pit legislators from the rural, western part of the state allied with those of the Eastern Shore against legislators from Baltimore and its suburbs. Because Republicans have made few gains in the Kentucky General Assembly, little partisanship exists there as well. Republicans are such a small minority that they are dependent on the majority, and they do not jeopardize their relationship.

But, overall, partisanship has grown. It has been on the rise in states where it had meant a lot, such as California, Michigan, New Jersey, and Wisconsin.[46] It has also been on the rise in states where it had meant relatively little, in Florida, for instance. The number of Floridians who identify with the Republican party has been increasing, as has Republican registration. By 1987 there had been a gradual build-up of GOP strength to 37.5 percent in both the house and senate, with the possibility that the senate might have a Republican majority in the foreseeable future. Texas is moving in the same direction, with Republicans now holding 37.3 percent of the seats in the house. The competition between the two parties for control of Texas was most sharply evidenced in 1987, when partisanship dominated a yearlong struggle over the budget and taxes.

What stimulates partisanship is the strong concern of both leaders and rank and file with the maintenance (or acquisition) of party majorities and leadership positions. A governor and legislature controlled by different parties can also be a stimulant. California is a case in point. Over the years partisanship has been intensifying (especially in the senate, which had once been a comradely institution—much more of a club). Willie Brown gained his assembly speakership with Republican support. Two years later, when he had consolidated his position within the Democratic caucus, he no longer needed support from Republicans. His treatment of them became less beneficent, and that exacerbated partisan feelings in the assembly. The sides hardened further because of the ideology and practice of the Republican governor. In California, partisanship has become mean spirited and is undoubtedly fueled by the Republican challenge to eighteen years of Democratic control of the legislature. The Democratic margin in the assembly has narrowed, and the number of California voters who identify with the Republican party now equals the number who identify with the Democratic party.[47] Whereas legislators used to fight one day and come together again the next, now they hold grudges. Elsewhere, too, partisanship is becoming nastier. In the Illinois house the speaker and the minority leader are bitter in their enmity, and members are frequently at one another's throats. Personalities help provoke partisan contention in Michigan also.

When Democrats and Republicans are ideologically at opposite poles on major issues, partisanship will be more intense. Along with other factors, patterns of policy difference can divide the parties sharply. A recent study of legislative voting in California shows that both the house and senate are polarized, with liberals and conservatives falling almost completely in opposite partisan camps. In the assembly, for example, not one Republican was more liberal than the most conservative Democrat, and in the senate only one Republican was more liberal than the most conservative Democratic.[48]

Whatever the ideological split, issues are also raised and used for electoral purposes, as vehicles in the quest of the parties for power. There is nothing new in the legislative parties taking into account the potential effects that their position vis-à-vis a bill will have on their electoral prospects. By way of illustration, there is the story of the legislative staffer who cautioned a party leader in Ohio: "If you pass this bill, you're going to screw up the state for the next thirty years." "We can't worry about the next thirty years," the leader replied. "We have to worry about the next election."

Beyond merely taking into account the electoral effects of legislative positions, the parties in the senate and house go further today. They raise and exploit issues, more than previously, to gain partisan advantage rather than to enact legislation to their liking. One way that a legislative party attempts to secure an edge electorally is by "making a record" that will help it, embarrass the opposition, or both. Floor amendments, requiring record votes, is the conventional device used. As one observer noted, "Clearly, efforts are made to establish records on which to run or on which to try to maneuver your opponents into an undesirable position." Typically, Democrats will try to get Republicans on record against teachers or environmental interests, while Republicans will try to get Democrats on record against economic development.

Partisan positioning has become routine in states such as California, Connecticut, Illinois, Iowa, Michigan, and Wisconsin. In some legislatures, it would seem, a large part of the floor session is managed at least partly with the next election in mind. Take Michigan, for example. At an earlier time, the custom was to forego record votes so that colleagues would not be embarrassed. Now, both sides call for roll calls to put the opposition on record. In the past, Michigan legislators quickly put out of mind the votes cast against them by their colleagues.

In more and more states—and particularly the larger, competitive, professionalized ones—winning power is becoming more important to legislators than exercising it. After all, if power cannot be won, it cannot be exercised. Thus, legislators can justify the efforts they devote to their reelection. No one else will do it for them, and there is so much to lose. But the impact of their activities is great. As one critic of the California legislature argues:

> [The system] has been politicized and corrupted by the pervasive influence of money in politics and government, politics as a career orientation, the need for legislators to reassure their reelection, and the lack of time to consider policy because time must be spent raising money.[49]

Other states may lag behind California, but there is no doubt that the politicization sweeping a growing number of legislatures is leaving its mark on the process and the institution.

Fragmentation

In any American state legislature power is highly decentralized. Some legislators have somewhat more power and others somewhat less, but essentially each elected representative has a vote and a say. Power is divided, not only among individuals but also between houses and parties and among committees, delegations, and other groupings. It is by no means easy in a legislature to reach agreement on a controversial issue.

The natural state of a legislature is fragmentation. But in a number of respects, the legislature is even more fragmented today than twenty years ago. Earlier, leaders were truly in command, and power was tightly held as compared with now. Partly as a consequence of modernization and reform, legislatures have been democratized.[50] Resources are more broadly distributed, and the gap between leaders and other legislators is narrower.

Committee systems have been strengthened significantly over the years. Now, standing committees are agencies of specialization, and the legislative workload is parceled out among them. Each committee rules over its own turf, with substantial power delegated to it. The chairpersons—or at least those who chair major committees—set their own agendas, shape their committee's decisions, and negotiate issues with one another. They are figures with whom lobbyists, executive officials, legislators, and legislative leaders must reckon. Ten or twenty standing committees, each in its own domain doing its own thing, constitute a formidable centrifugal force in a legislative body.

Legislative staff is far more dispersed than it used to be. Years ago, the dominant staff was the office of legislative council or an equivalent service agency. It provided information and research for the two chambers, both parties, every committee, and the entire roster of members. Recently, however, staffing patterns changed. First, partisan staffing for the legislative parties in each house was established in a dozen or so states, challenging the dominance of the nonpartisan centralized staffs. Second, in a number of places—most recently Louisiana and Oklahoma—agencies that worked for both the senate and house split up, so that each chamber wound up with its own base of support. Third, standing committees, in states such as California and New York, acquired their own professionals whose primary loyalty was to the committee, to the chair, and to a specific policy domain. Fourth, in a growing number of places legislators are being staffed as individuals at the capitol or in their districts, in response to their demands for help or as a reward for the backing they give their leaders. Whatever the pattern, practically everywhere current staffs are larger and more accessible to members. If the knowledge provided by staff constitutes power, then power within the legislature is shared among more members today.

Another fragmenting tendency results from the many groups and lobbyists promoting particularistic interests in the legislature. Their overall influence may or may not be greater than formerly, but their numbers and activities have grown substantially. Years ago relatively few interests were represented at the state level; now there are many. This is because of the growth in the political awareness and mobilization of previously uninvolved segments of the population; the substantial development of multistate business enterprises; the upsurge in ideological politics and single-issue groups; and the reduction of the federal government's role in various policy arenas and the increase in action at the state level. Most states have also witnessed an explosion of lobbyists, with the greatest growth among contract lobbyists who represent multiple clients and are resident in the capital.[51] As they seek to satisfy their concerns, lobbyists and their clients pull legislators in different directions.

Probably the greatest impetus toward institutional fragmentation is the constituency basis of legislative representation. Legislators owe their first and, nowadays, foremost allegiance to their constituents. They introduce local bills to benefit their districts; they endeavor to get more than a fair share for their districts from state aid formulas, and particularly the school aid formula; they seek to have funds for statewide programs spent in their districts; they try to get as much pork for their districts as they can; and, with or without personal staff and local offices, they manage to deliver more mail and more service to the folks back home. Add to all this the fact that the trend over the years has been away from multimember districts and toward single-member ones, thus encouraging greater parochialism on the parts of members. As a recent study of members of Congress observed, "Single-member district systems do not provide elected representatives with compelling personal incentives to pursue common interests."[52] Or from a state legislative perspective, the closer legislators are tied to their district, the more difficult it may be for them to consider statewide interests.[53]

These fragmenting tendencies buttress the individualism of members. Because of the candidate-centered nature of political campaigns, the opportunities offered them by television and other media, and the legislative resources at their disposal, the individualism of legislators has increased markedly. The media exerts a special appeal. It pays attention to members who are different—independents, mavericks, rebels. If members aspire to higher office and seek statewide name identification, individualism offers a most promising route.

Much of what today's legislators do is designed to prove themselves outside the legislature instead of within it. The *California Journal,* for example, went pretty far in referring to the legislature not as a single entity, but "more like an Oriental bazaar with 120 rug merchants . . . peddling their wares to colleagues, lobbyists, the governor and whoever else may come along." [54] Survival has become the primary consideration for members, and the personal dimension has assumed far greater importance in the legislative process. California legislators have come to identify with "what's mine," and not with "what's ours." The ascendancy of the individual is spreading throughout the states, especially in professional bodies but in citizen bodies as well.

Summary

Whatever the difficulties, if performance is the standard, then state legislatures are in better shape today than they were twenty years ago. They are effectively meeting their responsibilities as far as representation, participation, and production are concerned.

Legislatures are expected to represent the citizens of their state, with members linked to constituencies and groups. Legislatures are much more representative than before. Periodic reapportionment, the emergence of women and minorities in legislative ranks, and the close relationship forged by members with their districts have changed the composition and behavior of legislative bodies.

Legislatures are expected to participate in the making of public policy and the allocation of public funds, and they do. No longer does the governor propose and the legislature dispose. Although the governor still controls the agenda on priority measures in most places, in some states the legislature is almost as likely to initiate major policy as is the governor. Today legislatures are in the thick of the policy fray, and as a consequence they frequently come toe to toe with their governors. For the most part, they are able to work things out, although increasingly the courts are being asked to settle disputes. Legislatures also take on governors when it comes to the state budget. In recent years, thanks largely to the growth of their fiscal staffs, legislatures have flexed their budgetary muscle and expanded their budgetary role. Legislatures have even become involved in administration, by means of sunset processes, the review of administrative rules and regulations, and the conduct of program evaluations and performance audits.

Legislatures are expected to produce outcomes that respond to public demands and needs, command support, and prove effective in application. Although their record is by no means unblemished, legislatures generally have fashioned policies that are responsive to their various publics. Legislatures duck fewer issues; instead, they wrestle with the most contentious problems. They have adopted noteworthy measures in the areas of the environment, education, and social welfare. And they have raised taxes when additional revenues were necessary to do the job. Not every legislative policy succeeds because of the gap between policy pronouncement on the one hand and the level of funding and vigor of administration on the other. There is substantial room for improvement, but some progress is being made even in the area of implementation.

While the current legislative record in representation, participation, and production is a good one, there is an additional function that the legislature can be expected to perform. The legislature should provide a process that is authoritative, deliberative, and open—a process that is capable of resolving conflict and building consensus. That process and the legislature as an institution are in jeopardy.

Contemporary trends—professionalization of careers, preoccupation with elections, and fragmentation—are taking a toll. Individualism is in the ascendancy. Members run their own campaigns, promote the interests of the districts they represent, and pursue their personal political ambitions. The capital community of legislators, lobbyists, and other participants in the process is more diffuse. Few values are shared, and legislative norms are weaker than they used to be. Trust is still important, but as a bond it links fewer members today. A legislator's word is still binding, but not as binding as it once was.

The process remains a remarkably open one, but it is less deliberative than it should be. Given the goals of members, the demands of groups, and the heavy workload, deliberation gives way to expediency. Members frequently are unwilling to say no to their colleagues, lest their colleagues say no to them. They are adverse also to saying no to constituents, lest their constituents withdraw support from them. The process has become porous; much seeps through that probably should not. Standing committees do not screen the wheat from the chaff as diligently as they might.

In view of the individualism of members and the fragmentation of the institution, it is probable that the legislature will continue to enact policies that respond to constituents and interest groups. But will the legislature be able to sustain its capacity to make policies that benefit the states' entire citizenry? If the case of the U.S. Congress is an indication, then state legislatures also face the prospect of an unraveling of organizational coherence and approaching paralysis. The result would be a declining ability to fashion a consensus, not with respect to narrowly focused matters, but on statewide policies.[55]

Much today depends on the abilities of legislative leadership, for leadership may be the only glue that holds things together. The power of leadership in many places is eroding; in some places, however, leadership power is still impressive.[56] Overall, leaders are managing extremely well, particularly in view of the pressures upon them. They are standing up to the immediate demands, which is what they have to do to survive from day to day. They are satisfying the parochial and careerist needs of members, and, thus far, they have even been able to shape policies needed by the state.

But costs have been incurred. There is a cost when leaders devote themselves disproportionately to electoral politics, delegating policies to others. There is a cost when, to satisfy members' appetites, they give everyone a piece of the budget bill. There is a cost when they permit legislation to sneak by, because members want corners cut for the bills they have introduced. There is a cost when they expand the committee system to meet demands for more chairmanships. The cost of doing business is on the rise, and the legislative institution and process are diminished as a result.

Moreover, neither rank and file nor leadership has time or energy left for tending to institutional matters. Rules and procedures, the organization and performance of staff, the job being done by committees and on the floor, and the public's perception and understanding of the legislature are not immediate problems. Thus, they get short shrift.

The legislative process is suffering neglect, and the fabric of the legislative institution is wearing thin. The situation in the legislature today may be analogous to that of the infrastructure at the state and local level. The nation is spending too little on maintenance; facilities are running down. After a period of transformation and institution building in the late 1960s and 1970s, the legislature as an institution now seems to be eroding. American legislatures are undergoing further change, and perhaps another transformation.

Notes

1. See the poll by Louis Harris, commissioned by the National Conference of State Legislatures, as reported in Glenn Newkirk, "State Legislatures through the People's Eyes," *State Legislatures* (August-September 1979): 6-11.
2. For a brief account of the changed legislative role, see Lucinda S. Simon, "Legislatures and Governors: The Wrestling Match," *The Journal of State Government* 59 (Spring 1986): 1-6.
3. The following is adapted, in part, from Alan Rosenthal, "The Changing Character of State Legislators—Or: Requiem for a Vanishing Breed," *Public Affairs Review* (1985): 80-93.
4. Cited in *Wisconsin State Journal,* August 28, 1983, with data supplied by Wisconsin Legislative Reference Bureau.
5. It is interesting to note that in Minnesota, although 28 percent of the

members surveyed admitted to being full time, 88 percent believed the legislature should not be full time and 90 percent believed legislators should have another occupation. Charles H. Backstrom, "The Legislature as a Place to Work: How Minnesota Legislators View Their Jobs," Hubert H. Humphrey Institute of Public Affairs, University of Minnesota, December 1986, 5.

6. The percentages of full-time members reported here are estimates furnished by in-state sources. Those who identify their occupations as "legislator," as reported in state blue books and directories, tend to be somewhat lower. See National Conference of State Legislatures, *State Legislators' Occupations: A Decade of Change* (March 25, 1987), and Peverill Squire, "Career Opportunities and Membership Stability in Legislatures," *Legislative Studies Quarterly* 13 (February 1988): 75, 78.

7. Charles G. Bell and Charles M. Price, "20 Years of a Full-Time Legislature," *California Journal* (January 1987): 36-40.

8. For example, a member of the Florida house explained that demands on her time was one factor in her decision not to run for reelection in 1988. She found that she was spending 75 percent of her time away from home and would have to spend even more as she advanced in leadership.

9. Jerry Calvert, "Revolving Doors—Volunteerism in State Legislatures," *State Government* 52 (Autumn 1979): 179. See also Squire, "Career Opportunities and Membership Stability in Legislatures."

10. "Legislative Compensation Questionnaire Summary," prepared for Compensation Study Committee, Wisconsin, with memorandum dated February 13, 1984.

11. Cited in Lucinda Simon, "The Legislative Pay Puzzle," *State Legislatures* (July 1987): 14-19.

12. See *New York Times,* January 17, 1988.

13. See National Conference of State Legislatures, *State Legislators' Occupations,* 9.

14. As characterized by a member of the new breed, Speaker Tom Loftus, in "New Breed Legislator/Legislative Leader: Sun Spot Number One," Institute of Politics, John F. Kennedy School of Government, Harvard University, October 3, 1984, unpublished paper.

15. Marilyn Johnson and Susan Carroll, *Profile of Women Holding Office II,* Center for the American Woman and Politics, Rutgers University, 1978, 10A. Updated by 1981 data.

16. Bell and Price, "20 Years of a Full-Time Legislature," 38.

17. Quoted in the *Los Angeles Times,* January 29, 1984.

18. Calvert, "Revolving Doors—Volunteerism in State Legislatures," 175.

19. Gary L. Crawley, "Electoral Competition, 1958-1984: Impact on State Legislative Turnover in the Indiana House," *American Politics Quarterly* 14 (January-April 1986): 114. See also Lucinda Simon, "The Mighty Incumbent," *State Legislatures* (July 1986): 31-32; and Wayne L. Francis and John R. Baker, "Why Do U.S. State Legislators Vacate Their Seats?" *Legislative Studies Quarterly* 11 (February 1986): 119-126.

20. Steven D. Williams, "Incumbency in the Tennessee General Assembly,"

Comparative State Politics Newsletter 8 (June 1987): 22.

21. Crawley, "Electoral Competition, 1958-1984: Impact on State Legislative Turnover in the Indiana House," 107-108. See also Squire, "Career Opportunities and Membership Stability in Legislatures."

22. Bruce Cain, John Ferejohn, and Morris Fiorina, *The Personal Vote* (Cambridge, Mass.: Harvard University Press, 1987), 7. See also Lawrence C. Dodd, "A Theory of Congressional Cycles: Solving the Puzzle of Change," in Gerald C. Wright, Jr., Leroy N. Rieselbach, and Lawrence C. Dodd, eds., *Congress and Policy Change* (New York: Apathon Press, 1986), 3-44.

23. *New York Times,* March 1, 1987.

24. Neal R. Peirce, "State of the States," *National Journal,* June 4, 1988, 1494.

25. Jeffrey Kanige, "Money and Power: A Dangerous Brew," *New Jersey Reporter,* February 1988, 8.

26. See Don Noel, "Build a Building and Fill the Space," *The Courant,* September 4, 1987.

27. Letter to Joint Committee on Legislative Management, January 7, 1988.

28. Michael Oreskes, "Tandem Jobs: Legislative and Campaigns," *New York Times,* September 19, 1987.

29. Sherry Bebitch Jeffe, "For Legislative Staff, Policy Takes a Back Seat to Politics," *California Journal* (January 1987): 42.

30. Vincent R. Zarate, "Assembly Dems Sue 6 Republicans over Mailings," *Star-Ledger,* August 7, 1987.

31. See Malcolm Jewell, *Representation in State Legislatures* (Lexington: University of Kentucky Press, 1982): 9-10.

32. Richard F. Fenno, Jr., *Home Style: House Members in Their Districts* (Boston: Little, Brown, 1978), 109. See also Robert S. Erikson, "The Advantage of Incumbency in Congressional Elections," *Polity* 3 (Spring 1971): 395-405; and Cain, Ferejohn, and Fiorina, *The Personal Vote,* 135-194.

33. Williams, "Incumbency in the Tennessee General Assembly," 22.

34. John E. Chubb, "Institutions, the Economy, and the Dynamics of State Elections," *American Political Science Review* 88 (March 1988): 133-154. See also Crawley, "Electoral Competition, 1958-1984," 110.

35. Jeffrey E. Cohen, "Perceptions of Electoral Insecurity among Members Holding Safe Seats in a U.S. State Legislature," *Legislative Studies Quarterly* 9 (May 1984): 366-367.

36. Mark Simon, "Do Caucus Leaders Build Better Candidates?", *California Journal* 17 (August 1986): 388.

37. Tom Loftus, "The New 'Political Parties' in State Legislatures" (Address at the annual meeting of the Council of State Governments, 1984).

38. Alan Rosenthal, ed., *The Governor and the Legislature,* Eagleton's 1987 Symposium on the State of the States, Eagleton Institute of Politics, Rutgers, The State University of New Jersey, December 17-18, 1987.

39. As quoted in Frank Lupin, "Case against State Senators Linked to a Shift in Political Campaign Power," *New York Times,* September 17, 1987.

40. Tom Loftus, "The Wisconsin Budget Process," Lecture for the University of Wisconsin—Whitewater, March 17, 1986, 7.
41. Quoted in Bill Hurley, "Passing the Pork," *Milwaukee Sentinel,* September 3, 1987.
42. Joel A. Thompson, "Bringing Home the Bacon: The Politics of Pork Barrel in the North Carolina Legislature," *Legislative Studies Quarterly* 11 (February 1986): 91-108.
43. The following paragraphs on Florida are based on Alan Rosenthal, "The State of the Florida Legislature," *Florida State University Law Review* 14 (Fall 1986): 415-417.
44. "Campaigns Will Have Big Impact on Session," *St. Petersburg Times,* April 6, 1986.
45. Alan Rosenthal, "If the Party's Over, Where's All That Noise Coming From?", *State Government* 57 (1984): 50-51.
46. Partisanship also varies depending on how narrow the majority is in a legislative chamber. In Indiana, with the house in 1988 split fifty-two Republicans to forty-eight Democrats, partisanship is rather intense. It is less intense in the senate where the margin is not quite as narrow. Because the Republicans have the narrowest of edges in the Michigan senate, partisanship is intense there, too.
47. Ken Hoover, "A Change in the Wind," *California Journal* (April 1988): 170-174.
48. Elaine Guidoux, "Who's Conservative? Who's Liberal?", *California Journal* (June 1988): 242-245. See also Andrea Margolis and Richard Zeiger, "Bleeding Hearts, Stone Hearts," *California Journal* (January 1987): 30-32.
49. Sherry Bebitch Jeffe, "For Legislative Staff, Policy Takes a Back Seat to Politics," 42-43.
50. Fragmentation in the U.S. House is more attributable to careerism. See Dodd, "A Theory of Congressional Cycles," 12-18.
51. Charles G. Bell, "Legislatures, Interest Groups and Lobbyists: The Link beyond the District," *The Journal of State Government* 59 (Spring 1986): 14-15.
52. Cain, Ferejohn, and Fiorina, *The Personal Vote,* 209.
53. See Alan Rosenthal, "The Consequences of Constituency Service," *The Journal of State Government* 59 (Spring 1986): 25-30.
54. As quoted in *Los Angeles Times,* January 29, 1984.
55. Dodd, "A Theory of Congressional Cycles," 25-27.
56. See Alan Rosenthal, "Challenges to Leadership," *The Journal of State Government* 60 (November-December 1987): 265-269.

5. STATE SUPREME COURTS: ACTIVISM AND ACCOUNTABILITY

Lawrence Baum

Scholars and other observers of American courts focus most of their attention on the federal level. The United States Supreme Court is the most closely watched of all courts, and lower federal courts receive considerable scrutiny for their involvement in national policy making. In contrast, the courts of the states have conducted their work in relative obscurity.

This general inattention to state courts seems unjustifiable during any period. The majority of all cases are filed in state courts. In the areas in which courts touch the lives of most individuals—criminal law, divorce, and lawsuits over personal injuries—activity is concentrated primarily in state courts. And state supreme courts sometimes engage in a judicial activism comparable to that of the U.S. Supreme Court.

In recent years, the role of the judiciary in state politics and policy making has become more noticeable. As a result, state courts have begun to attract the attention that was denied to them for so long. These developments have centered on state supreme courts, whose activities in a number of states have made them increasingly visible. This chapter will survey recent developments that have enhanced the roles of the state supreme courts.[1]

The work of state supreme courts must be understood in relation to the systems of government in which they operate. Like other state political institutions, supreme courts operate in the context of federalism, both "vertical" (the federal-state relationship) and "horizontal" (relationships among states).[2] Their primary vertical relationship is with the U.S. Supreme Court. Under generally accepted legal doctrine, state judges are obliged to follow the Supreme Court's interpretations of federal law. More broadly, the policies of the Supreme Court—what it does and does not do—help to set the agendas of state supreme courts and influence the direction of their policies. Horizontally, a state supreme court stands alongside supreme courts in other states, courts that often face similar legal and policy issues. State supreme courts

serve as sources of policy cues to each other. While no court is obliged
to adopt the legal interpretations of courts in other states, judges may
choose to follow the initiatives of other courts and the trends in state
courts across the nation.

State courts also operate in an environment of other state political
institutions, which include the electorate as well as the legislature and
executive branch. These other institutions hold considerable power over
the courts, and this power helps them to influence judicial action. The
other institutions in state government also provide alternative forums
for those who seek to shape public policy. Interest groups that fail to secure what they want from other institutions may bring their demands
to the courts. Similarly, those who are unhappy with court decisions
may "appeal" to the legislature, the executive branch, or the voters.
This process sometimes involves the federal government as well.
Groups that seek certain judicial policies can turn to state courts, for instance, if they fail to gain what they want from the federal courts.

State supreme courts have engaged in a new wave of activism as
policy makers. In response, other institutions in state government have
given increasing scrutiny to the courts' work, thereby enforcing a
greater accountability on judges and courts.

Activism

State courts have always been active policy makers; this is an
inevitable product of their roles as interpreters of state law.[3] Historically, their power over policy has been greatest in the "common law"
areas of the law. In these areas, the basic legal rules were established
almost entirely by state courts rather than through statutes. Even
though legislatures had the power to make the rules themselves, they
exercised this power only to a limited degree and otherwise deferred to
the courts. Three common-law areas are particularly important. The
first is property law, the rules governing the ownership and transfer of
property. The second is contract law, the rules for the enforcement of
contracts. The last is tort law; this is a broad and ill-defined area that
centers on liability for wrongful acts that cause property damage,
personal injuries, or death.

Through their primacy in these areas, state supreme courts set
down fundamental legal rules that shape American economic and social
life in critical ways. It was the courts that did most to determine the
rights of property owners, the meaning of contracts, and the ability of
individuals to recover money for injuries. Had state courts done nothing
more, their decisions in the common-law fields would have ensured
them a significant role as policy makers.

The importance of the U.S. Supreme Court lies largely in its power of judicial review, under which it can declare statutes unconstitutional. State supreme courts can overturn statutes on the basis of both the federal and state constitutions, but many of them traditionally made limited use of this power. A 1954 commentary, for instance, concluded that "Judicial review in Utah has not played an important role in shaping public policy." [4] Other courts were more active; the New York court of appeals, the highest court in the state, struck down 136 statutes in the period from 1906 through 1938.[5] Such courts enhanced their roles in state policy making through the power of judicial review.

Judicial activism, then, is nothing new in the states. By such measures as numbers of laws declared unconstitutional, state supreme courts in the current era do not seem substantially more activist than in the past.[6] Nor is state-court activism of recent years fundamentally different in kind from past policy making.[7] What distinguishes the work of state appellate courts is the content of their activism. While generalizations over time and across states are very difficult, until recently it probably was accurate to describe the policies of state supreme courts as moderate to conservative. Groups such as landlords, creditors, and employers, for instance, have been more successful in winning cases than tenants, debtors, and employees.[8] In recent years, in contrast, the most visible activism of supreme courts has been predominantly liberal. This activism has been most concentrated and has received the greatest attention in two areas. In tort law, state courts have adopted new rules expanding the legal rights of people who have suffered personal injuries or property damage. In civil liberties, the courts have used provisions of state constitutions to expand individual rights.[9]

Tort Policy

State courts accomplished most of their work in creating the basic set of tort law rules during the nineteenth century. Inevitably, the rules that they established were diverse in ideological content and varied a good deal from state to state. Not surprisingly, scholars who review the work of state courts in this area differ in their conclusions about its overall direction.

One feature of early state tort policy is fairly clear. On a number of basic issues, most supreme courts adopted rules that limited legal liability for property damage, injuries, and death.[10] For instance, charitable institutions such as nonprofit hospitals were accorded general immunity from lawsuits. Employees were limited in their ability to sue their employers for injuries on the job by the fellow servant rule, under which employers had no responsibility for injuries caused by the conduct of fellow employees. Under the contributory negligence rule, an injured party who bore any share of the fault for the injury could not recover damages from someone who was primarily at fault. Not all supreme courts accepted all these rules fully, but the general pattern of judicial doctrine was favorable to tort defendants (those allegedly responsible for damage or injuries) rather than tort plaintiffs (those who sought compensation for losses that they had suffered).

Some historians argue that state courts adopted these rules largely to provide economic protection for developing industries. Whatever the motivation behind them, these rules gave an advantage to businesses and other large institutions as defendants against workers and consumers as plaintiffs. In that sense, there was a strong conservative thrust to the tort law created by state supreme courts.

Beginning in the first half of the twentieth century, and accelerating since the 1950s, this thrust has been largely reversed.[11] On issue after issue, supreme courts have eliminated traditional doctrines that limited tort liability, replacing them with doctrines that favor plaintiffs over defendants. The states have differed in the speed and extent of this reversal. However, every state has participated in this shift in tort law, and most have taken major steps to change their traditional doctrines.

The range of issues involved in this reversal of traditional doctrines is impressive. Courts in a majority of states altogether eliminated the immunity of charitable institutions from lawsuits, putting them on the same footing as other enterprises. More strikingly, a majority of states eliminated or greatly narrowed the long-standing immunity of state and local governments from lawsuits. Doctrines that limited the liability of contractors and builders for defective construction were widely abrogated. Even procedural rules were changed. For instance, in medical malpractice the statute of limitations (the time period beyond which suits cannot be filed) was altered in half the states so that it did not begin until the former patient discovered the problem or could have been expected to do so.

In adopting these doctrinal changes, courts frequently had to make sharp breaks with well-established legal principles. When the South Carolina Supreme Court in 1985 decided to abolish the immunity of state and local governments from lawsuits, it overruled at least 118 of its past decisions, handed down from 1820 through 1984.[12] The doctrinal changes in tort law are symbolized by what is perhaps the most dramatic set of changes: the adoption of strict liability rules for makers of defective products. As the twentieth century began, consumers were restricted in their ability to sue manufacturers by the privity doctrine, which did not allow suits against any party except the business that had sold the product directly to the consumer, and by the negligence rule, which required the consumer to prove negligence in the manufacture of a defective product. The effect of these rules was to make successful suits against manufacturers very difficult.

Beginning in 1913, state supreme courts began to establish exceptions to these rules for food and drink and for inherently dangerous products. After World War II, more courts adopted these exceptions. Then they began to overthrow the rules themselves. The first major steps were taken by the supreme courts of Michigan in 1958 and New Jersey in 1960. In a 1963 decision, the California Supreme Court went even further in eliminating the privity and negligence requirements. The court held that a manufacturer was strictly liable, whether or not proved negligent, for damages caused by defective products.[13]

The strict liability rule was a radical departure from traditional tort rules; in effect, it replaced one legal framework with another. Yet other states quickly jumped on the bandwagon. Within four years, courts in a dozen other states had followed California's lead; by 1976, thirty-seven states had established strict liability by judicial decision. Today, all but a few states operate under the strict liability rule. The speedy and overwhelming acceptance of this rule underlines the strength of the new wave in tort law.

The broadening of the rights of injured parties continues to be a strong trend in the 1980s. Some supreme courts that previously had rejected the new proplaintiff tort doctrines, such as those of Texas and Ohio, acted to catch up by reaching a series of decisions that overturned their old rules. Since 1981, according to one commentator, "the Texas Supreme Court has gone from being one of the most pro-defendant courts in the nation to being one of the most pro-plaintiff."[14]

In addition, state judges continue to produce new doctrines favorable to tort plaintiffs. One such doctrine, which illustrates the vigor of this continuing trend, concerns the identification of a product's manufacturer. Traditionally, it was the clear rule that a person injured by a defective product must identify and sue the company that produced it. If a prescription drug had been produced by several companies, and a person injured by the drug did not know which company's product had been used, a successful suit was impossible. But since 1979, a few supreme courts have allowed the injured person to sue one or more drug manufacturers in such a situation.

Another recent example concerns emotional distress. The traditional rule is that a person who suffers some kind of emotional damage as the result of another person's negligent act cannot recover money unless there was an accompanying physical injury. But, Hawaii in

1970 and several other courts in the 1980s ruled that people could bring lawsuits for the infliction of serious emotional distress in the absence of physical injury. Here, too, judges have been willing to overthrow long-standing doctrines to allow compensation to people who suffer injuries.

Acceptance of these changes in tort law has not been unanimous. Some courts and individual judges have objected to the substance of proposed doctrinal changes and to the courts' overturning of established legal rules. Support for doctrinal change has been sufficiently broad to produce something of a revolution in torts.

There is no single explanation for this plaintiff-oriented trend in the state courts. In part, it seems to reflect the liberal policy views of supreme court justices. The California Court, with a highly liberal membership through most of the postwar period, and the Michigan Court, which gained a liberal majority in the late 1950s, were among the leaders in tort liberalism. The Texas and Ohio Courts became supportive of tort plaintiffs after judges who were sympathetic toward the position of plaintiffs arrived on those courts.

The fact that the shift in tort law has been so widespread suggests that more than personal policy preferences are involved. It appears that societal views about accidents and injuries have changed, leading to greater sympathy toward individuals who seek compensation through the courts. One source of this change is the general availability of insurance to pay court judgments against defendants.[15] Inevitably, judges have shared this change in view and have adopted legal doctrines reflecting it.

Horizontal federalism also plays an important part in this revolution in the law, and its role merits exploration. State policy makers have always taken cues from their counterparts in other states. Indeed, Jack Walker and other scholars have documented a tendency for innovative legislation to "diffuse" from state to state. This process is understandable, because legislators in different states often face similar problems and look to other states for potential solutions.[16]

A similar process occurs in the courts, but with more powerful sources.[17] In part because of historical links between courts of different states, in part because of their own legal training in a "national" body of law, judges are strongly inclined to look to judicial opinions in other states for cues. They have little difficulty in keeping abreast of those opinions, which are published in a standard set of regional reports and are cited by lawyers whose positions they support. In this cue-taking process, a certain momentum may develop: if a doctrine has been adopted in a number of states, judges may come to view it as the accepted approach to a particular issue, and its widespread acceptance will influence additional courts to adopt it.

This diffusion of innovations has been particularly pronounced in tort law in recent years. Improvements in communication have increased judges' awareness of developments in other supreme courts, and their opinions often reveal a desire to follow a seemingly dominant trend in tort doctrines. Indeed, a court's opinion sometimes tallies up the number of courts taking either side on a doctrinal issue to show that the court is aligning itself with the majority or with most courts that recently considered the issue. This process is reflected in the surprisingly quick acceptance of strict liability as a general rule for product liability by the great majority of state supreme courts. More broadly, the general movement of state courts toward support for tort plaintiffs undoubtedly has exerted considerable influence on judges who did not want to be left behind.

As the state supreme courts have increased their support for victims of injuries, many observers have perceived a similar trend in trial courts. They report that juries are now more willing to rule in favor of tort plaintiffs and that the level of damage awards has increased tremendously. For the most part, these conclusions are based on limited and unsystematic evidence, such as the publicity given to very large awards in individual cases. More systematic evidence suggests that plaintiffs' success has indeed increased somewhat, though less than some observers have claimed. Data on jury decisions in San Francisco and Cook County (Chicago) from 1960 through 1984 show some tendency for plaintiffs to win more cases and larger awards in recent years, though the pattern is complex and differs among types of cases.[18] Whatever the reality, the perception of a change in jury behavior is politically important in itself.

Civil Liberties Policy

During the 1950s and 1960s, the U.S. Supreme Court gave unprecedented support to civil liberties. It broadened the scope of legal protection for freedom of expression, expanded the civil rights of racial minority groups, and established a series of new protections for criminal defendants. One important effect of the Court's work was to nationalize rights. The Court held that the Fourteenth Amendment extended nearly all of the prohibitions in the Bill of Rights to state governments, and it established standards for these rights that applied to all states as well as the federal government.

During this period, some state supreme courts opposed the decisional trend at the federal level. This opposition was especially widespread on issues of criminal procedure. In interpreting and applying major Supreme Court decisions that expanded defendants' rights, some state judges indicated their lack of sympathy with these decisions. While state supreme courts could not legally reject the U.S. Supreme Court's interpretations of the federal Constitution, they could—and some did—weaken the impact of the Court's decisions through narrow interpretations and sometimes outright evasion of the Court's commands. Such opposition was particularly strong on issues of racial equality, where some southern supreme courts worked to maintain the status quo of segregation.[19]

This opposition to the Supreme Court was consistent with the pattern of limited support for civil liberties exhibited by state supreme courts. On the whole, these courts traditionally were not strong protectors of individual rights. For instance, state courts in the twentieth century generally had been willing to restrict freedom of expression to protect what they saw as national security interests, sometimes evading Supreme Court decisions to do so.[20] On the basis of this history, the widespread skepticism toward the civil liberties innovations of the Warren Court was not surprising.

That skepticism also reflected tensions in the federal system. State legislators and administrators often expressed resentment of federal intervention into their traditional spheres of activity. Similarly, some state judges resented the Supreme Court's massive intervention into state legal policy, particularly in the criminal procedure field where state supreme courts had been dominant. Consciously or unconsciously, state judges resisted the doctrinal trend in the Supreme Court in part as a means to assert their independence.

The policy differences between federal and state courts during this period were highlighted by the activities of civil liberties groups such as the National Association for the Advancement of Colored People (NAACP) and the American Civil Liberties Union (ACLU). Such groups brought cases to federal courts whenever possible, because they saw the courts of most states as fundamentally unsympathetic toward civil liberties. In doing so, they were following the lead of other interest groups that had taken advantage of the federal system by directing their attention to the level of government that seemed most sympathetic.

The role of the Supreme Court in civil liberties, of course, has changed considerably in the 1970s and 1980s. As the Warren Court became the Burger Court, the Supreme Court became less supportive of civil liberties. This shift was sharpest in criminal procedure, where the Supreme Court increasingly has narrowed defendants' rights rather than broadening them.

In response, some state supreme courts began to take the lead in supporting civil liberties. They could do so by adopting broad interpretations of provisions in the federal Constitution, on issues on which the Supreme Court had not ruled definitively. But a more certain means to stake out an independent position is to interpret the state's constitution. If the U.S. Supreme Court holds that a right is not protected under the U.S. Constitution, a state supreme court can hold that the right does exist under a provision of its own constitution. Unless there is a conflict between that right and some federal right—and ordinarily there is not—the state decision and the state-protected right stand. It is easier to interpret a state law as providing broader protection than its federal equivalent when the two differ in wording, but even when the two provisions read exactly the same, a state supreme court can hold that the history of its state's own provision allows a broader interpretation.

This kind of action was rare before the time of the Burger Court; according to one count, there were only 10 decisions that supported rights on the basis of state constitutions between 1950 and 1969. But 36 such decisions were handed down in the 1970-1974 period and 88 from 1975 through 1979. The numbers continued to grow in the 1980s, with 177 decisions interpreting state constitutions to provide broader rights than those under the U.S. Constitution from 1980 through part of 1986.[21]

The use of state constitutions to expand civil liberties has been most common in the area of criminal procedure, because it is here that the Burger Court most quickly and most consistently cut back on the scope of rights. The largest concentration of cases concerns prohibitions against unreasonable searches and seizures. In the 1970s and 1980s, the Supreme Court found a broader range of police practices to be legally acceptable, and it also narrowed the circumstances under which illegally seized evidence can be excluded from use against defendants. Several state supreme courts have disagreed with the Supreme Court in both areas, and they have established broader protections for defendants under their own constitutions. State courts have expanded protections against compulsory self-incrimination and double jeopardy in the same way.

Action to protect other types of civil liberties has become more common in the 1980s. In some major areas, state supreme courts have been relatively inactive; the best example is racial equality, where few decisions have gone beyond protections established under the U.S. Constitution by the Supreme Court. In contrast, state courts have been quite active on issues of sex discrimination. This activity results primarily from the existence of equal rights amendments protecting sexual equality in about one-third of the state constitutions. Here, more than in most other areas, differences in the wording of the federal and state constitutions explain the activism of state courts. Some supreme courts have treated their states' equal rights amendments as narrow protections against sex discrimination, but others have used them vigorously to overturn state laws. The Pennsylvania Supreme Court has been especially vigorous.

It is largely the cumulation of dozens of individual decisions that gives significance to the use of state constitutions as means to expand rights. But some single decisions stand out as quite important in themselves. Among them are the following:

The U.S. Supreme Court held in 1973 that the Constitution did not prohibit inequalities in funding of education across a state as a result of reliance on the property tax. But several state supreme courts have held that such inequalities violate their own constitutions. In doing so, they have required fundamental changes in the mechanisms for financing education and in the actual distribution of funds.

Reversing an earlier decision, the Supreme Court ruled in 1976 that the Constitution's protection of freedom of expression did not apply to privately owned shopping malls. Three state supreme courts then found such protection in their states' equivalents of the First Amendment. These decisions reopened access to an increasingly important means to communicate with the public.

In search and seizure, the Supreme Court in the 1980s has narrowed the exclusionary rule by holding that under certain circumstances illegally seized materials could be used as evidence if the police officers involved had acted in "good faith." Some commentators view this line of decisions as a fundamental limitation on the exclusionary rule. Almost immediately, several state supreme courts ruled that no good faith exception existed under their own constitutions.

Especially striking are two recent obscenity decisions. Since it first addressed the issue in 1957, the Supreme Court has consistently held that obscenity is unprotected by the First Amendment of the U.S. Constitution, so that the publication and sale of obscene material may be subject to criminal penalties. But the Oregon Supreme Court, based on its own reading of history, held in 1987 that the equivalent of the First Amendment in its state constitution disallowed criminal prosecutions based on obscene material.[22] In 1988, the Hawaii Supreme Court held that a statute prohibiting the sale of pornographic material violated the right of adults to read or view such material in their homes under a state constitutional provision protecting privacy.[23]

The use of state constitutions as independent sources of protections for civil liberties has not occurred evenly across the states; to a considerable extent it is regionally based. The initial impetus occurred primarily in the West, and by one count the western states account for about half of all the rights-protecting decisions between 1950 and 1986. In the 1980s such activity has grown considerably in the Northeast, while it remains less common in the South and Midwest.[24] The extent of constitutional activism in the states also varies with their traditions and the membership of their courts. More liberal states and judges have played larger roles in this movement. California is a particularly clear example of the impact of membership. Until 1987, its supreme court had a consistently strong liberal majority, and the California Supreme Court was even more of a leader in civil liberties activism than it was in tort law.

Still, the use of state constitutions to protect liberties has been quite widespread; in the great majority of states, the supreme court has employed its constitution for this purpose in at least one instance. Like the trend toward expansion of the rights of injured parties, the movement to expand civil liberties has been broad in its membership.

In a way, state activism in civil liberties is even more striking than the state revolution in tort law. The state supreme courts, often viewed as obstacles to civil liberties as recently as the 1960s, now are viewed increasingly as protectors of liberties. How can this rapid shift in positions be explained?

At the outset, it should be noted that the shift is not as dramatic as it appears. Courts that generally accepted the Supreme Court's liberalism in the 1960s and those that largely accept its conservative policies on civil liberties since that time receive little notice, but such courts are not rare. Alongside the decisions in which supreme courts expand liberties are many other decisions in which they refuse to do so. Several courts, for instance, have rejected arguments that their states' systems for school finance were unconstitutional and that their constitutions protect freedom of expression in shopping malls. Indeed, looking beyond the most dramatic decisions to general patterns of policy, it is not at all certain that the state supreme courts as a whole are more favorable to civil liberties today than is the U.S. Supreme Court.[25] Still, the development of an unprecedented civil liberties activism in state supreme courts is an important phenomenon that requires explanation.

In part, it may be a generational phenomenon. State supreme court justices of the 1970s, and even more those of the 1980s, had the Warren Court as a model during the time prior to their reaching the bench. Undoubtedly, many came to accept the legitimacy and desirability of judicial activism on behalf of civil liberties. This would be particularly true, of course, for those with broadly liberal policy views—and such judges probably have become more common on state courts.

Further, the U.S. Supreme Court's drift toward greater conservatism in civil liberties created an opening for state judges to fill. Richard P. Nathan has pointed to a cyclical pattern in American history, a tendency for state governments to play active and innovative roles during periods of conservatism in the national government.[26] Such a pattern may be seen today in the courts. During the time of the Warren Court, state supreme courts probably had some difficulty in keeping up with judicial innovations at the national level, and to move ahead of the Supreme Court would have been very difficult. But as the Supreme Court has drawn back, an opportunity has arisen for state judges to take the initiative, to make their own marks in civil liberties. Indeed, Nathan and Martha Derthick have argued that "the Burger Court was to the judicial system what the Reagan Administration has been to the Presidency: a conservatizing force that deflected liberal effort to the state level." [27]

From this perspective, the growing number of speeches and articles by state supreme court justices on behalf of civil liberties activism is striking. In proselytizing for this policy role, judges often display a great pride in their independent contributions to the law of civil liberties. Resistance to the federal courts' innovations in this field provided a means for state judges to assert their own independence in the 1950s and 1960s; support for new rights and liberties provides an even better means for state judges to stand out as independent policy makers in the 1970s and 1980s. If the Supreme Court under Chief Justice William H. Rehnquist narrows civil liberties more substantially than in the past, this independent role may become even more attractive for state judges.

Inevitably, this shift in the relative positions of state and federal courts has influenced the strategies of interest groups. As state courts have begun to assert themselves as supporters of civil liberties, groups such as the ACLU have shifted their priorities somewhat and brought more cases to them. Undoubtedly, civil liberties groups already have encouraged the trend in state supreme courts by providing them with appropriate cases and by framing effective arguments for broad interpretations of state legal protections for civil liberties. If these groups continue to increase their attention to state courts, their impact should be enhanced further. At the same time, state officials bring more cases to the Supreme Court in which they challenge procivil liberties rulings by their own courts. Both the Reagan administration and conservative interest groups have also looked to the Supreme Court as a locus for efforts to narrow civil liberties.

The Supreme Court has given considerable scrutiny to decisions by state courts protecting civil liberties on the basis of state constitutions. In recent years, the Court's majority has been eager to overturn state decisions expanding civil liberties if the state court did not clearly base its decision on the state constitution instead of relying on the U.S. Constitution. This has been particularly true in criminal procedure.

The Court seemed to take a harder line on this matter in some 1987 decisions, refusing to allow state supreme courts to reconsider cases on the basis of state law after the Court reversed state court interpretations of federal law.[28]

In response, some state judges have expressed resentments similar to those of conservative state judges during the time of the Warren Court. After the Supreme Court returned a case to the Montana Supreme Court in 1983 asking whether the state decision was based on federal or state law, members of the Montana Court complained about the Supreme Court's action in heated terms; one justice wrote that in his earlier opinion for the court:

> I clearly made a mistake, for I did not recognize the extent to which the United States Supreme Court stood ready to intrude on the judicial affairs of this state in interpreting our own constitution.[29]

Such resentments encourage judges to depart from the Supreme Court's path in interpreting their own constitutions, and increasingly they have learned how to make the state-law basis of their decisions clear to insulate them from Supreme Court review.

Interestingly, the use of state constitutions to protect rights has been encouraged by some members of the Supreme Court itself. Members of the liberal minority on the Court, increasingly unsuccessful in convincing colleagues to support their positions in the 1970s and 1980s, see the state supreme courts as alternative institutions for strengthening of civil liberties. Indeed, a widely publicized article by Justice William Brennan provided one impetus for this use of state constitutions.[30] Like the support that some members of Congress and the federal executive branch give to states' rights, the actions of the Supreme Court's liberals underline the ideological character of the federal system. Participants in the policy-making process, whatever their own institutional positions, tend to favor the level of government whose policies they prefer.

Accountability

The relationship between state courts and other state institutions is complex. Courts are subject to considerable control by the other branches of government and by the electorate. Only in a few states do judges hold office for life, so the great majority of judges can be removed by other policy makers or by the voters. The other branches of government play a part in establishing court jurisdiction and budgets. Court decisions can be overturned by the legislature or, in some states, by the voters.

When judicial action arouses controversy, other institutions sometimes use their powers over the courts to exert control. The most extreme instance was the action by the Kentucky legislature in the 1820s to abolish its supreme court and replace it with a new court.[31] Far more common are minor attacks on the courts by the other branches, such as refusals to provide requested budgetary support. It is also common for legislatures and, occasionally, the voters to change the law in response to decisions that they oppose.

On the whole, however, other state institutions make sparing use of their powers over the judiciary. To a considerable extent, state courts have been left free from control even when they were making important policies. This freedom is symbolized by the infrequency with which judges are removed from office at the end of their terms. Thus, the position of state courts in relation to other political institutions has been a mixture of accountability and autonomy.

In recent years, state courts have been subject to increased accountability. Courts and judges have faced greater oversight and control from the legislature, the executive, and the electorate. This change is largely a result of the courts' liberal activism: opposition to the policy roles played by state courts has aroused other participants in the political process to attack the courts' policies and even the courts themselves.

State Legislatures versus State Courts

Both in tort policy and in civil liberties, the other branches of state government have acted to limit or overturn some of the policies adopted by supreme courts in recent years. They have been especially active, but have played a rather complicated role, in the tort field.

Torts. In tort law, legislatures actually have taken a good deal of action to reinforce the general proplaintiff trend in judicial doctrines, because legislators are influenced by the same changes in social thinking as judges. Frequently, when courts develop a new doctrine favoring plaintiffs, some state legislatures adopt that doctrine by statute instead of waiting for judicial action. This is true, for instance, of strict liability for defective products. Some courts, reluctant to change long-standing rules themselves, have deferred to the legislature; for example, the Wisconsin Supreme Court urged the legislature to liberalize the statute of limitations for medical malpractice actions, and the legislature did so.[32]

On some issues, legislatures play the dominant role. The most important of these issues is the replacement of the contributory negligence rule by comparative negligence. Under comparative negligence, if an injured party was partially at fault for the injury, that party is not automatically denied compensation by the other party. Instead, injured parties may recover partial compensation, based on the degree of their own fault. The significance of this change can be understood in the context of automobile accident cases, where frequently neither party was blameless. Under comparative negligence, one party can still sue the other and receive some compensation.

A few states had established some form of comparative negligence before 1969, and since that time most others have followed. By now, about forty states have discarded contributory negligence. It is striking that in all but four of these states, it was the legislature, not the supreme court, that changed the rules.

Since the mid-1970s, however, the primary activity of state legislatures in tort law has been to consider—and frequently to adopt— rules that narrow the legal rights of injured parties. When they do so, they are reacting in opposition to the general trend in state courts. In many instances, legislatures have directly reversed court decisions.

This legislative activity results chiefly from interest-group pressure, exerted by groups whose economic positions suffer when the rights of tort plaintiffs are expanded. These groups include those that appear as defendants in tort cases, such as manufacturers, physicians, and the insurance companies that usually pay for court judgments against defendants. They have perceived a threat to their interests in both the new tort doctrines established by state supreme courts and in a seemingly growing sympathy by trial juries for tort plaintiffs. In response, they have worked actively to limit both through legislation.

The efforts of these groups illustrate the impact of a system of overlapping governmental powers on interest-group strategies. In tort policy, as in many other fields, state courts and legislatures both hold significant power to make policy. A group that is unhappy with the policies of one branch can turn to another to seek redress. In torts, basically a nonconstitutional field, the legislature is supreme when it chooses to intervene; in most instances, it can simply supersede common-law rules by statute. Historically, state legislatures have been sympathetic toward business interests. For that reason, it is not surprising that business groups that are defendants in tort cases and insurance companies that pay their costs should seek legislative intervention on their behalf when the courts treat them unfavorably.

Much of the effort of these interest groups has been directed at establishing a favorable political climate for the legislation they support. They have sought to create a perception that a "liability crisis" exists, one in which lawsuits are burgeoning in numbers and jury awards to plaintiffs are increasing exponentially, with the result that manufacturers and service providers are driven out of business and the general public suffers. Insurance companies, for instance, have publicized what they portray as examples of juries' willingness to award damages to plaintiffs who have very weak or even crazy cases. Even more, they emphasize serious alleged consequences of such awards: companies cease producing football helmets, life-saving drugs are kept out of the market.

To a great extent, these groups have been successful in shaping public and legislative perceptions. The increasing attention given to the judicial expansions of plaintiffs' legal rights probably reflects their efforts in part. Until recently, even landmark tort decisions often were ignored by the mass media. The 1963 decision of the California Supreme Court that first established strict liability as a general rule, perhaps the most important tort decision of the century, was not reported in the leading San Francisco newspaper. Today, newspapers devote considerable space to major tort decisions.

The success of defendant groups in making tort law a public issue, combined with the considerable prestige and resources of business groups in the states, have given them a good start in securing changes in state law. Indeed, they have secured substantial changes through legislation. Doctrines favorable to injured parties have been cut back in one way or another in a large number of states. For instance, at least three legislatures overturned decisions that made social hosts liable for injuries caused by their guests who were operating under the influence of liquor served by the hosts. Some states have restored the immunity of government entities from suits, in whole or in part. Legislatures also have adopted a variety of statutes that do not overturn specific judicial doctrines but operate in other ways to strengthen the legal positions of defendants.

Defendant groups have enjoyed particular legislative success in the area of medical malpractice. In the mid-1970s and again in the mid-1980s, physicians and insurance companies argued that a serious crisis existed in malpractice. As depicted by these groups, the problem lay in a rapid growth in the numbers of malpractice suits and in a greatly increased willingness by juries to rule against doctors in those suits. New judicial doctrines favorable to plaintiffs sometimes were portrayed as aggravating the problem. These developments within the courts were blamed for a dramatic increase in malpractice insurance premiums and in some cases an inability of doctors to obtain insurance. In turn, it was argued, doctors were forced to practice "defensive medicine," and some were leaving or curtailing their practices.

Not everyone shared this view. As some critics saw it, there was no crisis in malpractice. Instead, the insurance companies that represent physicians were raising rates far more than their risks justified; the companies then enlisted doctors in an effort to protect insurance interests by securing more favorable legal rules. The scenario depicted by doctors and insurance companies was broadly accepted by the interested public and by legislators, and doctors created additional pressure with threats to withhold or limit their services in some places. The result was something of a legislative panic and a general willingness to adopt legislation protecting against malpractice suits.

The extent of such action is remarkable. During the perceived crisis of the 1970s, nearly every state legislature adopted some provisions sought by physicians, hospitals, and insurance companies. Widespread action is again being taken in the late 1980s. The substantive and procedural provisions adopted by states in the two periods are impressive in their range. Among them are ceilings on the amount of money that can be awarded in a malpractice case and on the proportion of an award that the plaintiff's lawyer can obtain as a fee, limits on the time period in which a suit could be brought after medical treatment, and creation of pretrial screening panels for malpractice cases. The variety of such provisions and the numbers of states adopting them indicate the strength of medical groups and insurance companies.

Tort defendants have faced increasingly strong opposition in state legislatures. Groups representing plaintiff interests, although generally less powerful than defendants, have their own influence over state legislatures. This is especially true of organizations of plaintiffs' lawyers, who enjoy a certain sympathy from the fellow lawyers who serve in state legislatures. In recent years these groups have recognized a threat to their court victories and have joined battle in the legislature, creating a closer contest. Notably, in both North Carolina in 1984 and California in 1985-1986, political action committees representing physicians ranked first in contributions to state legislative candidates, with associations representing lawyers for personal injury plaintiffs in second place.[33] Further, legislators' own attitudes increasingly are mixed, in part because of arguments by groups supporting tort plaintiffs that the alleged liability crisis is at least exaggerated.

The result has been to limit the success of insurance companies and their allies in state legislatures. By 1986, it was evident that legislatures were less willing to adopt statutes supported by tort defendants than in the recent past. Indeed, legislatures increasingly consider reversing the prodefendant changes that they had made. According to the head of one group representing defendants, 1988 was "a year that in many states we had to be on the defensive." [34] In some states, legislatures that are pressed to deal with increasing insurance rates have acted to regulate insurance practices as well as to revise tort law rules. (By mid-1988, the attorneys general of nineteen states also had joined antitrust suits against insurance companies for raising rates and limiting coverage for public agencies.) A closely fought battle is likely to continue across the states in the next several years.

Inevitably, the battle over tort rules has extended beyond state legislatures. Some statutes favoring defendants, such as limits on awards to plaintiffs in medical malpractice cases, have been challenged as unconstitutional in state and federal courts. At least eleven state supreme courts had struck down one or more provisions of prodefendant tort legislation by mid-1985.[35]

Business groups also have brought the battle to Congress. The federal government has the power to preempt state tort rules by establishing uniform national rules. While seeking favorable action in state legislatures, tort defendants have pressed for legislation establishing national rules on product liability. Significantly, their effort obtained the support of the Reagan administration. While proponents of federal preemption have argued that uniform rules are desirable in themselves, the rules that they propose generally would favor defendants' interests. One example is an overturning of strict liability for defective products. The simultaneous lobbying of state and federal legislatures on behalf of defendants' interests is still another manifestation of the multiple access points created by federalism.

Civil Liberties. In tort policy, state legislatures have played mixed roles because external pressures and their own members' attitudes are mixed. On civil liberties issues, both forces are much less favorable to the liberal direction of judicial policy. Both public and legislative opinion are generally unsympathetic to expansions of civil liberties, especially where such expansions are seen as threatening important values. This is clearly true of the rights of criminal defendants, which have been the most common subject of new rights created by state supreme courts in recent years. Thus, the strong legislative impulse is to work against the courts instead of taking the same direction. Groups that seek to protect civil liberties against legislative incursions, such as the ACLU, often are on the defensive.

But the legislature's legal position relative to the courts is weaker in civil liberties than in torts. Most important civil liberties decisions are based on constitutional provisions. Thus they cannot be overturned through simple legislation but require more cumbersome procedures for amendment of state constitutions—most commonly, proposal by the legislature and approval by the voters. As a result, unpopular supreme court decisions are less vulnerable in civil liberties than they are in tort policy.

Occasionally, legislatures formally propose constitutional amendments to overturn supreme court decisions. There are at least four instances of such action in recent years, on issues ranging from the death penalty to school busing.[36] The small number of these proposals, however, underlines the protection that is enjoyed by decisions based on state constitutions.

Legislatures also have acted against civil liberties decisions through statutes. As long ago as the 1950s, some state legislatures expressed their disapproval of civil liberties decisions by the U.S. Supreme Court with legislation purporting to void such decisions; this was the case, for instance, with southern legislatures after *Brown v. Board of Education.*[37] In a few instances, the same action has been taken after state supreme court decisions. The California Supreme Court held in 1981 that the legislature could not withhold financial support for abortions under the Medicaid program. Nonetheless, in its budgets in succeeding years the legislature did withhold such support, after which lower courts quickly voided the legislature's action.

Like Congress, state legislatures hold considerable statutory power over court jurisdiction. They can use this power to keep the courts out of certain areas. In New Jersey, a set of rulings culminating in 1983 made it unconstitutional for cities to adopt zoning rules that had the effect of shutting out low-income people.[38] The legislature responded in 1985 by passing legislation that largely removed the courts from this field, apparently in the hope that the administrative agency now given primary responsibility in the field would be more sympathetic to communities.

On one important policy issue, legislative action has been required to make a decision effective. Courts in several states have ruled that state systems for funding of primary and secondary education must be changed radically to provide more equal funding for school districts. In California and New Jersey, where such decisions were first made, legislators moved slowly and incompletely to implement those decisions. Nevertheless, after more than fifteen years funding inequities remain, and new challenges are working their way through the court.[39]

Legislative unhappiness with the civil liberties activism of judges has been reflected in some criticism of the judges themselves. In the most extreme case, a New Jersey legislator delayed the confirmation of the state's chief justice for reappointment, in part because of disagreement with the supreme court's decisions that opened up communities to low-cost housing. The major reason publicly stated for this opposition to the chief justice was his maintenance of a primary residence in New York, which he explained by the need to care for an ill wife. In reality, some of the opposition was based on unhappiness with the supreme court's activism: "I am convinced that the supreme court under the present chief justice is aggressively turning New Jersey into a judiciary state. . . ."[40] Only after a long battle was the chief justice confirmed.

Initiatives and Referendums

The electorate plays a critical role in amendment of state constitutions, both on referendums on amendments proposed by legislatures and—in states that provide for them—on initiative measures proposed through petitions. In a few states, the electorate has voted for one or more measures to amend state constitutions to overturn liberal court decisions on civil liberties. Not surprisingly, all but one of these decisions had expanded the rights of criminal defendants.[41]

In three instances, California voters have overturned liberal decisions. After the supreme court struck down the death penalty under the state constitution in 1972, the voters reinstated it later the same year. A 1976 decision that effectively brought about busing of students to achieve racial integration in Los Angeles was overturned by another measure. And in 1982 the voters approved a "victims' bill of rights" that limited criminal defendants' rights in a variety of ways; the most important provision prohibited the exclusion of evidence against defendants that would be acceptable under the U.S. Constitution.

Voters in three other states have overturned defendants' rights decisions. Massachusetts voters reestablished the death penalty in 1982. Florida in 1982 and Pennsylvania in 1984 overturned decisions that narrowed the range of evidence that could be used against defendants. Interestingly, Chief Justice Warren Burger used a 1983 opinion to applaud the Florida voters' action and encourage voters to overturn other state court decisions that expanded the rights of criminal defendants.[42]

Some states have adopted other proposals that limit defendants' rights, though not in reaction to specific court decisions. Voters in several states, for example, have approved new provisions that allow detention of criminal defendants prior to trial on the basis of their predicted dangerousness if they were released. In some instances, however, state voters have adopted constitutional amendments that broadened liberties; one example is the guarantee of equal protection of the laws that Georgia voters approved in 1982.[43]

When they take such action, voters do not always have the last word. Measures to restrict civil liberties are likely to require judicial interpretation, and frequently their constitutional legitimacy is challenged. Supreme courts have overturned some initiatives adopted by the voters, bringing about further conflict between the court and the rest of the political system.

Voters also have played some role on tort rules. In 1986, there were heated battles over ballot propositions in two states. In California, voters approved a referendum to abolish joint and several liability, under which one defendant could be assessed the full damages for which several parties were responsible. Arizona voters, however, defeated a proposed constitutional amendment with several provisions favorable to tort defendants. Total spending on these measures was about $5 million in Arizona, $10 million in California.[44] This level of spending indicates how important these issues are to the groups that support tort plaintiffs and defendants.

Judicial Elections

The primary forum in which voters pass judgment on the work of state courts is contests for judgeships. In most states, voters determine whether judges remain in office. The largest number of states hold "regular" elections with either a partisan or nonpartisan ballot, in which incumbent judges are subject to challenges by opponents. In a growing number of states, primarily those that use the "Missouri Plan," incumbents are subject to confirmation elections in which voters determine whether or not they should remain in office by voting "yes" or "no"; should an incumbent fail to gain the necessary support (usually a simple majority), another judge will be selected (usually by a commission and the governor).

Typically, incumbents have had an easy time remaining in office. In states with regular elections, incumbents often are unopposed, and most who face opposition have little difficulty winning their contests. In states with retention elections, the overwhelming majority of incumbents win voter approval—about 99 percent in major trial courts between 1964 and 1984.[45] Successful challenges to incumbents based on partisanship and policy issues occur from time to time, but they are relatively rare.

This general picture has not changed fundamentally in recent years. But serious opposition to incumbent judges has become more common; in some states more judges have suffered defeats, and policy issues have come to play a larger role in election contests. In particular, the liberal policies of state courts have become an important issue and a basis for challenges to sitting judges. Most often, in an atmosphere of widespread fear of crime, criminal justice issues figure in electoral challenges to incumbents.

At the trial court level, a judge's perceived overall position on criminal justice issues is most likely to influence the voters. Judges sometimes are identified as "soft on crime" by newspapers, police, and prosecutors, or simply by their opponents in elections. Because crime is such a salient issue to so many voters, an incumbent is likely to become vulnerable when perceptions of softness are widespread. In some states, organized groups, such as the Law and Order Campaign

Committee in California, have targeted judges for defeat on the basis of criminal justice issues, and they have enjoyed a degree of success. More broadly, criminal justice has become an implicit issue in many judicial contests, with both candidates proclaiming their support for strong law enforcement.

At the supreme court level, a line of decisions favorable to criminal defendants on a variety of issues may become the basis for opposition. Law-and-order groups, for instance, sought unsuccessfully to defeat a leading civil libertarian on the Oregon Supreme Court in 1984. But it is a single issue, the death penalty, that arouses opposition most frequently. Popular support for capital punishment is overwhelming in the 1980s, and the death penalty has gained a great symbolic importance for many people. Not surprisingly, it became a major issue in several supreme court races, including a 1984 Louisiana contest and a 1986 Oklahoma election. In a heated race for chief justice of North Carolina in 1986, opponents of Associate Justice James Exum attacked him strongly for his votes against death sentences. Capital punishment became the key issue in the contest, but Exum nonetheless won, probably because of his party advantage as a Democrat.

California provides the most dramatic example. The state supreme court's long-standing support for civil liberties fostered considerable unhappiness among California voters, and liberal justices won relatively narrow victories in retention elections from the late 1970s on. Voter unhappiness increasingly focused on the death penalty. After capital punishment was reinstated by initiative, the supreme court overturned a succession of death sentences on a variety of legal grounds, and this pattern of decisions garnered a great deal of negative publicity.

The most adamant opponent of capital punishment on the court was Chief Justice Rose Bird, who was alone in voting against every death sentence that came before her court. This stance reinforced opposition to Bird based on other grounds. She had been unpopular among conservatives since her appointment as chief justice in 1977, in part because of her relative youth, her gender, and her liberal views. During her time on the court, allegations of an abrasive personal style and a feud among justices that ultimately was aired in a series of public hearings damaged her further. And many people were never comfortable with her nontraditional style, symbolized by her advocacy of vegetarianism.[46] In her first retention election in 1978, she won only 52 percent of the vote, and conservatives later initiated three separate efforts to get a measure on the ballot to recall Bird from office.

In 1986, the majority of the court's justices came before the voters for retention, including Chief Justice Bird and two other strong liberals on the court. Massive opposition to these justices was organized. The court and the death penalty came to dominate races for other offices as well. For instance, a candidate for state controller was attacked because Chief Justice Bird had performed his wedding ceremony. Ultimately, the three liberals were all defeated, the first appellate judges in California to suffer that fate.[47] With three new appointments by Republican governor George Deukmejian, who had strongly opposed Bird, the court gained a conservative majority. This result has attracted the attention of conservatives in other states, and major campaigns to defeat liberal justices may become more common.

Tort law issues lack the visibility and emotional content of criminal justice issues, and their explicit role in electoral campaigns has been much more limited. But groups concerned with tort policy naturally would prefer to have a sympathetic supreme court, and in some states they have involved themselves in electoral campaigns. Their primary role has been to supply financial support for candidates that they prefer.

In 1986, groups involved in tort issues were quite active in at least four states with hotly contested supreme court elections. While the death penalty dominated public discussion of the races for the California Supreme Court, groups that supported or opposed the court's tort liberalism provided much of the funding for these contests. Supporters of Republican candidates in the 1986 North Carolina races raised funds on the basis of tort issues; one letter to physicians said that the election of the Democratic candidate for chief justice would result in a "medical malpractice crisis." [48]

In Ohio, the critical public issue was allegations of improper behavior by Frank Celebrezze, the incumbent chief justice. But the funding that fueled massive campaigns came largely from groups that reacted to the supreme court's recent tort liberalism. Chief justice Celebrezze received about $350,000 from labor unions. His opponent, Thomas Moyer, obtained more than $400,000 from businesses and the medical profession.[49]

The Texas Supreme Court has been strongly favorable to tort plaintiffs in recent years. (The court has no jurisdiction over criminal cases, so such issues are irrelevant to its elections.) Tort issues became the centerpiece of contests for several seats on the court in 1986, with groups on both sides contributing substantial amounts of money to candidates that they saw as sympathetic to their interests. (In addition, law firms involved in the lawsuit between the Pennzoil and Texaco companies, a case with enormous stakes that was expected to reach the supreme court in 1987, contributed nearly $400,000 to members of the court in 1985-1986.)[50]

As justices increasingly come under attack for their performance on the bench, the general atmosphere of judicial elections in many states has changed. The ethical rules that prohibit explicit discussion of policy issues in judicial contests are increasingly flouted directly and indirectly. Strong campaigns against incumbents have become more common. The level of spending by judicial candidates has increased markedly. In Ohio, for instance, the 1980 race for chief justice cost candidates a total of about $100,000; in 1986, total spending was about $2.7 million. More than $11 million was spent in the three California races in 1986.[51]

It should be emphasized that defeats of incumbent judges remain clearly the exception to the rule, and uncontested races are still quite common below the supreme court level. But the vulnerability of sitting judges and their accountability for their actions have increased.

The matter of accountability merits emphasis. In the past, most judges could feel that their actions were largely invisible and that they need not fear electoral consequences for their decisions. Liberal and conservative judges alike could follow the legal path that they preferred with little regard for the electorate. Today, judges have less reason to feel safe. Not only could they be called to account for their decisions, but at least in California they have been subjected to threats of electoral opposition if they decide pending cases to the dissatisfaction of the threateners. In 1982, for instance, Pete Wilson announced during his successful campaign for the U.S. Senate that if the state supreme court overturned an initiative limiting defendants' rights, he would support a recall of Chief Justice Bird.[52]

In states where they have been subject to the greatest pressures, judges recognize that they are now more accountable. One member of the California Supreme Court, in announcing his retirement in 1985, expressed his own sense of the change:

> You cannot ignore that there are elections, any more than you can ignore that there is a crocodile in your bathroom. It used to be that justices would be re-elected unless they screwed up. There was a consensus that judges were not to be kicked out of office because of the political tenor of their opinions—that seems to be going by the boards.[53]

Even though the removal of judges from the bench remains rare, the fact that some judges are now vulnerable sends a powerful message to the judiciary. Increasingly, judges who wish to maintain their positions will take into account the possibility of opposition from interest groups and from the electorate as a whole. In the current era, this means that electoral concerns may militate against continuation of the liberal policies that characterize much of the recent work of state courts.

Summary

State courts have always been important policy makers, and they have always been involved in state politics. In that sense, there is nothing new about recent events involving state courts.

But the activity of state supreme courts in the past several years has produced a policy role somewhat different from the one that prevailed for most of their history. The activism of the supreme courts on behalf of liberal tort and civil liberties policies probably is unique in its extent. In turn, this activism has enmeshed the state courts in state political processes to a degree that is unusual in American history. Judges have helped to make themselves an issue in state government and politics; in doing so, they have reduced their own freedom from control.

More broadly, the recent activism of state supreme courts and the reaction to that activism in other institutions illustrate the fragmentation of governmental power in the United States and its impact. Both the federal system and the overlapping powers of different government institutions create multiple points of access for interest groups that seek to influence policy. They also create a potential for conflict among institutions over policy issues on which they share power. Tort and civil liberties policy involved federal and state governments and several different institutions in state government. In these two areas, government policy is a complex and often contradictory aggregation of rules adopted at different levels and in different institutions.

The involvement of state supreme courts in politics and public policy is likely to increase further in the next few years. Civil liberties groups increasingly will focus their attention on state courts and state constitutions to win what they cannot win from a more conservative U.S. Supreme Court, and in reaction conservative groups that are less sympathetic to civil liberties undoubtedly will devote more of their energies to state cases. More and more, supreme court elections will become a battleground for groups concerned with judicial policies on torts and on criminal procedure. Students of state politics and of the courts will have even more reason to pay attention to state supreme courts.

Notes

1. The term "supreme court" will be used to refer to the highest court of each state. Most of these courts are officially known as supreme courts, but there are exceptions; for instance, in New York the court called the su-

preme court is a lower court and the highest court is the court of appeals. The supreme courts of Texas and Oklahoma hear only civil cases; each state has a court of criminal appeals that is in effect its supreme court for criminal cases. Where "Supreme Court" is capitalized, without any state designation, the reference is to the United States Supreme Court.

2. G. Alan Tarr and Mary Cornelia Aldis Porter, *State Supreme Courts in State and Nation* (New Haven, Conn.: Yale University Press, 1988), 2.

3. Bradley C. Canon, "A Framework for the Analysis of Judicial Activism," in *Supreme Court Activism and Restraint,* ed. Stephen C. Halpern and Charles M. Lamb (Lexington, Mass.: Lexington Press, 1982). As Canon has shown, the concept of judicial activism has several different dimensions. As used in this paper, the term "activism" will refer broadly to significant policy-making activities, particularly those that make substantial changes in existing policy.

4. Martin B. Hickman, "Judicial Review of Legislation in Utah," *Utah Law Review* 4 (Spring 1954): 50-64.

5. Franklin A. Smith, *Judicial Review of Legislation in New York, 1906-1938* (New York: Columbia University Press, 1952), 223.

6. Oliver Peter Field, *Judicial Review of Legislation in Ten Selected States* (Bloomington: Bureau of Government Research, Indiana University, 1943), 11-27.

7. Federal courts in recent years increasingly have engaged in a form of activism sometimes referred to as "institutional reform," in which judges require fundamental changes in the operation of such public institutions as schools, prisons, and mental institutions, and in which they often supervise closely the implementation of their requirements. In its extent, this type of activism represents a real departure from the past. Such action is considerably less prominent in state courts, whose recent activism has taken primarily traditional forms.

8. Stanton Wheeler, Bliss Cartwright, Robert A. Kagan, and Lawrence M. Friedman, "Do the 'Haves' Come Out Ahead? Winning and Losing in State Supreme Courts, 1870-1970," *Law and Society Review* 21 (1987): 403-445.

9. State supreme courts have been active in other areas as well. In some of these areas, their activism can be characterized as ideologically liberal; an example is the widespread weakening of traditional rules that gave employers almost complete freedom to fire their employees. Other forms of activism, such as the striking down of the legislative veto of administrative rules in several states, are more difficult to label ideologically.

10. Lawrence M. Friedman, *Total Justice* (New York: Russell Sage, 1985), 53-60.

11. The following discussion is drawn from Lawrence Baum and Bradley C. Canon, "State Supreme Courts as Activists: New Doctrines in the Law of Torts," in *State Supreme Courts: Policymakers in the Federal System,* ed. Mary Cornelia Porter and G. Alan Tarr (Westport, Conn.: Greenwood Press, 1982), 83-108.

12. *McCall v. Batson,* 329 S.E.2d 741 (South Carolina 1985).

13. *Greenman v. Yuba Power Products*, 377 P.2d 897 (California 1963).

14. Paul Burka, "Heads, We Win, Tails, You Lose: How a Group of Trial Lawyers Took Over the Texas Supreme Court and Rewrote State Law," *Texas Monthly* (May 1987): 138-139, 206.

15. Henry J. Steiner, *Moral Argument and Social Vision in the Courts: A Study of Tort Accident Law* (Madison: University of Wisconsin Press, 1987), 100-108.

16. Jack L. Walker, "The Diffusion of Innovations among the American States," *American Political Science Review* 63 (September 1969): 880-899.

17. Martin Shapiro, "Decentralized Decision-Making in the Law of Torts," in *Political Decision-Making*, ed. S. Sidney Ulmer (New York: Van Nostrand Reinhold, 1970), 44-75.

18. Deborah R. Hensler, "Trends in Tort Litigation: Findings from the Institute for Civil Justice's Research," *Ohio State Law Journal* 48 (1987): 479-498; and Mark A. Peterson, *Civil Juries in the 1980s: Trends in Jury Trials and Verdicts in California and Cook County, Illinois* (Santa Monica, Calif.: Rand Corp., 1987).

19. Tarr and Porter, *State Supreme Courts in State and Nation*, 74-82.

20. Carol E. Jenson, *The Network of Control: State Supreme Courts and State Security Statutes, 1920-1970* (Westport, Conn.: Greenwood Press, 1982).

21. Ronald K. L. Collins, Peter J. Galie, and John Kincaid, "State High Courts, State Constitutions, and Individual Rights Litigation since 1980: A Judicial Survey," *Publius* 16 (Summer 1986): 141-161.

22. *State v. Henry*, 732 P.2d 9 (Oregon 1987).

23. *State v. Kam*, 748 P.2d 372 (Hawaii 1988).

24. Collins, Galie, and Kincaid, "State High Courts, State Constitutions, and Individual Rights Litigation since 1980."

25. See Harold J. Spaeth, "Burger Court Review of State Court and Civil Liberties Decisions," *Judicature* 68 (February/March 1985): 285-291. State civil liberties decisions reviewed by the Burger Court in the 1969-1984 period had liberal results more often *after* the Supreme Court's decision than before.

26. Richard P. Nathan, "America's Changing Federalism," in *The New American Political System*, rev. ed., ed. Anthony King (Washington, D.C.: American Enterprise Institute for Public Policy Research, forthcoming).

27. Richard P. Nathan and Martha Derthick, "Reagan's Legacy: A New Liberalism among the States," *New York Times*, December 18, 1987, A39.

28. Ronald K. L. Collins, "High Court's Rights-Claims Record: A Challenge to 'New Federalism'?", *National Law Journal* (August 31, 1987): 26.

29. *State v. Jackson*, 672 P. 2d 255 (Montana 1983).

30. William J. Brennan, "State Constitutions and the Protection of Individual Rights," *Harvard Law Review* 90 (1977): 489-504.

31. Charles A. Johnson and Bradley C. Canon, *Judicial Policies: Implementation and Impact* (Washington, D.C.: CQ Press, 1984), 156.

32. *Hansen v. A. H. Robins*, 335 N.W.2d 578 (Wisconsin 1983)

33. Malcolm E. Jewell and David M. Olson, *Political Parties and Elections in American States,* 3d ed. (Chicago: Dorsey Press, 1988), 165. See also, Sheila Kaplan, "Justice for Sale," *Common Cause Magazine* (May/June 1987): 29-32.
34. Daniel B. Moskowitz, "Push for New Liability Laws to Heat Up," *Washington Post,* Washington Business section, January 25, 1988, 42.
35. United States General Accounting Office, *Medical Malpractice: No Agreement on the Problems or Solutions* (Washington, D.C.: Government Printing Office, 1986), 83.
36. Janice C. May, "Constitutional Amendment and Revision Revisited," *Publius* 17 (Winter 1987): 174-176.
37. *Brown v. Board of Education,* 347 U.S. 483 (1954).
38. *Southern Burlington County N.A.A.C.P. v. Mount Laurel,* 456 A.2d 390 (New Jersey 1983).
39. Richard Lehne, *The Quest for Justice: The Politics of School Finance Reform* (New York: Longman, 1978).
40. Chris Mondics, "Chief Justice in New Jersey Barely Reappointed," *National Law Journal* (August 18, 1986): 39.
41. May, "Constitutional Amendment and Revision Revisited," 153-179.
42. *Florida v. Casal,* 462 U.S. 637 (1983).
43. Ronald K. L. Collins, "Foreword: Reliance on State Constitutions— Beyond the 'New Federalism,' " *University of Puget Sound Law Review* 8 (Winter 1985): vi-xxvii.
44. Fred Strasser, "Both Sides Brace for Tort Battle," *National Law Journal* (February 16, 1987): 1, 36-37, 39-40.
45. William K. Hall and Larry T. Aspin, "What Twenty Years of Judicial Retention Elections Have Told Us," *Judicature* 70 (April/May 1987): 340-347.
46. Paul Obis, "Tipping the Scales: California Chief Justice Rose Elizabeth Bird on Diet and Cancer," *Vegetarian Times* (September 1985): 28-32, 58.
47. John T. Wold and John H. Culver, "The Defeat of the California Justices: The Campaign, the Electorate, and the Issue of Judicial Accountability," *Judicature* 70 (April/May 1987): 348-355.
48. "GOP Makes Its Pitch to Business, Doctors," *Raleigh News and Observer,* October 11, 1986, A1, A11.
49. Mary Grace Poldomani, "Insurance Lobby Dug Deep for Moyer," *Akron Beacon Journal,* June 14, 1987, A1, A8.
50. Bruce Hight, "Firms in Texaco Case Funded Eight Justices," *Austin American-Statesman,* February 26, 1987, A1, A6.
51. Sheila Kaplan, "Justice for Sale."
52. Larry Liebert, "Wilson's Warning if Proposition 8 Is Killed," *San Francisco Chronicle,* August 6, 1982, 8.
53. Alexander Stille and John C. Metaxas, "Bowing Out," *National Law Journal* (July 15, 1985): 2.

6. CUSTODY BATTLES IN STATE ADMINISTRATION

William T. Gormley, Jr.

State bureaucracies have paid a price for their growing importance, and that price is a loss of discretion. In recent years, state bureaucracies have become more permeable, more vulnerable, and more manipulable. They are subject to a growing number of controls, as governors, state legislators, state judges, presidents, members of Congress, federal bureaucrats, interest groups, and citizens all attempt to shape administrative rule making, public utility and business rate making, and adjudication at the state level. Of equal significance, state bureaucracies are subject to tougher, more restrictive, and more coercive controls.

In other words, state bureaucracies have become more accountable for their actions. In a sense, this is both understandable and desirable. Even state bureaucrats concede the virtues of accountability, at least in theory. Yet accountability is a multidimensional concept. Increasingly, the question is not whether but to whom state bureaucracies shall be accountable. A related question is how accountability can best be structured to avoid damage to other important values, such as creativity and flexibility.

This chapter summarizes the recent proliferation of controls that limit the discretion of state bureaucracies. It focuses primarily on legislative oversight, executive management, due process, and regulatory federalism. It also highlights the coercive character of certain controls and the consequences of coercion for bureaucratic performance. "Coercive controls" are contrasted with "catalytic controls," which may yield comparable progress with fewer adverse side effects. The emergence of "custody battles" that pit competing claimants against one another, in bitter struggles over authority, with state bureaucracies as the ultimate prizes will also be discussed. Increasingly, courts are being asked to resolve these disputes. Yet the courts are not disinterested claimants. Often the courts wish to shape the behavior of state bureaucracies. Thus, judges have emerged in recent years as key arbiters and managers, deciding custody battles in some instances, triggering custody battles in others.

The Proliferation of Controls

During the 1970s, politicians, judges, and citizens strengthened their leverage over state bureaucracies, which were growing in size and importance. They did so by institutionalizing a wide variety of control techniques. Some of these techniques, such as sunset laws and ombudsmen, were new. Others, such as executive orders and conditions of aid, were old but not much utilized in earlier years. Control techniques also differed in their directness, formality, durability, and coerciveness. However, they all shared a common purpose—to make state bureaucracies more accountable to other public officials or to the people.

Legislative Oversight

During the 1970s, state legislatures discovered oversight as a form of bureaucratic control. Legislative committees took an active interest in bureaucratic implementation or nonimplementation of state statutes and conducted hearings aimed at identifying and resolving problems. This became easier as the legislator's job became a full-time profession in most states and as legislative staffs became larger and more professional. More than their congressional counterparts, state legislators decided not to leave oversight to chance. Perhaps oversight needed an extra push at the state level. In any event, state legislatures established regular mechanisms for legislative review.

Following the lead of Colorado, approximately two-thirds of the state legislatures adopted sunset laws, which provide for the automatic expiration of agencies unless the state legislature acts affirmatively to renew them. Although the threat of extinction is far-fetched in the case of relatively large agencies, the threat of review must be taken seriously by all agencies. The sunset review process is especially important for obscure agencies that might otherwise escape scrutiny by legislative committees.

In addition to sunset laws, many state legislatures substantially upgraded the quality of their legislative audit bureaus. Gradually, these organizations came to place greater emphasis on program evaluation and policy analysis and less emphasis on auditing and accounting. To ensure careful, well-crafted evaluations, state legislatures augmented the staffs assigned to these organizations.

Finally, the overwhelming majority of state legislatures provided for legislative review of administrative rules and regulations. In sixteen of these states, legislative vetoes enable the legislature to invalidate an administrative rule or regulation. Through the legislative veto process, state legislatures have exercised closer scrutiny of administrative rule making. The U.S. Supreme Court ruled the legislative veto unconstitutional at the federal level,[1] and state courts have invalidated legislative vetoes in eight states.[2] Nevertheless, the legislative veto continues to be an important mechanism for legislative control in one-third of the states.

In thinking about legislative controls, it is useful to distinguish between inward-looking and outward-looking legislative changes. As Alan Rosenthal argues, state legislatures have become more fragmented, more decentralized, and less cohesive in recent years. In some sense, this might be characterized as "legislative decline." Yet a fragmented legislature is not necessarily weaker in its dealings with other units of government, such as state bureaucracies. Indeed, a highly fragmented legislature may provide more occasions for legislative oversight and more incentives for individual legislators to engage in oversight. Thus, as legislatures become weaker internally, they may become stronger externally. This is especially true of those forms of legislative control that do not require a legislative majority.

Executive Management

For years, governors have complained about the fragmented character of the executive branch. Many executive branch officials are elected by the people or appointed to office for fixed terms not coinciding with the governor's term. The very number of state agencies, boards, and commissions can be overwhelming and disconcerting. Also, agencies have their own traditions and habits and may be reluctant to follow the priorities of a new governor. All of these factors have inhibited executive integration, coordination, and leadership over the years.

During the 1970s many governors took steps to deal with these problems. Most governors spearheaded major reorganizations of the executive branch, striving for greater rationality and for a reduction in the number of boards and commissions. Minor reorganizations were also commonplace, as in environmental protection, where most states merged antipollution units in an effort to achieve greater integration. Some states went a step further, combining antipollution units with conservation units.

Governors also institutionalized cabinet meetings, subcabinet meetings, or both in an effort to secure greater coordination and integration. During the 1970s, approximately fourteen governors established a cabinet for the first time and approximately twenty-five governors established subcabinets to advise and coordinate in broad policy domains.[3] The hope was that these meetings would ensure that key executive branch officials marched to the same drumbeat.

In addition to these steps, governors relied on new budget techniques, such as zero-based budgeting, to increase their control over agency budget submissions and, ultimately, agency budgets themselves. Under zero-based budgeting, the previous year's budget base is not taken for granted, although it may be incorporated into alternative budget submissions. During the 1970s, approximately twenty-five states adopted a modified form of zero-based budgeting.[4]

At the same time, governors fought successfully for shorter ballots to bring more top state officials under gubernatorial control. During the 1970s a number of states shortened their ballots. Between 1962 and 1978 the number of elected state executives declined by 10 percent.[5] As a result of these reforms, governors today are more likely to deal with state agencies headed by gubernatorial appointees in whom they can have confidence.

Finally, executive orders have become more popular in recent years. In Wisconsin, Gov. Lee Dreyfus issued more executive orders in 1979 than his predecessors had issued during the 1960s and 1970s.[6] Dreyfus's successor, Anthony Earl, issued even more executive orders than Dreyfus.[7] Similarly, in Massachusetts, the number of executive orders issued between 1965 and 1980 rose 206 percent over the preceding fifteen years.[8] Many of these executive orders were aimed at controlling state bureaucracies.

Interest Representation

Unable or unwilling to control state agencies directly in every instance, politicians relied on surrogates to ensure better representation for favored points of view, such as consumers, environmentalists, and the elderly. McCubbins and Schwartz refer to this phenomenon as "fire-alarm oversight" because politicians in effect depend on citizens or other public officials to spot fires in the bureaucracy and to help stamp them out.[9] During the 1970s states took a number of steps to improve representation for broad, diffuse interests or other underrepresented interests, especially before state regulatory agencies; as a result, a "representation revolution" occurred.[10]

For example, many established "proxy advocacy" offices to represent consumer interests in state public utility commission proceedings, such as rate cases. In some instances, attorneys general served this function; in other instances, separate consumer advocacy offices were established. As a variation on this theme, Wisconsin established a Citizens Utilities Board, funded by citizens through voluntary contributions but authorized by the state legislature to insert membership solicitations in utility bills.[11] State legislatures in Illinois and Oregon subsequently established similar organizations, though without provisions for bill inserts.

Disappointed in the performance of occupational licensing boards, state legislatures mandated lay representation on such boards in the hope that it would result in fewer anticompetitive practices. Wisconsin law specifies that at least one public member shall serve on each of the state's occupational licensing boards. California goes even further. Since 1976, California has required that all occupational licensing boards must have a majority of public members, except for ten "healing arts" boards and the Board of Accountancy.[12]

Many state legislatures require public hearings in various environmental policy decisions. The California Coastal Act of 1972 requires a public hearing before a coastal zoning commission whenever a developer submits a construction permit request for a project that might have an "adverse environmental impact" on coastal resources.

Some interest representation reforms that occurred on the state level were mandated by or encouraged by the federal government. Thus, Congress required states to cooperate with the U.S. Environmental Protection Agency (EPA) in providing for public participation under the Federal Water Pollution Control Act, the Resource Conservation and Recovery Act, the Comprehensive Environmental Response, the Compensation and Liability Act, and other statutes. Through the Older Americans Act, Congress requires states to establish long-term-care ombudsman programs to investigate complaints by nursing home residents and to monitor the development and implementation of pertinent laws and regulations.

Regulatory Federalism

The dynamics of regulatory federalism differ significantly from those of interest representation reforms. In both cases, politicians exercise indirect control over state bureaucracies, relying on surrogates to articulate their concerns. However, regulatory federalism is much more intrusive than interest representation. If a consumer advocacy group recommends a new rule or regulation, a state agency may consider and reject it. If a federal agency instructs a state agency to adopt a rule or face a sharp cutback in federal funds, the state agency does not have much of a choice.

Regulatory federalism is a process whereby the federal government imposes conditions on state governments that accept federal funding. Regulatory federalism arose as an adjunct to the new social regulations of the 1970s and as an antidote to the laissez faire of general revenue sharing. Regulatory federalism includes a variety of tech-

niques, such as direct orders, crossover sanctions, crosscutting requirements, and partial preemptions.[13] Some of these techniques apply to
state legislatures, some to state agencies; many apply to both.

According to the Office of Management and Budget (OMB), the
number of crosscutting requirements enacted into law increased dramatically during the 1970s, nearly doubling over the previous decade.[14]
Examples include the Age Discrimination Act of 1975, the Rehabilitation Act of 1973, the Endangered Species Act of 1973, the Fair Labor
Standards Act Amendments of 1974, and the Archaeological and
Historic Preservation Act of 1974. These statutes contain requirements
that pertain to substantial numbers of agencies within all fifty states.

The number of crossover sanctions approved in recent years has
gone up significantly—although OMB has not attempted a precise
count. The federal government, for example, has threatened to reduce
highway assistance to states with serious air pollution problems that
fail to establish automobile emission inspection programs. Similarly, the
federal government has threatened to withhold federal highway funds
from states that fail to adopt a twenty-one-year-old drinking age.

In addition to crossover sanctions, the federal government has
imposed program-specific sanctions on states that fail to meet federal
cost-containment guidelines. These programs are often called quality
control or quality assurance systems, because they punish states for
erroneously awarding benefits to ineligible persons. During the 1970s,
Congress established comprehensive quality control systems for several
major entitlement programs, including Aid to Families with Dependent
Children (AFDC), food stamps, and Medicaid. In 1980, Congress
streamlined a preexisting quality control system for social security
disability payments.

Several regulatory federalism initiatives of recent years have been
challenged in court. However, the courts have routinely upheld the
federal government's right to impose constraints on state governments
accepting federal funds.[15] The courts have also upheld partial preemptions,[16] crossover sanctions,[17] and direct orders.[18]

Due Process

In addition to serving as arbiters in intergovernmental disputes,
federal judges have been active participants in efforts to control state
bureaucracies. They have intervened vigorously in pursuit of such
constitutional rights as "due process of law" and freedom from "cruel
and unusual punishment." Dissatisfied with progress at the state level,
they have gone so far as to seize state prisons and homes for the
mentally ill or the mentally retarded, substituting their managerial
judgment for that of state public administrators.

Wyatt v. Stickney was the first of a long line of institutional reform cases in which federal judges decided to play a strong managerial role.[19] Alabama's homes for the mentally ill and the mentally retarded were overcrowded, understaffed, dangerous, and unsanitary. In response to a class action suit, Judge Frank Johnson held that mental patients have a right to adequate and effective treatment in the least restrictive environment practicable. To secure that right, he issued specific treatment standards and ordered rapid deinstitutionalization.

Shortly after the *Wyatt* decision, Judge Johnson found himself embroiled in an equally bitter controversy over Alabama's prisons. By most accounts, conditions in the state's prisons were deplorable. Rapes and stabbings were widespread, food was unwholesome, and physical facilities were dilapidated. In response to inmate complaints, Judge Johnson issued a decree calling for adequate medical care, regular fire inspections, and regular physical examinations.[20] When conditions barely improved, he issued detailed standards, including cell-space requirements, hiring requirements, and a mandatory classification system.[21]

The Alabama cases set the stage for a large number of similar cases throughout the country. In state after state, federal judges mandated massive changes in physical facilities, staffing ratios, health services, and amenities. They specified the size of prison cells, the credentials of new employees, and plumbing and hygiene standards. They shut down facilities and prohibited new admissions, even where alternative facilities were not available.

The U.S. Supreme Court finally applied the brakes on mental health orders in *Youngberg v. Romeo*.[22] In that decision, the Supreme Court ruled that mentally retarded clients are constitutionally entitled to minimally adequate treatment and habilitation but that professionals, including state administrators, should be free to decide what constitutes minimally adequate training. Thus, the decision was viewed as a partial victory for state administrators.

The Supreme Court has yet to slow the tide of prison reform cases, which continue to drag on in many states. A good example is Texas, where Judge William Justice has been locked in a bitter battle with the Texas Department of Corrections since he called for sweeping reforms in *Ruiz v. Estelle*.[23] By 1988, thirty-seven states were under some kind of court order for their prisons. In nine states, the entire state prison system was under court order.[24]

Types of Controls

In thinking about recent efforts to control state bureaucracies, it is useful to imagine a spectrum ranging from catalytic controls, at one end, to coercive controls, at the other end, with hortatory controls falling in between. Catalytic controls stimulate change but preserve a great deal of bureaucratic discretion. Coercive controls require change and severely limit bureaucratic discretion. Hortatory controls involve more pressure than catalytic controls but more restraint than coercive controls.[25]

Most reforms can be classified according to this scheme. Moreover, different types of controls have different types of effects. Catalytic controls have been surprisingly effective, while coercive controls have been notably counterproductive.

Catalytic Controls

Catalytic controls require state bureaucracies to respond to a petition or plea but do not predetermine the nature of that response. As a result, such controls are action forcing but not solution forcing. They alter bureaucratic behavior, but they permit the bureaucracy a good deal of discretion and flexibility. Examples of catalytic controls include public hearings, ombudsmen, proxy advocacy, and lay representation.

Public hearings have enabled environmentalists to win important victories in their dealings with state bureaucracies. For example, citizens have used public hearings on state water quality planning in North Carolina to secure important modifications of state plans concerning waste water disposal, construction, and mining.[26] Similarly, citizens used public hearings before California coastal commissions to block permits for development projects that would have an "adverse environmental impact" on coastal resources.[27]

Ombudsmen have been active on several fronts in state politics but especially on nursing home issues. According to one report, nursing home ombudsmen have been effective in resolving complaints on a wide variety of subjects, including Medicaid problems, guardianship, the power of attorney, inadequate hygiene, family problems, and the theft of personal possessions.[28] Another study found that nursing home ombudsmen provide useful information to legislators and planners.[29]

Proxy advocates have effectively represented consumers in rate cases and other proceedings held by state public utility commissions. As a result of their interventions, utility companies have received rate hikes substantially lower than those originally requested. Proxy advocates have also been instrumental in securing policies on utility disconnections and payment penalties that help consumers who are struggling to pay their bills.[30]

Catalytic controls may be too weak in some instances. In several southern states, for example, public hearing requirements in utility regulatory proceedings have been pointless because consumer groups and environmental groups have not materialized to take advantage of such hearings.[31] Lay representation on occupational licensing boards has also been a disappointment. Lacking expertise, lay representatives have typically deferred to professionals on these boards.[32]

Overall, though, catalytic controls have been remarkably successful in making state bureaucracies more responsive to a wide variety of formerly underrepresented interests. In effect, they have institutionalized what political scientist James Q. Wilson refers to as "entrepreneurial politics" or the pursuit of policies that offer widely distributed benefits through widely distributed costs.[33] Moreover, catalytic controls have achieved results without engendering bureaucratic hostility and resentment. Studies show that state administrators welcome citizen participation[34] and interest group interventions.[35] At their best, catalytic controls provide state bureaucrats with ammunition to justify policies that promote the public interest.

Hortatory Controls

Hortatory controls involve political pressure or jawboning, usually by someone in a position of authority. They strike a balance between bureaucratic discretion and bureaucratic accountability. Some, such as sunset laws and administrative reorganizations, are relatively mild; others, such as partial preemptions and crossover sanctions, are relatively strong.

The strength of hortatory controls depends primarily on two factors: their specificity (are the goals of the controllers clear?) and the credibility of the threat (how likely is it that penalties will be invoked?). Thus, short ballots are relatively weak, even though they strengthen the governor's hand, because they do not push the bureaucracy in a clear substantive direction; sunset laws are relatively weak because the threat of termination is remote, except in the case of small agencies.

To argue that some hortatory controls are mild is not to say that they are ineffective. A study of legislative audit bureau reports reveals that they do lead to changes in legislation, administrative practice, or both. Indeed, research by legislative audit bureaus is more likely to be utilized by state legislators than other types of research.[36] The literature on administrative reorganizations reveals that they do not reduce government spending but they can promote coordination and integration if they are well crafted and well executed.[37] The key seems to be to put agencies with interrelated missions under the same roof.

Research on sunset laws roughly parallels the findings on administrative reorganizations. As a cost-containment device, sunset legislation has been a failure. However, as a mechanism for focusing legislative attention on agencies and issues low in visibility, sunset legislation has been a success. In a number of states, such as Connecticut and Florida, sunset laws have resulted in significant changes in statutes and agency rules.[38]

Stronger hortatory controls have been even more effective, though they have also been dysfunctional in some respects. In response to changes in Federal Financial Participation conditions, states have altered their welfare eligibility standards to conform to stringent new federal policies.[39] States have also reacted positively, albeit reluctantly, to crossover sanctions, such as the threat to withhold federal highway funds if automobile inspection and maintenance programs are not established.[40] Prodded by the federal government, states have established quality control systems for AFDC, food stamps, and Medicaid; and they have upgraded quality assurance systems for Social Security disability payments. Few states react cavalierly to a serious threat to withhold federal dollars.

Yet the side effects of these hortatory controls should not be ignored. In response to quality control systems in welfare, "errors of liberality" have declined, but "errors of stringency" have increased.[41] In effect, states have sacrificed accuracy for cost containment. States have also enforced federal regulations that they know to be unreasonable, in response to partial preemptions in environmental policy. For example, the Minnesota Pollution Control Agency enforced a rigid EPA definition of hazardous waste, even though it meant that a lime sludge pile could not be removed from a highway site, could not be used for waste-water treatment, and could not be used to clean an electric utility company's smokestack emissions.[42]

Strong hortatory controls place a premium on uniform standards and universal compliance with such standards. In some instances, such as civil rights, there may be no practical alternative to strong controls because local prejudices are too deeply ingrained to permit cooperation. In others, however, strong hortatory controls may impose premature closure, discouraging innovation and experimentation and making it difficult for the states to serve as "laboratories" for the nation and for other states.

Despite the new federalism, strong hortatory controls have been particularly prominent in intergovernmental relations in recent years. Although federal aid to state and local governments has declined, there has been no commensurate decrease in federal regulations. Richard P. Nathan cites state reforms in health, education, and welfare as evidence of a growing state role in a conservative era.[43] Yet state administrators cite precisely these issue areas, along with environmental policy, as ones in which federal influence is relatively strong.[44] It is, of course, possible that states are both innovating and responding. Or perhaps the state legislatures are innovating, while the state agencies are responding. In any event, regulatory federalism has not abated in recent years, even if the goals and purposes of federal overseers have changed during the conservative Reagan era.

Coercive Controls

Coercive controls rob state bureaucracies of their discretion. They compel a specific response, often within a specific time frame. Neither the solution nor the deadline may be reasonable, but the state bureaucracy does not have the luxury of responding reasonably. Immediate compliance becomes more important than rationality, and short-term "outputs" become more important than long-term "outcomes."

Coercive controls often trigger bureaucratic circumvention or resistance. In the former case, bureaucrats comply with the letter, but not the spirit, of a tough requirement. In the latter case, the bureaucracy goes to court. In both cases, an adversarial relationship develops that precludes cooperation, bargaining, and persuasion.

As a response to legislative vetoes, some state agencies have issued emergency rules, which are not subject to the usual legislative review process. In Wisconsin, for example, state agencies issued a total of fifty-four emergency rules during the 1985-1986 legislative session—a sharp increase over earlier years.[45] Reliance on emergency rules is especially unfortunate, because such rules do not involve public hearings. Thus, to escape highly threatening legislative vetoes, agencies have escaped less-threatening public hearings as well.

Court orders have triggered some of the more dysfunctional bureaucratic responses. When Judge Frank Johnson required state prisons to reduce their overcrowding, Alabama prison officials simply released large numbers of prisoners, forcing county jails to take up the slack. Unfortunately, county jails were poorly equipped for the task; they lacked adequate space and personnel. Consequently, many prisoners, shipped to county jails, were forced to endure conditions even worse than those they experienced in the state prisons.[46] Yet the state agency was technically in compliance with the court decree.

A key problem with coercive controls is that they place far too much emphasis on formal authority. In fact, many state agencies depend considerably on a series of informal understandings. This is especially true of prisons, where quick-thinking guards and cooperative inmates help to maintain a delicate balance between order and chaos. When that delicate balance is disrupted, tragedy may result. This is precisely what happened in Texas, where Judge Justice's court orders dissolved the informal networks that enabled the prisons to function on a daily basis. As guards became more timid, direct challenges to authority rose sharply. Disciplinary reports reveal abrupt and dramatic increases in incidents in which a guard was threatened or assaulted.[47] Inmates also turned on themselves, with their fists or with makeshift weapons. By generating rising expectations and undermining bureaucratic morale, Judge Justice created a temporary power vacuum that prison gangs quickly filled. The tragic result was a series of riots and violent episodes that left fifty-two inmates dead within two years.[48]

Coercion does not always beget violence, but it does often beget litigation. As a result, many coercive controls have resulted in bitter custody battles, as competing sovereigns have struggled over the right to serve as a state agency's legal guardian. Political disagreements have become legal disputes. Thus, when Gov. Brendan Byrne vetoed a legislative veto bill approved by the New Jersey state legislature, the legislature went to court. When President Reagan ordered National Guard troops to train in Central America, despite protests from governors, the governors went to court. When Judge Justice ordered the Texas Department of Corrections to adopt a large number of specific and costly reforms, the state of Texas went to court. These custody battles have become a recurring feature of state politics and intergovernmental relations.

Custody Battles

Custody battles have become more prominent in state politics for three principal reasons: (1) the proliferation of controls; (2) the intensification of controls; and (3) the judicialization of controls. As controls multiply, some are likely to be contradictory. Competing claimants emerge. As controls intensify, contradictory controls generate more friction. Competing claimants press their claims. As controls spill over into the courts, disputes are resolved according to legal criteria. Moreover, the courts themselves become active participants in custody battles. Frustrated with both state politicians and state bureaucrats, judges have decided that they can do a better job and that they are entitled to try under the U.S. Constitution, the state constitution, or both.

State Legislatures versus Governors

Custody battles between state legislatures and governors have erupted in recent years. Although such disputes are not new, they seem to focus increasingly on directives to administrative agencies. They also seem to focus increasingly on questions of legal authority instead of on questions of political preference. As a result, state judges have found themselves playing a key role in arbitrating disputes between governors and state legislatures.

Legislative vetoes have aroused considerable conflict between state legislatures and governors, even when the same party controls both branches of government. In New Jersey, for example, the Democratic state legislature and Democratic governor Brendan Byrne clashed in court over a generic legislative veto and a more specific veto, whereby certain building authority proposals must be approved by both houses or the presiding offices of the legislature, depending on the nature of the proposal.[49] The New Jersey state supreme court upheld the specific legislative veto[50] but ruled the generic veto unconstitutional, citing violations of separation of powers and the presentment clauses of the state constitution.[51] (Legislative vetoes have been ruled unconstitutional in seven other states.)

Executive orders have also triggered conflict between state legislatures and governors. In Pennsylvania, for example, Republican governor Richard Thornburgh issued an executive order "privatizing" the state's liquor control store system. The Democratic state legislature, which had just rejected such a plan, promptly took the governor to court. A Commonwealth Court judge ruled in favor of the legislature, noting that the governor's privatization plan was "without authority and contravenes the Sunset Act." He also accused both sides of playing an unseemly game of political football at the public's expense.[52]

Money, the "mother's milk" of politics, has fueled many disputes between state legislatures and governors. In Wisconsin, Republican governor Tommy Thompson refused to accept a decision by the Democratic state legislature to maintain welfare benefits at existing levels. Stretching the outer limits of his line-item veto authority, Thompson vetoed two digits and a decimal point from the state legislature's benefit formula, thereby effecting a 6 percent reduction in welfare benefits. The legislature promptly took the governor to court, but the Wisconsin Supreme Court upheld a generous interpretation of the governor's line-item power.[53]

The most striking aspect of custody battles between state legislatures and governors is that they often have a partisan edge, pitting a Republican governor against a Democratic state legislature or vice versa. As divided government has become more common at the state level, it becomes increasingly difficult for state agencies to know whether they are in Democratic or Republican hands. Thus, the voters' ambivalence has triggered important legal battles with high stakes.

Federal Politicians versus State Politicians

Increasingly, state bureaucracies are being asked to implement federal statutes, such as environmental protection statutes. Often these federal statutes contradict state statutes or the policy preferences of the state's governor. Under such circumstances, a showdown is likely, with the federal government citing the "commerce clause" or the "take care clause" of the U.S. Constitution, while the state government cites the Tenth Amendment.

The U.S. Supreme Court and other federal courts have routinely sided with the federal government in custody battles where the allocation of federal funds is at issue. If states accept federal funding, they must also accept the conditions the federal government attaches to those funds. However, many intergovernmental disputes do not involve federal funding but instead a federal effort to preempt state activity in a particular policy domain. Here also the U.S. Supreme Court has sided with the federal government, though with occasional exceptions.

In *National League of Cities v. Usery,* the Supreme Court surprised many observers by rejecting the federal government's attempt to extend minimum wage and maximum hour provisions to municipal employees.[54] In doing so, the court said that the Tenth Amendment prohibited any federal action that impaired "the State's freedom to structure integral operations in areas of traditional governmental functions." The decision was an important victory for both state and local governments.

In subsequent cases, the Supreme Court wrestled gamely with the "traditional governmental functions" criterion and offered further clarification. For example, in *Hodel v. Virginia Surface Mining and Reclamation Association,* the Court articulated a threefold test for determining when Tenth Amendment claims shall prevail.[55] Specifically, the Court extended protection to the states if federal regulations: (1) regulate the states as states; (2) address matters that are indisputably attributes of state sovereignty; and (3) impair the states' ability to structure integral operations in areas of traditional function. In *Hodel*—a strip mining case involving a partial preemption statute—the Court concluded that Congress had acted properly and with restraint.

Similarly, in *Federal Energy Regulatory Commission (FERC) v. Mississippi,* the Court applauded Congress for imposing modest constraints on state public utility commissions, when it could have preempted the field entirely.[56] Not every member of the Court joined in the applause. Justice Sandra Day O'Connor, supported by Justices Burger and Rehnquist, accused her colleagues of making state agencies "bureaucratic puppets of the Federal government" [57] and of permitting "Congress to kidnap state utility commissions into the national regulatory family." [58] Nevertheless, Justice O'Connor's concerns failed to sway the majority in *FERC v. Mississippi* or in *Equal Employment Opportunity Commission (EEOC) v. Wyoming.*[59]

Finally, after years of painful efforts to distinguish between "traditional government functions" and other functions, the Supreme Court abandoned that doctrine outright in *Garcia v. San Antonio Metropolitan Transit Authority*.[60] Writing for the majority, Justice Harry Blackmun concluded that "State sovereign interests . . . are more properly protected by procedural safeguards inherent in the structure of the federal system than by judicially created limitations on federal power." [61] In effect, the states would have to protect themselves through vigorous lobbying on Capitol Hill. The Supreme Court would no longer invoke a rule that was "unsound in principle and unworkable in practice" [62] to protect the states from excessive federal control.

Although most custody battles between federal and state politicians have focused on the commerce clause, one celebrated dispute involved the Constitutional provision (in Article I) that the states shall have the authority to train state militia. A number of governors, opposed to the Reagan administration's Central America policies, objected to White House orders, backed by Congress, to use the National Guard for training exercises in Honduras. The governors feared that their troops would directly or indirectly support the contras' efforts to overthrow the Sandinista government in Nicaragua. Gov. Rudy Perpich of Minnesota and ten other governors sued the federal government to protest the deployment of National Guard troops without gubernatorial consent. The governors did not dispute the president's authority to federalize the Guard to deal with a national emergency, but they noted pointedly that no state of emergency existed.

On August 5, 1987, a federal district court upheld the federal government's right to deploy National Guard units while the Guard is on active duty. In the words of Judge Donald Alsop, "All authority to provide for the national defense resides in the Congress, and state governors have never had, and never could have, jurisdiction in this area." [63] Here, as in other disputes between federal and state politicians, the federal government has been successful in establishing its preeminence.

Federal Judges versus State Politicians

In custody battles between federal politicians and state politicians, federal judges have served as arbiters. In other disputes, however, federal judges have served as both arbiters and combatants. In numerous institutional reform cases, federal district court judges have ordered sweeping changes that are attainable only if state legislatures allocate more money than they wish to spend in a particular policy domain. These decisions have had tangible effects on state budgets.[64] The decisions have also raised important questions concerning both federalism and the power of the purse.

Confronted by shocking conditions in Alabama's prisons, Judge Frank Johnson ordered the entire prison system overhauled. He required immediate action to provide adequate food, clothing, shelter, sanitation, medical attention, and personal safety for inmates. He ordered individual cells, with each cell being at least 60 square feet in diameter. He required educational and rehabilitative services. And to ensure swift implementation, he established human rights committees.

Other federal judges have acted with equal vigor. Judge William Justice, appalled by conditions in Texas prisons, ordered an end to quadruple cells, triple cells, and double cells. He restricted the use of force by prison guards and ordered an end to the state's "building tender" system, in which inmates in effect guarded other inmates. In addition, he ordered sharp improvements in health care, fire, and safety standards. He also insisted on prompt punishments for violations of constitutional rights.

In other institutional reform cases, federal judges have ordered sweeping reforms of state treatment of the mentally ill and the mentally retarded. In New York, Judges Orrin Judd and John Bartels ordered sweeping changes at the Willowbrook Developmental Center on Staten Island, including more ward attendants, eighty-five more nurses, thirty more physical therapists, and fifteen more physicians. They prohibited seclusion of patients and called for the immediate repair of broken toilets. They also ordered a sharp decrease in the Willowbrook population, stressing the advantages of deinstitutionalization. To implement these reforms, they appointed and preserved a Willowbrook Review Panel, which developed into a powerful agent of change.

In Pennsylvania, Judge Raymond Broderick went even further, after learning of unsanitary, inhumane, and dangerous conditions at the Pennhurst State School and Hospital for the mentally retarded. In a strongly worded opinion, Broderick ordered the eventual closing down of the Pennhurst facilities, with residents being relocated in community facilities. In the meantime, he insisted on clean, odorless, and insect-free buildings; no new admissions; and less reliance on forcible restraint and unnecessary medication. To achieve these results, he appointed a special master and set deadlines for compliance.

More often than not, custody battles between federal judges and state politicians have been won by federal judges. In reviewing lower court decisions, appeals court judges and the U.S. Supreme Court have agreed that "cruel and unusual punishment" is intolerable in state prisons and that the mentally ill have a constitutional right to "treatment" if admitted to a state facility. However, appeals courts have also raised questions about the extraordinarily detailed and specific remedies mandated by federal district court judges.

In *Newman v. Alabama,* the U.S. Court of Appeals for the Fifth Circuit ruled that Judge Johnson went too far in specifying the size of new prison cells, in appointing human rights committees, and in insisting on rehabilitation opportunities for all prisoners.[65] In the words of the court: "The Constitution does not require that prisoners, as individuals or as a group, be provided with any and every amenity which some person may think is needed to avoid mental, physical and emotional deterioration." In *Ruiz v. Estelle,* the same court ruled that Judge Justice went too far in outlawing double cells in Texas prisons (but supported his ban on triple and quadruple cells).[66] In *New York State Association for Retarded Children v. Carey,* the U.S. Court of Appeals for the Second Circuit concluded that Gov. Hugh Carey could not be held in contempt of court for failing to provide funding for the Willowbrook Review Panel.[67] In *Pennhurst State School and Hospital v. Halderman,* the U.S. Supreme Court ruled that there is a right to treatment only if a state accepts federal funds and if federal conditions of aid are clearly and unambiguously stated.[68] In *Youngberg v. Romeo,* the Supreme Court ruled that even when a right to treatment exists, it should be operationalized by qualified professionals, not judges.[69]

Thus, custody battles between federal district court judges and state politicians have given way to similar custody battles between federal district court judges and federal appeals court judges. On questions of constitutional rights, the appeals court judges have generally deferred to federal district courts, to the chagrin of the states. On questions of remedies, however, the appeals courts have cautioned lower courts against excessive specificity that stretches the limits of judicial expertise.

Summary

State administrative agencies once enjoyed considerable autonomy. Ignored by virtually everyone but clientele groups, they were "semi-sovereign" entities. In the early 1970s, that began to change. As state budgets grew and state bureaucracies increased in importance, this era of independence came to a close. In an effort to make state agencies more accountable, politicians and judges institutionalized a wide variety of reforms. Through direct and indirect means, they attempted to bring state bureaucracies under control.

Ironically, this occurred at precisely the same time as the growing professionalization of state agencies. Thanks to civil service reforms, budget increases, rising education levels, and growing pressure for specialization, state bureaucracies acquired greater experience and expertise. They are now more adept at problem solving than ever before and arguably more deserving of discretion. Thus, they chafe at external pressure, particularly when it is highly coercive.

General agreement exists that state agencies ought to be accountable. Even state bureaucrats cheerfully concede that point. However, consensus on the need for bureaucratic accountability has given way to "dissensus" on lines of authority. If governors and state legislators both claim an electoral mandate, who is right? If presidents and governors both cite constitutional prerogatives, who is correct? If federal judges and state politicians disagree on spending priorities, who really deserves the power of the purse?

In the 1980s, state agencies are living in a different world—one characterized by growing emphasis on hierarchy, oversight, and judicial review. State agencies are more accountable to their sovereigns than they used to be. Yet accountability has become a murky concept. Principal-agent theories of politics work only when the principal's identity is clear to the agent.[70] In numerous policy areas, state bureaucratic agents face dual principals or even multiple principals.

Thus, custody battles rage, as competing sovereigns press their claims. As one might expect in a federal system, different actors have won custody battles in different settings and at different times. Increasingly, however, federal judges are settling the most difficult of these custody battles. In the process of resolving these disputes, federal judges have themselves become interested parties. Ultimately, federal judges decide how accountability shall be defined, how authority shall be structured, and how power shall be wielded in a federal system. If custody battles persist, the judicialization of state administration is the most probable result.

Notes

1. *Immigration and Naturalization Service v. Chadha*, 462 U.S. 919.
2. L. Harold Levinson, "The Decline of the Legislative Veto: Federal/State Comparisons and Interactions," *Publius* 17 (Winter 1987): 115-132.
3. Lydia Bodman and Daniel Garry, "Innovations in State Cabinet Systems," *State Government* 55 (Summer 1982): 93-97.
4. Thomas Lauth, "Zero-Base Budgeting in Georgia State Government: Myth and Reality," in *Perspectives on Budgeting,* ed. Allen Schick (Washington, D.C.: American Society for Public Administration, 1980), 114-132.
5. Larry Sabato, *Goodbye to Good-time Charlie: The American Governorship Transformed,* 2d ed. (Washington, D.C.: CQ Press, 1983).
6. Susan King, "Executive Orders of the Wisconsin Governor," *Wisconsin Law Review* (1980): 333-369.

7. Justin Kopca, "Executive Orders in State Government," Madison, Wis., May 1987, unpublished manuscript.

8. E. Lee Bernick, "Discovering a Governor's Power: The Executive Order," *State Government* 57 (1984): 97-101.

9. Matthew McCubbins and Thomas Schwartz, "Congressional Oversight Overlooked: Police Patrols v. Fire Alarms," *American Journal of Political Science* 28 (February 1984): 180-202.

10. William T. Gormley, Jr., "The Representation Revolution: Reforming State Regulation through Public Representation," *Administration and Society* 18 (August 1986): 179-196.

11. Involuntary bill inserts were later ruled unconstitutional in a California case that effectively invalidated a key provision of the Wisconsin law. See *Pacific Gas and Electric v. Public Utilities Commission of California*, 106 S. Ct. 903 (1986).

12. Howard Schutz, "Effects of Increased Citizen Membership on Occupational Licensing Boards in California," *Policy Studies Journal* 2 (March 1983): 504-516.

13. Advisory Commission on Intergovernmental Relations, *Regulatory Federalism: Policy, Process, Impact and Reform* (Washington, D.C.: Advisory Commission on Intergovernmental Relations, 1983).

14. Office of Management and Budget, *Managing Federal Assistance in the 1980s* (Washington, D.C.: Government Printing Office, 1980).

15. *Massachusetts v. U.S.*, 435 U.S. 444 (1978); *Connecticut Department of Income Maintenance v. Heckler*, 105 S. Ct. 2210 (1985).

16. *Hodel v. Virginia Surface Mining and Reclamation Association*, 452 U.S. 264 (1981); *FERC v. Mississippi*, 456 U.S. 742 (1982).

17. *South Dakota v. Dole*, Slip Opinion No. 86-260, U.S. Supreme Court, June 23, 1987.

18. *EEOC v. Wyoming*, 460 U.S. 226 (1983); *Garcia v. San Antonio Metropolitan Transit Authority*, 105 S. Ct. 1005 (1985).

19. *Wyatt v. Stickney*, 324 F. Supp. 781 (M.D. Ala., 1971).

20. *Newman v. Alabama*, 349 F. Supp. 278 (M.D. Ala., 1972).

21. *James v. Wallace*, 406 F. Supp. 318 (M.D. Ala., 1976); *Pugh v. Locke*, 406 F. Supp. 318 (M.D. Ala., 1976).

22. *Youngberg v. Romeo*, 102 S. Ct. 2452 (1982).

23. *Ruiz v. Estelle*, 503 F. Supp. 1265 (S.D. Tex. 1980).

24. Joel Rosch, "Will the Federal Courts Run the States' Prison Systems?" in *State Government: CQ's Guide to Current Issues and Activities 1987-88*, ed. Thad Beyle (Washington, D.C.: Congressional Quarterly, 1987): 165-168.

25. William T. Gormley, Jr., *Taming the Bureaucracy: Muscles, Prayers, and Other Strategies* (Princeton, N.J.: Princeton University Press, 1989).

26. David Godschalk and Bruce Stiftel, "Making Waves: Public Participation in State Water Planning," *Journal of Applied Behavioral Science* 17 (October-December 1981): 597-614.

27. Judy Rosener, "Making Bureaucrats Responsive: A Study of the Impact of Citizen Participation and Staff Recommendations on Regulatory

Decision Making," *Public Administration Review* 42 (July/August 1982): 339-345.

28. U.S. Department of Health and Human Services, Administration on Aging, *National Summary of State Ombudsman Reports for U.S. Fiscal Year 1982* (Washington, D.C.: Government Printing Office, 1983).

29. Abraham Monk et al. *National Comparative Analysis of Long-Term Care Programs for the Aged* (New York: Brookdale Institute on Aging and Adult Human Development and the Columbia University School of Social Work, 1982).

30. William Gormley, Jr., *The Politics of Public Utility Regulation* (Pittsburgh, Pa.: University of Pittsburgh Press, 1983).

31. Gormley, *The Politics of Public Utility Regulation.*

32. Gerald Thain and Kenneth Haydock, "A Working Paper: How Public and Other Members of Regulation and Licensing Boards Differ: the Results of a Wisconsin Survey," Madison, Wis., Center for Public Representation, 1983, unpublished manuscript.

33. James Q. Wilson, ed., *The Politics of Regulation* (New York: Basic Books, 1980).

34. Cheryl Miller, "State Administrator Perceptions of the Policy Influence of Other Actors: Is Less Better?" *Public Administration Review* 47 (May/June 1987): 239-245.

35. Glenn Abney and Thomas Lauth, *The Politics of State and City Administration* (Albany: SUNY Press, 1986).

36. David Rafter, "Policy-Focused Evaluation: A Study of the Utilization of Evaluation Research by the Wisconsin Legislature" (Ph.D. diss., University of Wisconsin, 1982).

37. Kenneth Meier, "Executive Reorganization of Government: Impact on Employment and Expenditures," *American Journal of Political Science* 24 (August 1980): 396-412; and Karen Hult, *Agency Merger and Bureaucratic Redesign* (Pittsburgh, Pa.: University of Pittsburgh Press, 1987).

38. Doug Roederer and Patsy Palmer, *Sunset: Expectation and Experience* (Lexington, Ky.: Council of State Governments, June 1981).

39. Sanford Schram. "The New Federalism and Social Welfare: AFDC in the Midwest," in *The Midwest Response to the New Federalism,* ed. Peter Eisinger and William T. Gormley, Jr. (Madison: University of Wisconsin Press, 1988): 264-292.

40. James Gosling, "Transportation Policy and the Ironies of Intergovernmental Relations," in *The Midwest Response to the New Federalism,* 237-263.

41. Evelyn Brodkin and Michael Lipsky, "Quality Control in AFDC as an Administrative Strategy," *Social Service Review* 57 (March 1983): 1-34.

42. Eric Black, "Why Regulators Need a Don't-Do-It-If-It's-Stupid Clause," *Washington Monthly* 16 (January 1985): 23-26.

43. Richard P. Nathan, "The Role of the States in American Federalism" (Paper delivered at the annual meeting of the American Political Science Association, Chicago, September 3-6, 1987).

44. Richard Elling, "Federal Dollars and Federal Clout in State Administra-

tion: A Test of 'Regulatory' and 'Picket Fence' Models of Intergovernmental Relations" (Paper delivered at the annual meeting of the Midwest Political Science Association, Chicago, April 17-20, 1985).

45. Douglas Stencel, "Analysis of Joint Committee for Review of Administrative Rules Caseload 1985-86," Madison, Wis., April 1987, unpublished manuscript.
46. Tinsley Yarbrough, *Judge Frank Johnson and Human Rights in Alabama* (University: University of Alabama Press, 1981).
47. James Marquart and Ben Crouch, "Judicial Reform and Prisoner Control: The Impact of *Ruiz v. Estelle* on a Texas Penitentiary," *Law and Society Review* 19 (1985): 557-586.
48. Aric Press, "Inside America's Toughest Prison," *Newsweek*, October 6, 1986, 46-6l.
49. Levinson, "The Decline of the Legislative Veto," 121.
50. *Enourato v. New Jersey Building Authority*, 448 A. 2d 449 (N.J. 1982).
51. *General Assembly v. Byrne*, 448 A. 2d 438 (N.J. 1982).
52. Gary Warner, "Despite Ruling, Future of Liquor Stores Up in Air," *Pittsburgh Press*, December 30, 1986, 1.
53. Charles Friederich, "Lawmakers to Sue Thompson over Budget Vetoes," *Milwaukee Journal*, September 2, 1987, 3B; and Doug Mell, "Thompson Vetoes Win in Court," *Wisconsin State Journal*, June 15, 1988, 1.
54. *National League of Cities v. Usery*, 426 U.S. 833 (1976).
55. *Hodel v. Virginia Surface Mining and Reclamation Association*, 452 U.S. 264 (1981).
56. *FERC v. Mississippi*, 456 U.S. 742 (1982).
57. 456 U.S. 783 (1982).
58. 456 U.S. 790 (1982).
59. *EEOC v. Wyoming*, 460 U.S. 226 (1983).
60. *Garcia v. San Antonio Metropolitan Transit Authority*, 105 S. Ct. 1005 (1985).
61. 105 S. Ct. 1018 (1985).
62. 105 S. Ct. 1016 (1985).
63. Robert Whereatt, "State Loses Guard Suit," *Minneapolis Star and Tribune*, August 5, 1987, 1.
64. Linda Harriman and Jeffrey Straussman, "Do Judges Determine Budget Decisions?" *Public Administration Review* 43 (July/August 1983): 343-351.
65. *Newman v. Alabama*, 559 F. 2d 283 (5th Cir. 1977).
66. *Ruiz v. Estelle*, 679 F. 2d 1115 (1982).
67. *New York State Assn. for Retarded Children v. Carey*, 631 F. 2d 162 (1980).
68. *Pennhurst State School and Hospital v. Halderman*, 101 S. Ct., 1531 (1981).
69. *Youngberg v. Romeo*, 102 S. Ct. 2452 (1982).
70. Jonathan Bendor and Terry Moe, "An Adaptive Model of Bureaucratic Politics," *American Political Science Review* 79 (September 1985): 755-774.

7. THE PERSISTENCE OF STATE PARTIES

Samuel C. Patterson

It is difficult to overstate the pervasiveness of political parties in American state politics. All of the fifty state governors are either Democrats or Republicans. The other statewide elected officials are unanimously adherent to one of the two major parties. All of the 7,461 state legislators are Democrats or Republicans, except for the members of Nebraska's unicameral legislature and a handful of independents. Democrats and Republicans dominate local politics, which are not legally nonpartisan. In national politics, splinter party presidential electors have occasionally succeeded, but the citizens of the states elect only Democrats or Republicans to represent them in the U.S. Congress. The two major parties monopolize state political offices.

To make such an observation might imply that lying behind the Democratic and Republican monopolies of offices are highly organized and well-oiled party organizations. This is not so and never has been. In general, a political party may be thought of as "any group, however loosely organized, seeking to elect governmental office-holders under a given label."[1] The state parties are loosely organized structures of committees and leaders drawn together in efforts to capture public offices.

American party politics are broad in the scope of their coverage. Almost all elected public offices are occupied by Democrats or Republicans. These are about the only organized parties, and the vast majority of Americans identify with one of them. But, American party politics are shallow: as organizations they do not seem especially robust; in government, party cleavage may be episodic and ephemeral; among voters, loyalty may evanesce briefly during periodic elections.

To say that party politics are shallow in certain ways is not to say they are inconsequential. Ultimately it is important to know how shallow and with what they are compared. American parties may not compare unfavorably with the parties of other Western democracies, as is so often assumed.[2] American electoral politics, however, are not merely shadow and symbol, with no grounding in political party organization. Organized parties operate in every state, more-or-less endowed with leadership, managerial resources, staff, sufficient budgets, local organization, and loyal followers. What are these state party organizations like?

The Organized State Parties

State party organizations vary in size and shape, but they are similar enough to permit a general analysis. The distinguishing features of these organizations are to be found in their organizational formats, their purposes, their decentralization, their tenacity, and the extent to which they are regulated by government.

Organizationally Manifested

The states have organized their parties in a remarkably similar fashion. State parties are organizations of leaders and committees. Each has a governing committee presided over by the state party chairperson. This Democratic or Republican State Central Committee is made up of party activists who oversee party efforts at the state level. The state party chairs, elected by the state committees in three-fourths of the states, and by the state party conventions in the rest, provide leadership and management for their state organizations. These state chairs may be the state's principal political leaders, or they may be agents of, and perhaps even handpicked by, the governor.

In the smallest political unit of the state, the precinct, reside the grass-roots party leaders—the precinct committee members. Between the precinct leadership at the base of the organization and the state committee at its peak lies a range of party committees. Typically, party committees are established in congressional districts, state legislative districts, towns, cities, and wards. Party committees are not laid out in the form of a hierarchy. They are not centralized in the state capital, with orders flowing from the top down, like a bureaucracy or a firm. Instead, the organizational committees form autonomous layers, connected together, but each layer maintains its own structure and functions. This layering feature of American parties has been called "stratarchy" to denote the presence of "layers, or strata, of control rather than one of centralized leadership from the top down."[3]

State party organizations are organizationally manifested in party activists who are formed into committees in every state and most communities. Few political scientists have sought to make contact with party organizations and their leaders across the board. However, about ten years ago a team of scholars conducted interviews and collected mail questionnaire data from state and local party leaders throughout the country. They gathered data on state parties from about three-fourths of the sitting state chairpersons, two-thirds of the 560 men and women who served as state chair from 1960 to 1978, and from about 4,000 of the 7,300 local party leaders.[4] Scholars sought and found a substantial number of state and local party leaders.

The state parties are mainly defined by the cadre of leaders and activists who fill their leadership and committee posts. In fact, these parties are called cadre parties, or skeletal organizations, because they feature relatively small groups of leaders and activists and lack a "regularized, dues-paying membership commonly found among parties in other nations and among almost all nonparty organizations."[5]

Purposive Organizations

The state parties serve a variety of purposes for those who are actively involved in them. Prominent among these purposes are (1) giving systemic meaning to individuals' preferences about policy issues or their ideological predispositions, (2) facilitating the transformation of public opinion into governing policy, and (3) providing important avenues for social activity. The thousands of people involved in state party activity may wish to do a variety of things, operate on the basis of diverse motives, or have divergent axes to grind.

The job of the state party organizations is electorally oriented. The party organization embraces "a group of persons who consciously coordinate their activities so as to influence the choice of candidates for elective office," says one scholar.[6] Another offers a more succinct definition: a party is "a team seeking to control the governing apparatus by gaining office in a duly constituted election."[7] This does not mean that, in seeking to win elections, parties are single-minded and always make the right choices. These parties are purposive enough, though it often seems they may best be described as "forms of organized trial and error."[8]

Organizationally Resilient

"Organizations," says James Q. Wilson, "tend to persist."[9] The American state parties certainly are resilient. They have proved to be adaptive to changes in resources, political fortunes, electoral realignments, campaign technology, and influence. The extent of state party organizational tenacity should be the focus of empirical inquiry. Accounting for the persistence of the state parties should be a major task of inquiry about American political life. Oddly enough, the state parties seem to have been organizationally persistent at a time when they were said to be decomposing, declining, or perhaps even dying.[10]

The resiliency and persistence of the state parties lie partly in the extent of the decentralization of American party organization. The parties are mainly organized to capture state and local offices. Only the president, vice president, and 535 members of Congress are elected to national office; thousands of elective offices are available in the states. Accordingly, the political parties have taken on a federal organizational structure, mirroring that of the federal government. Some have advocated national centralization of the parties,[11] and indeed some party nationalization has taken place since 1968. In the Republican party it has occurred largely through dispensation to the states of financial largesse, and in the Democratic party, mainly through adoption of national party rules regulating the selection of national party convention delegates.[12] Despite the importance of these nationalizing tendencies, they are limited in effect; the state parties remain quite autonomous over most of the range of their activities, and the aggregate system remains primarily federated.

The state party's resiliency, its adaptability, and thus its persistence may also be due to its skeletal character. Without a large number of paid employees, or a body of politicians primarily dependent upon the organization for their livelihoods, the parties are more free to compromise so as to exploit their office drives. They are much less tied to the protection of vested interests in organizational maintenance efforts.[13]

Regulated Organizations

Scholars often note that political parties were eschewed by the founders of the republic, and that they are not mentioned in the national constitution. However, this truth should in no way be taken to suggest that American parties are not controlled by law. In fact, the state parties are highly regulated, so much so that Leon Epstein refers to them as public utilities.[14] For approximately one hundred years, the state parties have not been considered private, voluntary associations under state laws. On the contrary, like the electric company or the water works, political parties are conceived in state laws as agencies providing public services, affected with a public interest, and subject to state regulation.

State laws define what constitutes a political party. Ohio's law is typical in its legalistic detail and long-windedness:

> A political party ... is any group of voters which, at the last preceding regular state election, polled for its candidate for governor in the state or nominees for presidential electors at least five per cent of the entire vote cast for such office or which filed with the secretary of state, subsequent to any election in which it received less than five

per cent of such vote, a petition signed by qualified electors equal in number to at least one per cent of the total vote for governor or nominees for presidential electors at the last preceding election, declaring their intention of organizing a political party, the name of which shall be stated in the declaration, and of participating in the next succeeding primary election, held in even-numbered years, that occurs more than one hundred twenty days after the date of filing. . . . When any political party fails to cast five per cent of the total vote cast at an election for the office of governor or president it shall cease to be a political party.[15]

The scope of state regulation of parties varies among the states, but in all but five (Alaska, Delaware, Hawaii, Kentucky, and North Carolina), there is some kind of regulation dictating how the state parties are organized, their membership, and their internal operations. In 1984, the federal Advisory Commission on Intergovernmental Relations (ACIR) conducted a thorough analysis of state statutes regulating political parties.[16] Here is a summary of what they found:

Regulation	*Number of states*
How state central committee members are selected	36
Who may serve on state central committees	32
State central committee's meeting dates and location	15
Party internal rules and procedures	28
How local party committee members are selected	35
Composition of local party committees	34
Local party committees' internal rules, procedures, and activities	45

In addition to widespread state regulation of party organizations, the states also oversee the involvement of parties in the electoral process. These legal constraints include requiring nomination of candidates by primary elections, determining whether parties may engage in preprimary endorsements of candidates, regulating who can vote in party primaries, deciding whether primary losers can run in the general election under the label of another party, and establishing whether the ballot will permit straight party voting. Moreover, federal and state regulation of party campaign finance practices has had a major impact upon state party organization.

In some states, regulation leads to a strong party role in the electoral process. For example, states in which laws allow preprimary endorsement, provide for closed primaries, or facilitate straight-ticket voting foster strong parties. But the ACIR study concluded that "most states do not provide a legal environment conducive to the development or maintenance of strong state and local party roles in the electoral process." [17]

Strengths and Weaknesses of State Parties

There has been uninformed speculations about the strength of state party organizations. Claims about party effectiveness, and more common assertions about party decline, are usually strident, impressionistic, often confined to some national perversity unrelated to the state parties, and inclined to exaggerate the impact of technology on politics. The notions are presumptive of some golden age of strong parties based on the model of a few urban political machines or the disciplined socialist parties of western Europe.

Recently, a few scholars have undertaken an investigation of state and local party organizations empirically, gathering data and observing party performance first-hand.[18] Such empirical observation belies the notion that the state parties have been innervated—nationalized, swamped by political action committees (PACs), decimated organizationally, overcome by media technology or modern "snake oil" public relations, or even altogether nonexistent.

The balanced assessment is that state party organizational strength has not been impressively high for many decades and was never high for most states. Much diversity exists today among states in the strength of their party organizations. The best general conclusion about state party strength is this:

> . . . there is mounting evidence that political parties, far from becoming doddering relics on the verge of extinction, are undergoing a complex process of adaptation to new electoral conditions and are emerging in many states as vigorous entities capable of performing a mix of both modern and traditional tasks.[19]

Resources of the Party Organizations

The resources available to the state party organizations can be described from the data gathered by two major investigations, one lead by political scientist Cornelius Cotter, and the other by the staff of the Advisory Commission on Intergovernmental Relations. These two field studies show that:

> Most state parties have permanent headquarter offices in the state capital; about a fifth of the county party organizations have permanent headquarters; and more than half the county parties have offices during the campaign season.

Most state headquarters are staffed by at least one full-time staff member, and about 15 percent have ten or more staff. Republican state parties are substantially better staffed than Democratic state parties.

The state parties now have significant budgets for operations, and considerably more than two decades ago. In 1984, nearly two-thirds of Democratic state parties had budgets under $250,000; more than half the Republican state parties' budgets were over $500,000. This budgetary disparity occurs partly because state Republican parties receive more help than their Democratic counterparts from the national party, and partly because the state Republicans have effectively exploited modern fund-raising methods such as direct mail and telephone solicitations.

These resources in office facilities, staff, and budgets allow the state parties to engage more fully in campaign politics. A sizeable majority of the parties provide money and fund-raising assistance to state and congressional candidates (see Table 7-1). Moreover, most can provide a range of technical assistance to state candidates, such as assistance with polling, media use, or coordination of contributions from PACs.

When it comes to state party services, on the average, the Republican parties have a substantial edge over the Democratic parties. It is only with respect to fund-raising assistance for congressional

Table 7-1   State Party Contributions to Candidates, 1984 (in percentages)

Type of assistance or service	Democrats	Republicans
Campaign contributions to		
State candidates	70	90
Congressional candidates	56	70
Fund-raising assistance to		
State candidates	63	95
Congressional candidates	63	63
Polling services	50	78
Media consulting	46	75
Campaign seminars	76	100
Coordinating PAC contributions	31	52

SOURCE: Advisory Commission on Intergovernmental Relations, *The Transformation in American Politics: Implications for Federalism* (Washington, D.C.: Advisory Commission on Intergovernmental Relations, 1986), 115.

candidates that state Democratic party leaders report levels of activity equal to that of Republicans.

Diversity of Party Strength

There is wide variation among the states in the organizational strengths of their state and local parties (see Table 7-2). Two sets of indicators were used by Cotter and his colleagues to measure party organizational strength: organizational complexity and programmatic capacity. Organizational complexity is measured through indicators of accessibility to party headquarters, staffing, and budgets; programmatic capacity is measured through indicators of institutional support, such as fund-raising, electoral mobilization, polling, providing information, and candidate-directed activity, which includes financial contributions to candidates, providing services, and preprimary endorsements.[20]

It is apparent from the data presented in Table 7-2 that, in general, state Republican parties are organizationally stronger than their Democratic counterparts. Of the ten strongest state parties, eight are Republican. Both parties are more-or-less equally strong in only four states—California, Michigan, Minnesota, and Pennsylvania. In these states, the county party organizations were rated "strong" as well. That the California parties are rated as relatively strong parties is perhaps indicative of the loose character of state party strength in the United States. Students of the California parties often speak of the formal party organizations as weak and ineffectual but attribute considerable strength to voluntary party organizations and influence on the state's politics to the legislative parties.[21]

Massachusetts has the weakest pair of party organizations; most of the other weak parties are Democratic parties in southern states, and both parties in the mountain west.[22] Recent investigations of party organizations in Florida and South Carolina indicate significant growth in organizational strength in these states, especially in light of their traditional partisan torpidity.[23]

Although there is some correlation between party strength at the state and local levels, parties strong at one level are not necessarily strong at the other. For instance, Ohio Republicans are rated strong at both state and local levels, but Ohio Democrats are organizationally weak at the state level while maintaining relatively firm local party control. In some southern states, the Republicans have developed impressive, centralized state party organizations without grass-roots party organization of parallel strength.[24]

State parties appear to be organizationally stronger in states where the legal environment is supportive and where minimal party regulation exists. Where state laws support parties and regulation is light, the

Table 7-2   Strength of State Party Organizations

	State Party Strength			
	Strong		Weak	
	Democratic	Republican	Democratic	Republican
Strong local parties	California	Arizona	Alaska	Hawaii
	Florida	California	Connecticut	Rhode Island
	Michigan	Connecticut	Delaware	West Virginia
	Minnesota	Illinois	Idaho	Wyoming
	North Dakota	Indiana	Illinois	
	Pennsylvania	Iowa	Indiana	
	Rhode Island	Maine	Maine	
		Michigan	Maryland	
		Minnesota	New Hampshire	
		Nevada	New York	
		New Mexico	North Carolina	
		New York	Ohio	
		North Carolina	Tennessee	
		North Dakota	Utah	
		Ohio	Washington	
		Pennsylvania		
		Tennessee		
		Washington		
		Wisconsin		
Weak local parties	Georgia	Alabama	Arizona	Idaho
	Kentucky	Colorado	Arkansas	Kentucky
	Nebraska	Florida	Colorado	Louisiana
	South Dakota	Georgia	Iowa	Massachusetts
	Virginia	Kansas	Kansas	Utah
	Wisconsin	Mississippi	Louisiana	Vermont
		Missouri	Massachusetts	
		Montana	Mississippi	
		Nebraska	Missouri	
		New Hampshire	Montana	
		Oklahoma	Nevada	
		Oregon	Oregon	
		South Carolina	South Carolina	
		South Dakota	Texas	
		Texas	Vermont	
		Virginia	West Virginia	
			Wyoming	

SOURCE: Cornelius P. Cotter, James L. Gibson, John F. Bibby, and Robert J. Huckshorn, *Party Organizations in American Politics* (New York: Praeger, 1984), 28, 52.

NOTE: These state parties could not be classified because of insufficient data: Democrats in Alabama, Hawaii, New Jersey, New Mexico, and Oklahoma; and Republicans in Alaska, Arkansas, Delaware, and Maryland.

parties (62 percent) tend to be organizationally strong. But, where the legal climate is unsupportive and regulation of parties is heavy, the state parties (57 percent) tend to be organizationally weak.

Financing the Parties

Research is only beginning to be conducted on state political campaign spending that would allow reliable generalizations about the sources of political money and its effectiveness. The state parties have been increasingly active in fund raising and in investment decisions. Party campaign spending runs a poor third to individual contributions and PAC expenditures. Nevertheless, state party campaign spending is not insignificant. Indeed, state parties have shown "they were able to maximize their financial role in the campaign process through skillful management of party resources." [25]

A number of states provide for financing parties and candidates through some system of public funding. Begun in 1973, public funding in eleven states developed through a tax-checkoff system. Taxpayers in these states indicate on their income tax return whether or not they want a contribution of state funds to go to the state Democratic or Republican party (in Iowa, the taxpayer may choose "both," in which case half a dollar goes to each party), to candidates, or to both. Eight states have an "add-on" system of public funding. Here, the taxpayer must accept an additional tax liability to make a contribution to a party or candidate.

The scope of these state public funding systems varies widely. In the twenty states operating with public funding, ten provide that the funds go to the state political parties.[26] These ten states are: Alabama, California, Idaho, Iowa, Kentucky, Maine, North Carolina, Rhode Island, Utah, and Virginia. In the main, public funding has had only a small effect upon campaign efforts by the state parties, partly because the amounts are fairly small and partly because the parties have tended to use the public funds for operational or organizational maintenance purposes. Moreover, taxpayer participation in these programs seems to be declining. The future of public funding practices may be in doubt. Nevertheless, public funding is one technique for supporting and strengthening the state parties, and in some states this effect has been considerable.

A recent striking development in state political financing has been the growth of campaign fund-raising through the legislative parties. This phenomenon was pioneered by California assembly speaker Jesse Unruh in the early 1960s. Today, in at least half the states, the legislative party leaders raise campaign war chests and distribute funds to legislative candidates.[27] In Illinois during 1986-1987, the Republican legislative campaign committees spent $1.8 million, and the Democratic committees spent about $1 million on state legislative candidacies.[28] To a considerable extent, this development embraces the channeling (or "laundering," to some) of PAC money. Major state interest groups find this kind of contributing more permissible or more effective than making direct contributions to candidates.

The national parties used to levy monetary assessments against the state parties as a way of raising their own money. Times have changed. Political money raising has been centralized a great deal in the 1980s. The national Republicans have taught a clear lesson about national party fund raising and the investment of national party funds in the state parties. In 1983-1984, a large majority of Republican state party chairs reported they had gotten financial help from the national Republican party. Seventy percent said the state party or state candidates had received national party financial aid; three-fourths reported getting fund-raising assistance from the national party. Democratic state chairs reported national party financial assistance was given to the state party as well, but on a much smaller scale. Only 7 percent reported national party financial aid to the state party, although 13 percent said national funds had gone to state candidates and 20 percent reported fund-raising assistance from the national party.[29]

Another source of national party funding for campaign efforts in the states is provided by the Federal Election Campaign Act. This act coordinates expenditures and the so-called agency agreements that permit the national parties to fund congressional and senatorial campaigns in behalf of the state parties. Coordinated expenditures do not count as contributions to candidates, nor are they considered expenditures by the candidates. They are party expenditures coordinated with a candidate's campaign and spent on behalf of the candidate.

In 1986, the coordinated expenditure limitation was $21,810 for U.S. House districts. For Senate races (and for House seats in states with only one representative), expenditure limits depend on state populations; these amounts ranged in 1986 from a minimum of $43,620 in a number of small states to a high of $851,680 in California.[30] Since the state parties also may spend up to these limits in congressional campaigns, where the national party serves as the agent of the state party its contributions are, in effect, doubled. These practices mean much larger amounts of money are available in the states to finance congressional elections. But, how much this development has actually helped or hindered the state parties is not known. Because the national Republican party has, so far, taken advantage of these strategies for intergovernmental party finance, much more than the Democrats have, the effects on the state parties have been felt mainly on the Republican parties.[31]

The 1979 amendments to the Federal Election Campaign Act incorporate putative efforts to assist the state parties, or at least stem the tide of party financial nationalization. These amendments allow the state parties to buy campaign material (for example, buttons and bumper stickers) and conduct voter registration drives unfettered by limits on campaign expenditure for national offices. The effects of the 1979 amendments on the state parties are highly debatable; some think they have helped the state parties, others think the state parties have been weakened. It does seem to be agreed that the reporting and accounting provisions of the federal law are so complex that they have further encouraged the state parties to stay away from national candidates and concentrate on races for governor and the state legislature.[32]

What the Parties Do

An array of state parties could be imagined that persisted organizationally but that performed no significant political role or engaged in no relevant activities. Such organizational shells would, like the human appendix, merely be vestiges of a late lamented existence. There are those who come close to speaking of the parties in this fashion, as if they had been fully superannuated by "candidate-centered" campaigning, media madness, and cold-eyed political consultants. But party organizations at the American grass roots do perform politically relevant activities, and there are live, breathing human beings actively engaged in state and local party politics.

Campaign Activities

Typically, scholars who have gathered empirical evidence about state and local party efforts find that a good deal of party activity goes on. Often, these investigators speak of these activities in a voice of surprise, since the conventional wisdom directs that they should find little party effort. When Cotter and his colleagues gathered their data about state parties in 1980, they found party activists impressively engaged in party organizational maintenance activities, despite the personalized, nonbureaucratic structure of the local parties.[33] They also uncovered substantial campaign activity on the part of state and local parties.

Perhaps the most striking showing of substantial campaign activity performed by the state parties draws from the 1984 data gathered by Gibson for county party leaders.[34] Comparing 1984 reports of party leaders with the data gathered in 1980, Gibson and his associates demonstrate significant increases in party activity in the states. This study indicates that well over 90 percent of county parties have a complete set of officers, with most having precinct chairs filled. More than 80 percent of both Democratic and Republican county chairs report they spend six hours a week or more engaged in party business; two-thirds indicate that their county committee meets twice a month or more during the election season; and about 70 percent maintain a campaign headquarters. But, almost no county chairs receive a salary, and only a minority have a staff or a regular annual budget. Consider the following sampling of local party activities reported by party leaders in 1984.[35]

Local party activity	*Democrats*	*Republicans*
Worked with state legislative candidates on campaign strategy	93%	92%
Worked with congressional candidates on campaign planning and strategy	87	84
Involved in recruiting candidates for state legislature	76	81
Involved in recruiting candidates for Congress	61	66
Distributed campaign literature	89	91
Arranged fund raisers	84	85
Contributed money to candidates	69	77
Organized telephone campaigns	78	78
Sent mailings to voters	66	75
Conducted registration drives	78	78
Canvassed door-to-door	67	68
Bought radio or television time	36	35
Conducted public opinion polls	23	25

The two parties differ very little in the aggregate in conducting local party activity, but the data indicate interesting variations among states. Most marked is the significant increase in the level of activity among southern Democratic parties, presumably striving to catch up with the greater activity of Republicans in their states since 1980.

Moreover, these local parties obviously are more intensively and pervasively engaged in recruiting candidates, planning campaigns, and making traditional campaign efforts than they are in buying and using mass media or opinion surveys. To be sure, some proportion of local parties are inert; although most have officers, some of these local party leaders apparently are not actively involved in campaigning. But, reported levels of local party activity are, overall, substantial and impressive. These cross-sectional findings are confirmed in recent intensive studies of party activism conducted in Middlesex County, N.J., in Cuyahoga County, Ohio, and in five major cities.[36]

Party Activists

Who are the activists who provide the core of state and local party organizations? Two definite responses can be given to this question. One response has to do with the types of people who become activists and the other has to do with their attitudes.

Invariably, studies of party activists show that they are drawn from the higher reaches of the socioeconomic scale. They are mostly college graduates and have relatively high incomes. They are about equally divided by gender. Racial and ethnic minorities are poorly represented among party activists in general, however their representation is better in states with large minority populations.[37] The two parties do not differ significantly in the socioeconomic status of their party activists. It is fair to say that the two American parties recruit their local party activists from about the same social classes.

Party activists tend to be ideologically more committed than the average citizen and much more strongly identified with their party.[38] The ideological difference between Republican and Democratic party activists is especially striking. Studies of grass-roots party leaders consistently show sharp ideological differences between the two parties. Republicans are markedly conservative while Democrats are decidedly liberal. For instance, a study of more than seventeen thousand state convention delegates in eleven states in 1980 showed "the consistent liberalism of the Democrats and the consistent conservatism of the Republicans," irrespective of the state in which the activists resided.[39] Even in Indiana, a state reputed to have a notoriously job- or patronage-oriented politics, a recent study of party activists shows sharp ideological differences between Republicans and Democrats.[40] Moreover, in Indiana and elsewhere, Republican activists appear as ideologically homogeneous, while Democratic activists often exhibit an ideological mix.[41] The same sharp ideological differences are to be found among state party activists who become national convention delegates.[42]

There is plenty of evidence that these grass-roots party activists are deeply involved in mobilizing voters to win elections. The activists of the two parties think of themselves as rival teams seeking control of political offices. Competitive activists appear, on the whole, to be thriving in many states—and in such contrasting contexts as traditionally partisan Michigan or reputedly organizationally weak California.[43]

Do State Parties Matter?

The case for the persistence of the state parties is weakened if it is true—as prophets of party demise imply—that even if there remain local party organizations, and even if they are active in campaign politics, this party effort makes no difference.

Impact on Nominations

State parties matter. They have an effect on the nomination of candidates. The advent of the direct primary has not kept the state parties from affecting nominations. Informally, party leaders may channel competition for primary nominations, in essence slate making within the context of the direct primary system.[44] In a number of states, the parties may officially endorse candidates in primaries. Where primary candidates are endorsed by state party conventions, the endorsed candidates are advantaged in garnering the support of activists and developing an effective organization.

The primary election in endorsement states may become largely a formality. A thorough study of gubernatorial nominations in selected endorsement states in 1982 showed, for instance, that "when endorsements are made, there are fewer contested gubernatorial nominations and, if there is a contest, the endorsee wins about three-fourths of the time." [45] Even if preprimary endorsement is not officially sanctioned, state parties may endorse candidates. This is exemplified by the Minnesota parties' impressively effective extralegal endorsement process.[46]

Effect on Elections

The effectiveness of the state parties bears upon the outcome of elections. "The relationship between electoral success and party organizational strength is," as John F. Bibby correctly says, "exceedingly complex." [47] In states where one party historically has enjoyed electoral dominance, there is little incentive for either party to organize. But where the competitive situation opens opportunities for electoral successes, organizational efforts by the state parties can bear handsome rewards, as the recent experience of the southern Republican parties attests.

The existing systematic study of the impact of state parties on electoral outcomes supports two assertions. First, state-level party organizational strength substantially affects state elections for governor and legislator but has a much smaller impact on presidential and congressional contests.[48] It is not surprising that state party efforts bear electoral fruit mainly in state elections. Presidential and congressional races usually follow national party campaigns.

Second, when party organizations gain strength, their electoral clout is greater, ceteris paribus. Cotter and his associates were able to establish a significant state-level organization effect on the outcomes of gubernatorial races in the 1975-1980 period.[49] Gibson and his colleagues investigated county party organizational changes and election outcomes from 1980 to 1984.[50] Although the electoral effect they demonstrate for county party organization strength is not great, it is certainly large enough to affect winning or losing elections.

Engendering Competitive Politics

Finally, the state parties matter because they contribute to competitive politics. Party activity may engender competitive politics by stimulating political participation.[51] On the whole, interstate patterns of party competition for state offices—governor and state legislature—has been very stable in the post-World War II era.[52] However, interstate variations in partisan competitiveness have been substantial. States differ in their levels of party competition because of socioeconomic differences among them. Where there is socioeconomic diversity, partisan competitiveness is keen. Also interstate variations in competitiveness are due to urbanization and the effects of population size. The largest metropolitan states have tended toward relatively uncompetitive politics. Cross-state differences in competitiveness also reflect the traditional political differences between North and South, a difference that, to some extent, still persists.

Even when these significant influences are brought to bear on interparty competition, variations among the states in political party organization strongly influence competitiveness levels as well (see Figure 7-1).

One multivariate analysis of the variables affecting state party competition from 1970 to 1980 concluded:

> No one doubts for a moment that partisan competition has a profound grounding in socio-economic complexity, in the sheer size of political units such that the probability of opposing coalitions is enhanced, and in the politico-cultural differences between regions. What is equally important and often overlooked . . . is that active effort by organized political parties contributes extensively to the generation of competitive politics.[53]

State politics and elections can become more competitive by enhancing the organizational strength of the state political parties.

Figure 7-1   Contribution of Party Organizational Strength to
Interparty Competition

Partisan competition

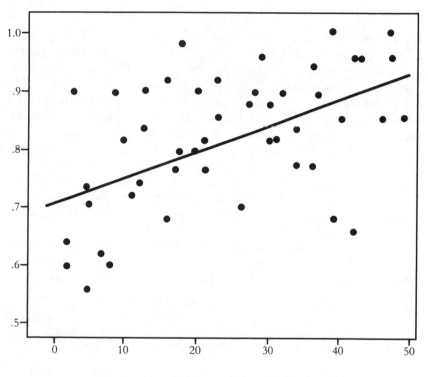

Party organizational strength

SOURCE: Samuel C. Patterson and Gregory A. Caldeira, "The Etiology of Partisan
Competition," *American Political Science Review* 78 (1984): 701.

Summary

When it comes to organizational vitality, the American state
parties are a diverse lot. In some places, parties are strong and vigorous;
in other places, they are sluggish; in yet others, moribund. But on
balance, the state parties appear remarkably vibrant. Clearly, party
strength has waned in the electorate—fewer Americans think of
themselves as "strong Democrats" or "strong Republicans" than in the
1950s, and more say they are political "independents." How can it be
that the state party organizations—and the national parties—are

stronger when, at the same time, party identification among voters is weaker? The answer may lie in the incentives that the less committed electoral marketplace presents to those who seek to capture political offices.

If the voters' response to candidacies is preordained, as in the classic "safe seats" or in the old "solid South," there is little incentive for parties to organize; the candidates of the dominant party will win without organization, and the candidates of the hopeless minority party cannot win through organization. But, where there is greater uncertainty in the electoral response, parties have an incentive to organize and behave competitively. Ironically, diminution of party strength in the electorate may have a fairly powerful role to play in stimulating party organizations to get organized, recruit competitive candidates, find adequate financial resources, mobilize voters, and compete vigorously for the control of offices.

The state parties are in need of much encouragement and improvement. Their organizational strength is still unevenly distributed. Efforts to stimulate further organizational development certainly should be encouraged. Laws conducive to party effectiveness should be passed in the states. The state parties should be stimulated to adapt themselves, where they have not already done so, to the new campaign technologies. It would be well if all the state party chairs could echo the report of Indiana Republican party chairman Gordon Durnil:

> We decided to teach ourselves the new campaign technology. The Republican organization developed a capacity for direct mail and handling demographics and other aspects of modern campaigning. As a result, politics in Indiana has remained party-oriented.[54]

Public funding of electoral politics should be reinvigorated and renewed. State public funding laws should be made effective and provide the public funds to the parties, instead of to the candidates. State and federal laws should encourage party channeling of private money and stimulate PACs to contribute their political money to the parties. Candidate-centered politics is "Made in the U.S.A.," and it need not be diminished. Partisan campaigning can and should be "candidate-oriented." Candidate- and party-centered politics are not inimical to one another; candidate-centered politics should also be party-centered. State parties are becoming more, not less, capable of supporting effective candidacies. Running for office in the states is a more professional endeavor than it used to be. There is no reason why the state parties cannot come to do a professional job in electoral politics. They should be encouraged to do so.

If the state parties were to become professionalized and competitive campaigning and governing organizations, then political scientist Elmer E. Schnattschneider's wildest dreams of "party reconstruction" would, at least partly, have come true.[55] Certainly the state parties can be stronger organizationally than they are today.

American state parties are what they are. Conditions for the development of party organizational strength vary across the land. In the twentieth century, the state parties have, in general, never been particularly strong. They are not, and never have been, close to the model for responsible party government found in the socialist parties of western Europe before they succumbed to "parliamentary cretinism." The skeletal organizations that constitute most state parties in the United States are, nevertheless, important to the American political process.

To the foreign eye it might seem that American politics is a nonparty politics, because the parties look so weak. But in American terms, the state parties have an important role to play. Their nonbureaucratic organization belies their effectiveness. They engage in a remarkable array of relevant organizational and electoral activities, and they have an independent, potentially decisive impact on political outcomes. And there is a very good chance they can become considerably stronger. In this sense, American state parties persist.

Notes

1. Leon D. Epstein, *Political Parties in Western Democracies* (New Brunswick, N.J.: Transaction Books, 1980), 9.
2. Epstein, *Political Parties in Western Democracies,* 122-129.
3. Samuel J. Eldersveld, *Political Parties in America* (New York: Basic Books, 1982), 99.
4. Cornelius P. Cotter, James L. Gibson, John F. Bibby, and Robert J. Huckshorn, *Party Organizations in American Politics* (New York: Praeger, 1984), 171-184.
5. Leon D. Epstein, *Political Parties in the American Mold* (Madison: University of Wisconsin Press, 1986), 144.
6. James Q. Wilson, *Political Organizations* (New York: Basic Books, 1973), 95-96.
7. Anthony Downs, *An Economic Theory of Democracy* (New York: Harper, 1957), 25.
8. Joseph A. Schlesinger, "On the Theory of Party Organization," *Journal of Politics* 46 (1984): 369-400; and Joseph A. Schlesinger, "The New American Political Party," *American Political Science Review* 79 (1985): 1152-1169.
9. Wilson, *Political Organizations,* 30.

10. William Crotty, *American Parties in Decline,* 2d ed. (Boston: Little, Brown, 1984).

11. E. E. Schnattschneider, *Party Government* (New York: Rinehart and Company, 1942); James MacGregor Burns, *The Deadlock of Democracy* (Englewood Cliffs, N.J.: Prentice Hall, 1963); and Austin Ranney, *Curing the Mischiefs of Faction: Party Reform in America* (Berkeley: University of California Press, 1975).

12. William Crotty, *Party Reform* (New York: Longman, 1983); and Gary D. Wekkin, "Political Parties and Intergovernmental Relations in 1984: The Consequences of Party Renewal for Territorial Constituencies," *Publius: The Journal of Federalism* 15 (1985): 19-37.

13. Schlesinger, "On the Theory of Party Organization," 369-400.

14. Epstein, *Political Parties in the American Mold,* 155-199.

15. *Ohio Revised Code,* 3517.01.

16. Advisory Commission on Intergovernmental Relations, *The Transformation in American Politics: Implications for Federalism* (Washington, D.C.: Advisory Commission on Intergovernmental Relations, 1986), 128-144.

17. Advisory Commission on Intergovernmental Regulations, *The Transformation in American Politics,* 128.

18. Advisory Commission on Intergovernmental Regulations, *The Transformation in American Politics;* Cotter, Gibson, Bibby, and Huckshorn, *Party Organizations in American Politics;* and Malcolm E. Jewell, *Parties and Primaries: Nominating State Governors* (New York: Praeger, 1984).

19. Timothy Conlan, Ann Martino, and Robert Dilger, "State Parties in the 1980s: Adaptation, Resurgence and Continuing Constraints," *Intergovernmental Perspective* 10 (1984): 6-13.

20. Cotter, Gibson, Bibby, and Huckshorn, *Party Organizations in American Politics.*

21. Charles G. Bell, "Is Party Allegiance Growing in California?" *Comparative State Politics Newsletter* 5 (1984): 5-7; and Richard Zeiger, "Future Uncertain for State's Democrats," *California Journal* 18 (1987): 120-123.

22. Alexander P. Lamis, *The Two-Party South* (New York: Oxford University Press, 1984); and John G. Francis, "The Political Landscape of the Mountain West," in *The Politics of Realignment: Party Change in the Mountain West,* ed. Peter F. Galderisi, Michael S. Lyons, Randy T. Simmons, and John G. Francis (Boulder, Colo.: Westview Press, 1987), 19-32.

23. Lewis Bowman, William E. Hulbary, and Anne E. Kelley, "Party Organization and Behavior in Florida: Assessing Grassroots Organizational Strength" (Paper delivered at the annual meeting of the American Political Science Association, Chicago, September 3-6, 1987); and Robert P. Steed, Laurence W. Moreland, and Tod A. Baker, "The Nature of Contemporary Party Organization in South Carolina" (Paper delivered at the annual meeting of the American Political Science Association, Chicago, September 3-6, 1987).

24. Stella Z. Theodoulou, *The Louisiana Republican Party, 1948-1984: The Building of a State Political Party* (New Orleans: Tulane University

Studies in Political Science, 1985).

25. Ruth S. Jones, "Financing State Elections," in *Money and Politics in the United States,* ed. Michael J. Malbin (Chatham, N.J.: Chatham House Publishers, 1984), 193.

26. Herbert E. Alexander and Mike Eberts, *Public Financing of State Elections* (Los Angeles: University of Southern California Citizens' Research Foundation, 1986).

27. Malcolm E. Jewell, "A Survey of Campaign Fund-Raising by Legislative Parties," *Comparative State Politics Newsletter* 7 (1986): 9-13.

28. Richard R. Johnson, "Partisan Legislative Campaign Committees: New Power, New Problems," *Illinois Issues* 13 (1987): 16-18.

29. Advisory Commission on Intergovernmental Relations, *The Transformation in American Politics,* 120.

30. *Federal Election Commission Record* 12 (April 1986): 1-2.

31. Gary C. Jacobson, "The Republican Advantage in Campaign Finance," in *The New Direction in American Politics,* ed. John E. Chubb and Paul E. Peterson (Washington D.C.: Brookings Institution, 1985), 154-160.

32. Advisory Commission on Intergovernmental Relations, *The Transformation in American Politics,* 271-278.

33. Cotter, Gibson, Bibby, and Huckshorn, *Party Organizations in American Politics,* 20-26, 43-49.

34. James L. Gibson, John P. Frendreis, and Laura L. Vertz, "Party Dynamics in the 1980s: Changes in County Party Organizational Strength, 1980-1984" (Paper delivered at the annual meeting of the Midwest Political Science Association, Chicago, April 17-20, 1985).

35. Gibson, Frendreis, and Vertz, "Party Dynamics in the 1980s," Table 1.

36. Kay Lawson, Gerald Pomper, and Maureen Moakley, "Local Party Activists and Electoral Linkage: Middlesex County, N.J.," *American Politics Quarterly* 14 (1986): 345-75; Ronald J. Busch, "Ambition and the Local Party Organization" (Paper delivered at the annual meeting of the Ohio Association of Economists and Political Scientists, Columbus, May 2, 1987); and William Crotty, *Political Parties in Local Areas* (Knoxville: University of Tennessee Press, 1986).

37. Ronald B. Rapoport, Alan I. Abramowitz, and John McGlennon, *The Life of the Parties: Activists in Presidential Politics* (Lexington: University Press of Kentucky, 1986), 44-58.

38. Malcolm E. Jewell and David M. Olson, *Political Parties and Elections in American States,* 3d ed. (Chicago: Dorsey Press, 1988), 56-62.

39. Rapoport, Abramowitz, and McGlennon, *The Life of the Parties,* 50. For results from the 1984 state convention delegates in twelve states, see Barbara Burrell and James Carlson, "Issue Coalitions and Cleavages among Party Activists" (Paper delivered at the annual meeting of the Midwest Political Science Association, Chicago, April 9-11, 1987).

40. Robert X. Browning and William R. Schaffer, "Leaders and Followers in a Strong Party State," *American Politics Quarterly* 15 (1987): 87-106.

41. Alan Ware, *The Logic of Party Democracy* (New York: St. Martin's Press, 1979), 130-152.

42. Warren E. Miller and M. Kent Jennings, *Parties in Transition: A Longitudinal Study of Party Elites and Party Supporters* (New York: Russell Sage Foundation, 1986), 161-188.
43. Samuel J. Eldersveld, "The Party Activist in Detroit and Los Angeles: A Longitudinal View, 1956-1980," in *Political Parties in Local Areas,* ed. William Crotty (Knoxville: University of Tennessee Press, 1986), 89-119.
44. Paul M. Green, "The Democrats' Biennial Ritual: Slatemaking," *Illinois Issues* 12 (1986): 12-14, 39.
45. Jewell, *Parties and Primaries,* 273.
46. Joseph A. Kunkel III, "Party Endorsement and Incumbency in Minnesota Legislative Nominations," *Legislative Studies Quarterly* 13 (1988): 211-213; and David Lebedoff, *The 21st Ballot: A Political Party Struggle in Minnesota* (Minneapolis: University of Minnesota Press, 1969).
47. John F. Bibby, *Politics, Parties, and Elections in America* (Chicago: Nelson-Hall, 1987), 107.
48. James L. Gibson, "The Role of Party Organizations in the Mountain West: 1960-1980," in *The Politics of Realignment: Party Change in the Mountain West,* ed. Peter F. Galderisi, Michael S. Lyons, Randy T. Simmons, and John G. Francis (Boulder, Colo.: Westview Press, 1987), 206-213.
49. Cotter, Gibson, Bibby, and Huckshorn, *Party Organizations in American Politics,* 100-103.
50. John P. Frendreis, James L. Gibson, and Laura L. Vertz, "Local Party Organizations in the 1984 Elections" (Paper delivered at the annual meeting of the American Political Science Association, New Orleans, August 29-September 1, 1985).
51. Timothy Bledsoe and Susan Welch, "Patterns of Political Party Activity among U.S. Cities," *Urban Affairs Quarterly* 23 (1987): 249-269.
52. Samuel C. Patterson and Gregory A. Caldeira, "The Etiology of Partisan Competition," *American Political Science Review* 78 (1984): 691-707; and Frank B. Freigert, "Postwar Changes in State Party Competition," *Publius: The Journal of Federalism* 15 (1985): 99-112.
53. Patterson and Caldeira, "The Etiology of Partisan Competition," 703-704.
54. *Brookings Review,* Vol. 5 (Winter 1987): 24.
55. E. E. Schnattschneider, *The Struggle for Party Government* (College Park: University of Maryland Program in American Civilization, 1948), 27-43.

8. THE TRANSFORMATION OF STATE ELECTORAL POLITICS

Barbara G. Salmore and Stephen A. Salmore

The most massive change in federal campaigns for the presidency and Congress over the past few decades has been the emergence of candidate-centered campaigns. In most of these contests, candidates have been able to use television, radio, and direct mail to communicate messages about themselves directly to voters. As a result, candidates' personal qualities and records in office have become voting cues equal to or more important than the party labels that traditionally determined most voters' decisions.

Candidate-centered voting was slower to take hold in state gubernatorial and legislative elections because, being less visible and their victories seemingly less consequential, candidates for these offices were less able to get their message directly to voters. Party labels and organizations remained critical factors in determining election out-election outcomes.

However, as state government has become more important and visible in policy terms, it attracts increasingly able and ambitious politicians. There is more at stake in state-level elections, more political players are interested in their outcomes, and more resources are available to wage campaigns. It is thus no surprise that party-line voting is declining and candidate-centered campaigns are becoming markedly more prevalent at the state level as well.[1] This chapter examines gubernatorial and legislative campaigns in the states and considers the extent to which they have come to resemble those for federal office.

Gubernatorial Campaigns and Elections

Three interrelated developments help to understand the character of recent gubernatorial contests: the "presidentialization" of gubernatorial elections, the increased decoupling of partisan outcomes in state and national executive races, and trends in the financing of gubernatorial election contests.

Candidate-Centered Campaigns

The forced withdrawal of presidential candidates Gary Hart and Joe Biden from the 1988 Democratic nomination race months before any actual votes were cast, because of personal "character flaws," is a graphic example of the increasingly candidate-centered nature of American presidential contests. Voters find presidential candidates' images more salient than their party labels and substantive issue positions.[2] The result has been an explosion in split-ticket voting in the past two decades.

Candidate-centered rather than party-centered presidential appeals have led to candidate-centered campaign organizations as well. Presidential candidates increasingly choose to separate their central campaign organizations from the national party organization. The campaign finance laws of the 1970s—providing for public funding of the general election and partial public funding of individual candidates in the nomination phase, funneled through individual campaign organizations and not the parties—reinforced this inclination. Many recent candidates not only separated themselves from their national party organizations but also practically divorced themselves from their fellow partisans running for other offices.

Presidents seeking reelection continued such "presidential" behaviors during the actual campaign season. Paid advertising emphasized their accomplishments in office. They proclaimed themselves too busy to debate their opponents very often, making it difficult for voters to compare the candidates or get the idea that the challenger might be as accomplished as the current chief executive.

In short, both the presidential campaign and presidential office became the province of individual entrepreneurs, relying on their own skills and their own resources more than those of their political parties. With only the briefest time lag, these developments were mirrored in the campaigns of many governors.

Split-Ticket and Cross-Party Voting

A variety of aggregate data suggests that split-ticket and cross-party voting has become rampant in recent gubernatorial elections.[3] During the 1950s, the governor's party on average controlled both houses of the state legislature in 68 percent of cases, and neither house in only 20 percent of cases. Partisan homogeneity was a consequence of the state electorates' patterns of party identification. Usually, when split control did occur, it was the result of legislative gerrymandering and malapportionment. By the 1970s, although Supreme Court decisions had ended malapportionment and blatant gerrymandering, the governor's party controlled both houses 53 percent of the time, and neither 35 percent of the time. By 1986, 46 percent of the thirty-seven states where one party controlled both legislative houses had a governor of the other party.

Detailed survey data available for presidential and congressional elections that permit precise charting of individual split-ticket voting are not widely available for state-level elections, but what is known confirms the spread of candidate-centered voting at the state level. A Gallup poll of the Texas electorate in 1986, investigating the reasons for voters' choices, found that only 11 percent of the supporters of Republican Bill Clements and 16 percent of those choosing Democrat Mark White cited the candidate's party in an open-ended multiple-choice question. Conversely, 61 percent of Clements's supporters and 75 percent of White's backers mentioned such candidate-centered reasons as prior record in office, managerial skills, and personal attributes. A 1985 New Jersey exit poll showed massive ticket splitting for gubernatorial and legislative candidates, clearly related to other polls' findings that many voters knew little about the challenger but had large amounts of positive information about the incumbent.[4]

Another indicator of candidate-centered voting in gubernatorial elections is the increase in partisan turnovers. In the 1950s, 24 percent of elections resulted in partisan turnovers in the governor's office; a figure that rose to more than a third in the 1970s and 1980s. Moreover, party turnovers were much more likely in contests without incumbents. As party identification in the electorate and party organizations in campaigns became less important, candidates of either party had a better shot of winning. The races most likely to be competitive—those for open seats—were much more likely to attract strong challengers.

Meanwhile, a popular and seemingly invulnerable incumbent is likely to attract only the weakest of challengers, particularly if the governor is of the majority party, but often even with more balanced party competition. Incumbent governors in such situations seem to barely acknowledge that there is a campaign going on. Consider, for example, the 1986 races in Maryland, Massachusetts, and New York, where each incumbent or "heir apparent" racked up a historic landslide victory.

In heavily Democratic Maryland, the Democratic candidate, Baltimore's longtime mayor William Schaefer, frightened off all but one entrant in the Republican primary. His Republican opponent, Thomas Mooney, dubbed the "Moonman," was a gadfly state legislator and recent Republican convert, best known for sponsoring eccentric legislation such as banning pay toilets and prohibiting moviegoers from bringing their own popcorn into theaters.

Not only did Schaefer ignore his opponent entirely, but so did Mooney's fellow Republicans and the state's journalists. When President Reagan visited the state to campaign for the Republican senate candidate, Mooney, despite heading "Maryland Democrats for Reagan" in 1984, was pointedly not invited. The state's leading newspapers did not cover Mooney, but it did publish articles describing Schaefer's transition team and proposed legislative agenda well before the actual election was held. Even when Mooney had a friend don an Abe Lincoln costume to complain that Schaefer was hurting the democratic process by refusing to debate, no television stations chose to cover this colorful "media event."

Things were not much better in Massachusetts, as the Republicans struggled to find an opponent for incumbent Democratic governor Michael Dukakis. Dukakis's first opponent departed the race when it was discovered that he had lied about his military service record. The second withdrew when the press reported he had been observed talking to himself on the phone in his office while in the nude. Governor Dukakis's positive, issue-oriented television advertising about his own record ignored his opponents entirely. The incumbent also was unable to find time to debate his eventual final challenger, except on one occasion coinciding with the seventh game of a World Series that determined the fate of the Boston Red Sox. The state's leading newspaper, the *Boston Globe,* did not even run a story on the debate, claiming it needed to hold the front page open for the sports story.

Although the Republican challengers in Massachusetts and Maryland faced the double whammy of being both the nominees of the clear minority party in those states and the challengers to immensely popular incumbents or heir apparents, things were not so ostensibly bleak in New York state.[5] Republican senator Alfonse D'Amato was regarded as a shoo-in for reelection, and incumbent Democratic governor Cuomo had won only a narrow open-seat victory in 1982. However, four years later, Cuomo had achieved at least the appearance of invincibility, and his frustrated opponent, Westchester County executive Andrew O'Rourke, was unable to persuade the incumbent to debate, or even campaign, until the last week of the race. O'Rourke took to carrying around a life-size dummy of the incumbent, which he "debated" in public appearances and television advertising. New York voters found the ploy amusing but unconvincing.

In contrast, less secure incumbents and candidates for open seats must fully engage their opponents. Maine's four-way 1986 open race (with two credible independent candidates as well as Democratic and Republican ones) featured five debates before the end of October. Tennessee's hard-fought open contest saw three debates by mid-

October, as did Wyoming's. In Wisconsin, where incumbent Gov. Tony Earle was in obvious trouble, there were four debates and three joint appearances between the candidates by the third week of October.

Thus, competition between the gubernatorial candidates often outweighs generalized party competition in a given state, just as it does in presidential contests. Nationally, the Republicans have never surpassed the Democrats as the majority party in terms of voters' identification, but they have still elected presidents in the majority of recent contests. In Wyoming, for example, where Republicans have had a virtual hammerlock on legislative contests at both the federal and state level for the past quarter century, voters chose a Democratic governor in 1986, as they have in a majority of years in that same period.

Split-ticket and cross-party voting have contributed to the establishment of freestanding campaign organizations by presidential candidates—and by gubernatorial candidates. Until a few decades ago, the relationships between many governors and their state party organizations were intimate indeed. In the extreme case, in 1913, state party bosses in New York could spearhead the successful impeachment of a governor of their own party who refused to do Tammany Hall's bidding on patronage distribution.[6]

The Rise of Direct Primaries

The spread of the direct primary has had the same negative effect on party control of gubernatorial nominations and campaigns that it had on presidential contests. Virtually all gubernatorial candidates have their own personal campaign organizations and personal band of political consultants. In only sixteen states is there even provision for preprimary endorsements by state parties in gubernatorial contests, and there is little evidence they regularly count for much.[7] Primary elections can be remarkable free-for-alls, with the state party organization helpless to control events, as demonstrated by several of the 1986 gubernatorial elections.

The Arizona gubernatorial contest was perhaps the extreme case. The Republican "organization" candidate was Burton Barr, for twenty years the leader of the majority in the lower house of the state legislature, which one writer described as "89 people surrounded by Burton Barr."[8] Barr had the strong endorsement of both the state party organization and President Reagan. However, although Barr could not have been better known or more respected in party circles, he was much less known by the general public than his primary opponent, Evan Mecham—a perennial candidate who frequently appeared in television commercials for his car dealership. Barr spent more than a million dollars on his primary campaign, mostly for eye-catching but vapid TV advertising extolling Arizona as a "great place to live," but telling viewers nothing about himself, his record, or his opponent. Mecham spent a fifth as much, mostly on newspaper-like tabloids mailed into every Republican household, detailing Barr's alleged conflicts of interest. On election day, he defeated Barr in the primary by eight percentage points.[9]

The Florida gubernatorial race the same year provides almost as chaotic an example. Democratic primary winner Steve Pajcic, representing "cosmopolitan" south Florida, had been opposed for the party nomination by state legislative leader Jim Smith, the candidate of the northern "natives." The loser was hardly supportive of Pajcic after his primary victory. Smith's daughter and wife announced their endorsement of the Republican candidate, with cryptic references to the "condominium vote" and with the comment that "real Floridians would like for Smith to be their governor."[10] Three Democratic members of the state senate who supported Smith, including two former senate presidents, also announced they were backing the Republican. The Republican primary victor, Tampa mayor Bob Martinez, was himself no stranger to these "renegade" Democrats, since he had been elected mayor as a Democrat and switched parties just in time to compete for the more available Republican gubernatorial nomination.

Although Arizona and Florida are both examples of states where party organization has always been weak or factionalized, historically strong party states were also subject to similar events in 1986. In Illinois, home of the legendary Cook County machine, Democratic primary voters elected supporters of Lyndon LaRouche as the official party nominees for lieutenant governor and secretary of state. This made it necessary for the "real" party candidates for various statewide offices to run on three separate lines, requiring massive expenditures instructing voters to "punch three" on the computerized voting machines. These efforts were not enough to save the hapless Democratic gubernatorial candidate, Adlai Stevenson, from a landslide defeat by the Republican incumbent he had come within five thousand votes of defeating in 1982.

In Ohio, the strong Republican organization was unable to persuade the elderly and erratic three-time former governor, Jim Rhodes, that it was time to give younger blood a chance to defeat the scandal-tarred Democratic incumbent, Dick Celeste. Rhodes conducted a bizarre campaign, centered around the argument that Celeste's support of gay rights was responsible for the spread of AIDS in Ohio. Republican state senator Paul Pfeifer, a Rhodes primary opponent, told the state's leading newspaper:

I've tried to make it my business not to comment, but this is too much. My initial reaction was we ought to get the Republican leaders together and disavow the SOB for doing this, but I thought better of it. The voters will take care of it.

At an election night party where Republican leaders almost celebrated Rhodes's landslide defeat, a Republican member of Congress was heard to proclaim "Free at last!" [11]

Not all states exhibit such extreme candidate-centered campaigns. In Kansas, for example, 1986 Republican general-election winner, Mike Hayden, and his campaign were cut from the traditional mold. Hayden had been speaker of the Kansas house. His campaign chairman was the state senate majority leader and had been the running mate of Hayden's chief primary opponent. His finance chairman was a Topeka city councilman and former county party chair. Hayden made do with only six paid staff, as compared with sixteen for his Democratic opponent. During the campaign, thirty Republican state legislators formed a "truth squad," appearing around the state to comment on the alleged costs of programs proposed by the Democratic candidate.

The stronger state parties also participated in other ways in several gubernatorial elections, particularly in encouraging voter mobilization on election day. Nevada and Pennsylvania Republicans mailed absentee ballots to likely Republican voters. Both state parties in Ohio made sizable contributions to various statewide races. South Carolina's Democratic party, in conjunction with Democratic congressional candidates, financed a substantial get-out-the-vote effort in heavily black (and Democratic) voting precincts. The Illinois state party and its legislative leaders paid for much of the "punch three" educational campaign. The Republican National Committee, in addition to contributing directly to some candidate campaigns, paid for full-page newspaper advertising the Sunday before the election in states such as California and Florida.

The Powers of Incumbency

Gubernatorial races, particularly in the larger states, are increasingly candidate-centered, and governors often appear to have trouble remembering that they are running at the top of the ticket. Legislative truth squads supporting the governor are less common than the complaints of the New York legislators, seeking to take control of the state senate, that popular incumbent Mario Cuomo "did less and did it later" (for example, taking five weeks to respond to a request to make radio ads for Democratic senate candidates). Cuomo was further described by the state's Democratic U.S. senator, Daniel Patrick

Moynihan, as having a "nonaggression pact" with Republican senator Alfonse D'Amato, up for reelection at the same time. Similarly in New Jersey, Republican state legislators running alone in the 1983 state midterm elections were vocally unhappy about Republican governor Tom Kean's expensive TV ads. They nominally supported the legislative candidates, while cementing Kean's favorable image for his own reelection contest two years hence. They gave few convincing reasons to cast a Republican vote for the legislature.

Governors who do choose to be more responsive to the needs of their fellow partisans often command comparable or greater personal resources than those available to the state parties. Ohio governor Richard Celeste reached into his own ample coffers to finance television advertising for other statewide Democratic candidates. California Republican George Deukmejian loaned $200,000 to political action committees established by his state's Republican legislative caucuses. In Massachusetts, with much of his party's legislative majority unopposed for reelection, Gov. Michael Dukakis hosted a fund raiser for the Democratic gubernatorial challenger in neighboring New Hampshire.

Part of the advantage of gubernatorial incumbency is related to structural enhancements of the office. The almost universal adoption of the four-year term (now enjoyed by forty-seven of the fifty governors, as opposed to only thirty-five in 1964) permits the building of stronger and more visible records. Additionally, more governors are eligible to run for multiple terms—also up to forty-seven, as opposed to thirty-five of the forty-eight governors as recently as 1950.

There is a clear correlation between the strengthening of the governor's position and the proportion of incumbents both seeking reelection and gaining it. Between 1900 and 1930, the percentage of governors (who were legally able to do so) seeking reelection ranged from under one-half to less than two-thirds; beginning in the 1960s, it rose to average more than three-quarters. And those who sought to stay in office were more successful. Whereas a third suffered defeat through the 1960s, 76 percent were successful in 1982, and 89 percent in 1986.[12] Each of the nine governors who enjoyed victories of more than 60 percent of the vote in 1986 was an incumbent, and more than half of all incumbents running that year were able to achieve victories of that magnitude.

However, executive incumbency, because of its visibility, has also traditionally been fraught with dangers. Vincent Breglio, a consultant who has worked in many gubernatorial contests, likens voters' views of governors to

> a microcosm of the presidential race. They see in that chair all the power to make good things happen or bad things happen. . . . For a

governor it's meat and potatoes—what's his or her record? If the farmers haven't had rain, the governor's going to get blamed.[13]

Unlike legislators, who work in relative obscurity and are able to control most of their press coverage and other publicity, governors are more in the spotlight. Newspaper statehouse bureaus cover them intensively. Television does, too, particularly when the state capital is in a major media market. As a political consultant who works in many gubernatorial contests puts it:

> In Mississippi, say, 50 percent of the people are in the Jackson media market, and they all know about state government. It's the same with Denver and Colorado. New York State is very well covered by TV, but state politics isn't because Albany is a jerkwater town. In a state like West Virginia, only about a quarter of the population lives in that [capital] media market. An incumbent has the opportunity to tell people what his record is during a campaign, whereas in other states they already know.[14]

But governors, like presidents, have learned how to use media attention and official resources to their benefit. They are able to obtain extensive media coverage unfiltered by reporters. More and more governors appear in "nonpolitical" public service and tourism ads, often broadcast to their own constituents rather than vacationers from other states—such as the ads featuring incumbent Tom Kean that ran in New Jersey throughout his 1985 reelection campaign. Visitors to state historical commission sites in Pennsylvania shortly after the 1986 election found an exhibit lavishly and favorably detailing the political history of newly elected governor Robert Casey, described in an accompanying glossy brochure as "an ongoing effort to record the commonwealth's history and collect artifacts illustrating our past."

An extraordinarily direct use of parallel state government "public service" advertising and gubernatorial campaign advertising occurred in the 1986 Illinois contest. Late that summer, incumbent James Thompson ran paid commercials showing him signing legislation committing state lottery profits to education (the ads of course did not mention that he had previously twice vetoed the same measure). Starting October 1, the Illinois State Lottery Commission spent $288,000 for a statewide TV advertising buy on the same topic.

Additionally, the Illinois State Department of Commerce and Community Affairs bought $73,000 worth of radio advertising on the Chicago Bears' radio network during the football (and election) season for messages promoting Illinois's standing as the nation's third-ranking state for high-tech industry—another Thompson campaign theme. Referring to the state-financed television advertising, Thompson's outraged opponent complained, "The governor is trying to brainwash people with their own money.... This commercial is nothing more than a gift to Thompson's campaign from the taxpayers." Governor Thompson, acknowledging the parallel advertising themes in the "state" and "campaign" commercials responded, "That's true. Well, I'm the governor, and part of a governor's campaign talks about what's going on in the state under his administration." [15]

Decoupling Federal and State Elections

The ability of governors to run candidate-centered campaigns is also aided by the states' growing practice of holding gubernatorial elections in nonpresidential years. Currently, only twelve states hold gubernatorial elections in presidential years, as compared with the thirty-four that did so in 1932. Three of these, which still have two-year gubernatorial terms, are also among the thirty-six states that elect their chief executives in midterm years. An additional five states insulate state level elections from national ones even further by holding their gubernatorial contests in odd-numbered years, when there are no federal elections at all.

The absence of a concurrent presidential election in so many states makes it easier for gubernatorial candidates to focus voters' attention on their own appeals. Not only is actual coattail voting impossible in the thirty-eight states where presidential and gubernatorial elections never coincide, but the kinds of casual voters that traditionally come out in presidential years and are most prone to engage in coattail voting are also absent from the midterm and odd-year electorates. On average, in the eighteen states that have held both midterm and presidential-year gubernatorial elections since 1960, turnout is a full 18 percent lower in the former than the latter.[16]

However, there is strong evidence that the effect of candidate-centered appeals further transcends the mere structural changes of moving most gubernatorial elections out of the presidential-year cycle. First, the 1986 elections broke an apparently "iron law" of midterm gubernatorial elections since 1950—that the president's party loses gubernatorial seats in the midterm. Between 1950 and 1982, the president's party lost gubernatorial chairs in every midterm election except 1962 (when there was no change). The average loss in this period of 6.2 seats was heavier for Republicans (who averaged 7.4 such losses) than Democrats (who averaged 4.7).[17] In 1986, however, the president's Republican party gained eight governorships.

The longstanding pattern of midterm losses for the president's party has been attributed to national trends, particularly the state of the national economy. For their own electoral purposes, presidents attempt to manipulate the economy so that there is "good news" in presidential years and "bad news," if unavoidable, in the off years, or midterm. Voters attribute the state of the local economy more to the president than to the governor but take it out on the governor in the midterm anyway. The Republicans' typically heavy losses in the recession year of 1982 were widely ascribed to this tendency.[18]

However, in 1986, Republican governors did best in some of the places where the economy was in the worst shape. Some Republican U.S. senators in farm states such as South Dakota may have lost because of the depressed rural economy, but the Republican gubernatorial candidate won. It was difficult to blame Texas Democratic incumbent Mark White for the drop in oil prices that devastated that state's economy, but his Republican opponent (a victim himself in 1982) won anyway.

South Dakota was also an example of the remarkable 1986 disjuncture between Senate and gubernatorial outcomes. In state after state—particularly the largest ones (Florida, California, New York, Illinois, and Pennsylvania)—there were split results in the gubernatorial and senatorial contests. In the South, Republicans picked up gubernatorial seats (in South Carolina, Texas, Florida, and Alabama) that they had seldom or never won since the Civil War. On the other hand, they lost every southern Senate race they contested (in Alabama, Georgia, Florida, North Carolina, South Carolina, and Louisiana), including the seats of several incumbents. Democrats picked up as many net Senate seats as they lost gubernatorial ones. It is difficult to ascribe these results to national trends instead of to the appeal of individual candidates.

Another and even stronger indicator of the decoupling of partisan outcomes in national and state politics is evident in the minority of gubernatorial races that do take place in presidential years. Both the 1936 Roosevelt Democratic presidential landslide victory and the 1952 Eisenhower Republican one resulted in victories for 90 percent of their fellow partisans running for governor in the many states they carried. This was almost identical to the results in presidential and gubernatorial elections from 1896 to 1908. Split presidential-gubernatorial outcomes were still less than 20 percent from 1912 to 1924. However, in the candidate-centered period since 1960, they have averaged around 40 percent.[19]

Thus, the structural changes—moving gubernatorial contests out of the presidential year—have also helped to reinforce the increasingly candidate-centered nature of gubernatorial races, and the two together have notably decoupled presidential and gubernatorial partisan outcomes.

Campaign Finance

The growing advantages of gubernatorial incumbency have resulted in more incumbents running and more incumbents winning with bigger electoral margins. Three recent trends in gubernatorial campaign finance have strengthened the incumbent advantage specifically and candidate-centered campaigning generally. These are dramatically higher campaign expenditures; increasingly heavy campaign contributions from the recipients of official patronage; and public financing in a few states.

The campaign "hyperinflation" (far exceeding increases in the general cost of living) that has struck recent U.S. Senate races is only too evident in gubernatorial contests. As recently as 1978, spending of $3 million by at least one of the gubernatorial candidates occurred in only three states—California, Florida, and Texas. Total expenditures were below $500,000 for both candidates in ten states that year.

In the following two election cycles, expenditures in the same three "leading" states approached or exceeded combined totals of $20 million, and the "$3 million candidate" became the norm rather than the exception in many states. An open-seat race involving only a few hundred thousand dollars on both sides was still possible in South Dakota in 1986, where the winner was reported to have personally knocked on more than sixty-five thousand doors, and each of the two candidates in Wyoming also managed to get by with $500,000 or less. But such contests are becoming positively quaint, as other relatively small states such as Maine, Tennessee, Kansas, and Kentucky saw record multimillion-dollar media contests. The most expensive races occur in large states with many media markets and closely contested open seats (such as Florida in 1986 and New York and California in 1982) or potentially vulnerable incumbents (such as Texas in 1982 and 1986 and Louisiana in 1987).

In states where strong front-runners have deflected serious competition, their financial advantage is almost embarrassing. In Maryland in 1986, the popular William Schaefer raised more than $3 million— three times as much as any previous Maryland gubernatorial candidate. His opponent—the hapless state legislator known as "Moonman"—raised less than $20,000 and garnered under a fifth of the vote; it was the worst showing in the entire country that year. In Massachusetts, also in 1986, incumbent Michael Dukakis took in almost $3 million by early October and seemed to have a different Republican opponent almost weekly. After the first two "self-destructed," the third managed to raise only $37,000 by October and was unable to qualify for the state's modest matching funds. Dukakis's subsequent landslide reelection paved the way for his 1988 presidential bid.

The war chests of well-financed incumbents and candidates in hotly contested open seats bulge with the contributions of recipients of official state patronage. Finance reports document massive contributions by those seeking to get or keep state contracts, jobs, or favorable regulatory decisions. Attorneys, contractors, developers and realtors, the financial community, health interests, and unions figure heavily in every state, and agricultural interests in many.

Out-of-state residents who happened to be employees of bond-writing brokerage houses such as Kidder, Peabody or Bear, Stearns were heavy 1986 contributors in Kansas, Ohio, California, and Florida. Ohio incumbent Richard Celeste even traveled to New York to hold a Wall Street fund raiser. Nevada governor Richard Bryan was impressively supported by the state's hotel and casino interests, as he amassed a treasury ten times as large as his opponent's. Both candidates in Kansas's close open race received contributions from interests hoping the new governor would legalize greyhound racing in the state. For the most part, such contributors are pragmatic, ignoring ideology and partisan preferences to support the likely winner (usually the incumbent), or playing both sides in close contests.

In the wake of the Watergate scandal, which brought taxpayer-funded presidential general election campaigns and partially funded nomination contests, a number of states made some provision for public funding of state-level races. Currently, nineteen states have some provision of public money from either a state income tax checkoff or a small voluntary add-on, but in only four states do the sums involved approach significance—New Jersey, Michigan, Wisconsin, and Minnesota. All four use the checkoff provision to raise funds that are funneled directly to individual candidates. Gubernatorial elections (both primary and general) in New York and Michigan are largely funded by public money, in systems similar to the federal procedure for presidential contests.[20]

Experience with public funding in the states reaches back barely more than a decade, but to date, it appears to have two principal effects: it does serve to hold down expenditures; and it very likely advantages incumbents. When the pioneering New Jersey system was first used in its 1977 elections, the sums provided seemed adequate for a state with no commercial television stations of its own, and no tradition of media-based campaigns. However, the collapse of the traditional party organizations, which became painfully evident that year, unleashed an escalating spiral of expenditures—mostly directed at the expensive New York City and Philadelphia media outlets necessary to reach the state's voters. By 1985, gubernatorial candidates in New Jersey spent more than three-quarters of all their funds on television-related expenses.[21] However, the total of about $4.2 million allotted to both gubernatorial candidates in 1985 was less than what any one of the victorious U.S. Senate candidates spent in the three contests between 1982 and 1988. Similarly, Michigan's candidates in 1986 each spent less than $1 million in their contest, as compared with the more than $5 million expended by the two 1984 U.S. Senate candidates.

Unlike presidential campaigns, where candidates receive extensive news ("free media") coverage for two years preceding the election, neither of the two states with substantial gubernatorial public financing has yet demonstrated that a challenger can defeat an incumbent when they are on a level financial playing field, especially when the levels are set rather low. In New Jersey, incumbents have won in landslides in both of the races in which they have figured in the public finance era.[22] In Michigan, incumbents also won their two races in landslides. Only in Wisconsin has a challenger prevailed against an incumbent with public funding limits—Tommy Thompson in 1986.

These results point to the necessity for challengers at virtually all levels to spend more than incumbents. They must spend more to offset incumbents' greater recognition levels and electorally useful official resources. In all recent gubernatorial election cycles, the bigger spender has won much more often, and most of the time, that individual was also the incumbent. However, even in the relatively few cases where they are outspent, incumbents (particularly Democrats) still win more than half the time.

Thus the "presidentialization" of gubernatorial contests, the delinking of state and national politics, and trends in campaign finance all contribute to the growth of candidate-centered campaigns for state chief executives. Have their compatriots in the state legislatures followed the path of their legislative colleagues in the U.S. Congress and also moved down the road to candidate-centered campaigns?

State Legislative Campaigns and Elections

If gubernatorial contests have become "presidentialized," there is also some evidence that legislative races in the states are becoming "congressionalized"—taking on the attributes that federal congressional campaigns have increasingly exhibited in the past few decades.

Dimensions of Congressionalization

The outcome of most congressional elections through the 1960s could be explained by a "surge and decline" pattern related to presidential coattails and performance.[23] Beginning in the 1970s this pattern substantially broke down. More voters cast their vote more often for the candidate than the party in legislative elections. Since much less information was usually available about challengers to sitting legislators, voters often chose "the devil they knew"—the incumbent. To have any chance of winning, challengers had to become almost as well-known and favorably regarded as their opponents.[24] Additionally, challengers found they had to disseminate unfavorable information about their opponents. Otherwise, voters faced with two equally acceptable choices tended to adopt an "If it ain't broke, don't fix it" mentality, resulting in incumbent victories.[25] Three closely interrelated developments contributed to incumbents' advantages and thus increasingly candidate-centered congressional races: more entrepreneurial behavior on the part of incumbents, growing official resources, and the sources of congressional campaign money.

The entrepreneurial congressional candidate is a product of the decline of the party as vote cue. When congressional candidates could no longer depend on their party labels to assure victory or president's coattails to help them in marginal districts, they began to feel electorally insecure no matter how large their previous victories.[26] As a result, they became inclined to rely almost exclusively on their own efforts to win reelection. Further, other candidates who for one reason or another could not have expected party organizational support in the past, and hence did not run, saw greater chances of success and were more likely to get into races. As one member of Congress observed in 1983:

> You can look around the floor of the House and see a handful—twenty years ago you saw a lot of them—today you can see just a handful of hacks that were put there by the party organization, and there are very, very few of them left. It is just mostly people that went out and took the election.[27]

"Taking the election" in this way required that candidates make electorally effective use of official resources and raise their own campaign money.

Informational newsletters and targeted mailings enormously drove up the use and cost of the congressional postal frank. More staff and staff time were detailed to constituency service. District offices were established or expanded to provide it. A full-time press secretary, previously quite rare, became a fixture of the staff. Seeking committees for electoral rather than policy reasons became an increasing obsession. The House committee system was reorganized to make it easier for more members, and more junior members, to acquire chairmanships and their attendant perks and publicity. More time in session was spent on position taking than legislation.[28]

Federal legislators also acted to change the campaign finance laws in a variety of ways that, intentionally or not, served their electoral ends. Publicly financed presidential elections freed huge sums for contribution to legislative campaigns. The creation of political action committees (PACs) channeled much of this money in distinctive ways. Most came from pragmatic economic concerns more interested in access than ideology. Thus, legislators on committees overseeing or regulating particular economic sectors could expect large numbers of PAC contributions. Much of the rest of the money came from issue-oriented groups whose support could be had by judicious position taking.

The limits placed on political party contributions relegated them to third place behind individuals and PACs. Although able to contribute far more heavily than any single individual or PAC, in combination individuals and PACs outweighed parties at least four to one in incumbents' war chests. Further, because nonparty contributions are so much more dispersed and individually such a small part of the total, incumbents are beholden to no one in particular.

Since PAC money went so overwhelmingly to "properly" placed incumbents, and party money was not that important to them, the political parties increasingly targeted their funds to the relatively few open seats and strong challengers. Once the beneficiaries of their largess were elected, they became incumbents, too, and were no longer beholden, to the extent they ever were, to their party organizations.[29]

Thus, "congressionalization" makes congressional incumbents relatively autonomous actors. Official resources build favorable recognition among constituents and give incumbents the ability to raise money from grateful individuals and political action committees. Challengers rely more on party money but need to demonstrate that they have a realistic chance of winning to get the party's limited resources. To what extent has congressionalization taken hold in state legislative elections?

What Encourages Congressionalization?

In the states, three sets of developments are clearly parallel to those at the federal level. Legislative professionalization results in greater official resources that can be used for electoral purposes; incumbency is replacing party as a voting cue; and, more and more campaign money comes from PACs. However, in most states none of these processes is as far advanced as in the U.S. Congress. Further, campaign finance needs, the campaign technology that money buys, and the need for that technology differ in important ways from the federal situation.

For much of the twentieth century, as the power and scope of the federal government grew, state government languished. However, the "new federalism" espoused by the Nixon and Reagan administrations made state government more important, more powerful, and more interesting to competent and ambitious politicians. The "one-man, one vote" court reapportionment decisions that ended malapportionment and blatant gerrymandering also changed the nature of representation in the state legislatures, the possible levels of party competition, and the nature of the contestants.

As in Congress, stronger institutions produced more official resources, at least in the larger states. Staff, particularly partisan staff attached to new or stronger legislative caucus organizations, grew apace. Computers analyzed policy alternatives but also generated newsletters, form letters to constituents, and targeted mailing lists. The number of states holding annual legislative sessions to deal with increased official business grew from nineteen in 1962 to forty-three in 1986. Legislative salaries increased to the point that in ten states, they reached median family income by 1979.[30]

Larger state budgets and a heavier legislative workload in many states produced additional official perquisites—increased expense accounts, budgets for personal legislative aides and district offices, and the chance to gain more visibility (and still more official resources) through leadership positions and committee chairmanships.

Unsurprisingly, in the face of these developments, more legislators found it attractive to stay in office, and more aspiring politicians wished to gain office. From the 1930s to the 1960s, average turnover in state lower houses dropped by half, to about a third, and fell below a third in the 1980s.[31]

Working harder at their jobs and having more interest in keeping them, incumbents not only chose to run for reelection more often but also were more often successful. In the 1960s and 1970s, typically fewer than a fifth of all legislative incumbents were defeated. In the 1980s, this number rarely approaches a tenth and is frequently close to zero.[32] Nor do large numbers of incumbents have close races. The record-setting performance of the U.S. House in 1986, when three-quarters of incumbents received at least 60 percent of the vote, is regularly matched and often exceeded in many state house elections. More than half of the legislators in a sizable number of states run unopposed.[33]

All the things that incumbents do to solidify their positions is reflected in the increase in split-ticket voting in legislative elections. Although the heavily candidate-centered contests for governor are more responsible for the sharp rise in split partisan control than are individual legislative races, it must be the legislators themselves who are responsible for the growing number of instances in which partisan control of the two legislative houses is split.

Between 1961 and 1983, the number of states in which different parties controlled the two legislative houses ranged from four to nine. This number rose to eleven in 1985 and twelve in 1987. Split-ticket voting is by definition an indication of the waning power of party as a vote cue. Although incumbency and party effects are impossible to entirely disentangle, partisan turnover is more than twice as likely to occur when a legislative race is for an open seat.[34]

The growing role of PAC money in legislative campaigns follows a similar trend for congressional elections. Even in those states where professionalization has barely made a dent, turnover (mostly voluntary) still approaches a third, and campaigns are still cheap, PACs are growing very rapidly as a major source of campaign funds. Typically, about a third of all campaign contributions and a majority of incumbents' war chests come from PACs. This was the case in recent elections in Arizona, Iowa, Kansas, and Missouri.[35]

What Limits Congressionalization?

It would be a mistake to think that congressionalization is complete everywhere, or indeed, almost anywhere. A number of factors limit its development. First, official resources that are useful for individual state legislative contests are fewer. To begin with, legislative districts—even those in the upper house—are much smaller than congressional ones almost everywhere. California state senate districts, which are larger than U.S. House districts, are the only exception. For example, a U.S. representative in a large state such as Ohio or Illinois serves about 550,000 constituents; the state assembly counterpart serves 110,000 in the Buckeye State and about 97,000 in Illinois. These are rather large assembly constituencies—the comparable figures are 45,000 in Wisconsin, 23,000 in Connecticut, and a mere 2,500 in New Hampshire, which has the largest lower house in the nation to serve the eighth smallest population.

Although many state legislative budgets are growing rapidly, nowhere do they resemble the commitment the federal government makes to the upkeep of its legislature. There are more than four times as many dollars behind each member of the federal legislature as there are behind those who serve New York state (by far the best-financed legislature both absolutely and per capita in the nation), and ten times as many as those supporting the New Jersey legislature, still at the upper end of the national spectrum. California's senate staff allowance of almost $400,000 is comparable to that of a U.S. House member with a slightly smaller constituency, but in the vast majority of states, an allowance of a tenth that size, to support perhaps one personal aide and a secretary, is extraordinarily generous. It would be unimaginable to the

Nevada legislator whose perks consist of $60 for postage and $1,000 for telephone calls over a two-year period, or to the New Hampshire representative who is paid $100 per year. And no state legislator enjoys the most prized of all congressional perks—the unlimited postal frank.

Although the advantages of incumbency are growing for state legislators, fewer official resources make it a more difficult proposition than for those in Congress. The effects of coattails on state legislative outcomes has diminished by half in the 1970s and 1980s as compared with the 1940s through 1960s, but they are still present to some extent.[36] Fewer official resources also make it more difficult for state legislators to achieve the recognition levels of their federal peers. Although systematic data on this point are sparse, in New Jersey, for example, recognition levels of legislators have doubled over the past ten years but are still half the levels achieved by members of Congress.[37] In these relatively low-information, low-turnout elections, party identification counts for more, as fewer of the casual "independent" voters bother to come out, or make their way to the bottom of the ballot when they do.

Individual candidates also do not have the advantage of economies of scale for high-cost, high-tech campaign techniques that are so crucial to nurturing candidate-centered voting. Accurate poll samples are no smaller for a legislative race than a congressional one. Media advertising depends on the size of a station's market, not the size of a candidate's constituency. Television, the best medium for building recognition quickly, is grossly cost-inefficient for almost all legislative candidates because stations cover so many legislative districts. News coverage is scarce enough for federal legislative candidates, let alone those for the state legislature, and the free "advertising" made possible by the federal frank is not available either.

Further, although an entrepreneurially minded state legislator needs to build personal recognition just as much as a federal legislator does, the payoff is simply not the same in the vast majority of cases. The federal candidate is seeking more prestige, more perquisites, and a higher step on the ladder of political ambition. Despite the longer and more frequent state legislative sessions, most state legislators will still spend less time in the state capitol than federal legislators spend in Washington.

Although campaign costs at the state level are going up astronomically in many cases, increases even in the larger states do not usually approach the costs at the federal level. Currently, a hotly contested race in one of the larger states involves individual candidate spending on the order of $300,000. In 1986, twenty U.S. House winners spent at least $900,000 on their contests. Aside from contested races in California, and a few seats in the Ohio senate (which is so closely balanced that party control has shifted five times in the past fifteen years, and where there is a media market pattern that is conducive to television advertising), spending such sums—and having to raise them—is, as of now, unfathomable.

All these factors make congressionalization of state legislative elections far from complete, and significantly less complete than the presidentialization of gubernatorial elections. However, state-level legislative candidates have been creative in casting about for ways to deal with these shortcomings.

The Role of Political Parties

The key difference between federal and state legislators is that members of Congress are better able to operate as independent entrepreneurs than their counterparts in the states. Their ability to use official resources as campaign resources when party resources failed them has led to the description of congressional offices as individual enterprises.[38] Almost all individual state legislators lack the access to such official resources.

Therefore, the obvious solution to the problem state legislators have is to band together in some larger organization that will have the resources they lack. There has always been such an organization—the political party. In the past, state legislative candidates benefited from voters' psychological attachments to the parties more than the work of party organizations. The state organizations were more interested in the governor's office, and county and local organizations were more interested in positions at those levels. Both the governor and county officials had what legislators lack—access to the patronage jobs that are the lifeblood of traditional party organizations.

Some observers believe that revitalized state party organizations, particularly on the Republican side, now emulate the national party organizations. They have a new interest in legislative races, since governors have lost most of their patronage powers and no longer need the state parties to run their own races. Elaborate studies detail growing state party budgets, larger staffs, and provision of campaign services to legislative candidates. Much is also now written about the national Republicans' plans to aid state parties in their quest to capture more state legislatures by 1990 and thus control more redistricting; much was written in the same vein several years ago about similar plans for 1980.

A close look at these studies casts some doubts on the state parties' efficacy. Although some are performing some "service bureau" functions, the research indicates that their budgets have actually decreased over the past few decades once inflation is taken into account; more importantly, there is no relationship between the state parties' organizational strength and either the number or closeness of legislative victories.[39] There has thus been an inverse correlation between Republican party efforts in the states and their performance in legislative elections. Republican control of the ninety-eight partisan state legislative houses dipped steadily from thirty-five in 1980 to twenty-nine in 1986. Democrats, whose state party organizations were often bankrupt, performed better in these elections.

Many state legislative candidates favor a solution to their problems that is already in place in many cases—help from their own fellow legislators in legislative party caucuses instead of from the traditional party organizations.

California pioneered the initiative and referendum, the use of political consultants, and the election of celebrities to office. California Assembly leader Jess Unruh also created, almost twenty years ago, the first legislative caucus devoted principally to the winning of state legislative elections. Now, legislative caucuses in more than thirty states raise funds to support legislative campaigns. In at least twelve of these (and most of the largest states), the amount of funds raised is enough to exert a significant effect on campaigns; in at least fourteen states these funds are a source of power for the legislative leadership, which controls the caucuses' campaign activities.[40]

Although fund raising is carried on by both minority and majority party caucuses, it is obviously easier for the majority to attract contributors, particularly the political action committees that provide a large portion of such funds. Generally speaking, state PACs give individual contributions very heavily to incumbents and anticipate that challengers will be supported by the large sums they also contribute to legislative caucus campaign committees. With the Democrats in control of about two-thirds of all state houses throughout the 1980s, an important explanation of their electoral success emerges.

Some examples give an idea of the scope of these enterprises. Democratic California Assembly leader Willie Brown and his senate counterpart had already reported raising well over $5 million for 1986 California legislative campaigns by mid-October. The Republican minority caucuses had raised another $2.5 million. The funds provided by the legislative caucuses and other intercandidate transfers eventually provided about 24 percent of the $56.3 million contributed to legislative races in the Golden State that year. Such fund raising permitted Brown to dole out $725,000 to a Sacramento-area assembly open-seat hopeful—considerably more than most California incumbent members of Congress spent on their reelections. In Illinois, where the most expensive campaigns for contested seats (of which there were few) cost in the range of $100,000 in 1986, the four party caucuses raised and spent almost $3 million. This doubtless exceeded the 23 percent of all campaign funds for which the caucuses were the source in the previous election cycle. By the fall of 1987, the House Republican Campaign Committee had already raised more than $500,000 for 1988 races.[41]

One advantage to candidates of funds controlled by the legislative leadership is that leaders want nothing more from the recipients than their vote to organize the chamber and reelect them to their positions. Wisconsin house leader Tom Loftus was particularly candid when he described the criteria he employed to disburse caucus funds to promising assembly challengers:

> Our only test is that a candidate is in a winnable seat and he or she is breathing, and those two requirements are in order of importance. . . . We don't care if this person believes in the principles of the Democratic party or if he or she belongs to the Democratic party. We know if they make it they will vote with the Democrats to organize, and that's the goal we care about.[42]

Campaign money is not the only valuable resource the legislative leadership controls. Desirable committee assignments, which provide not only visibility but electorally useful staff and access to individual campaign contributions, are also within the power of many to dispense. California's Willie Brown describes his use of this power in much the same way as Tom Loftus: "The Speaker in California has an awesome amount of power over House organization, and I don't use it based on party participation or party loyalty; I use it based on speaker loyalty." [43]

In addition to the interests of the leadership and the rank and file in using campaign funds and organizational resources for mutual benefit, there are also electorally useful government appropriations the leadership can often distribute. Besides the normal kinds of "pork barrel" legislation, a few legislatures specifically reserve discretionary funds that members, through the leaders, can use in their districts. Alan Rosenthal noted the "worthy legislative projects" that comprised almost 5 percent of Maryland's legislative budget, and the "special entries" awarding slush funds of $100,000 and $50,000 to North Carolina's senators and assembly members, respectively, in 1985.

Both pale in comparison to the "member items" in the New York state legislative budget, which have run as high as $1.8 million per member. Member items are sums that may be spent on district items entirely at a legislator's discretion. The Democratic House Speaker, who resides in Brooklyn but maintains eleven of his own district offices around the state, uses member items for partisan purposes far from his district. For example, he awarded an ice-making machine to upstate Utica (represented by Republicans in both houses) and then sent out a districtwide mailing to make sure residents knew it was a gift of the Democrats.[44]

Observers of the legislative caucuses' activities often note the extent to which they have taken over the electoral functions of what is conventionally thought of as "the party organization." This usually occurs because of the weakness of those organizations. In New York "the two houses of the legislature have in many ways assumed the functions of statewide party organizations" because "the influence of local political leaders has waned."[45] In others, it is because the state parties offer no or minimal assistance. In Oregon, the majority of state party money goes for staff salaries and overhead, and "candidates in partisan contests are left in the lurch."[46] Of a state party role in Wisconsin legislative races, Speaker Loftus says:

> Let me assure you that the expression of that sentiment would be an alien formation from the lips of those controlling the Wisconsin Democratic party. You might get some agreement that the purpose of the party is to help the candidate for governor or president. But a blank stare would greet you should you suggest some relationship with the jerk on the ballot who has happened to run under the banner for the legislature.[47]

The caucuses therefore assume many of the electoral functions once carried out by party organizations. In Ohio, for example, the House Republican Campaign Committee holds a two-day "issues seminar" for all Republican House nominees immediately after the primary. It also sponsors, in conjunction with its senate counterpart, a campaign management seminar covering video training, pointers on targeted mail, and the like. It is during this seminar that the members of the campaign committee and their staff decide which candidates will be "targeted" for financial and in-kind assistance later in the campaign. For the first time in 1986, this organization also hired professional consultants to produce radio and TV advertising and targeted mail for five races and one incumbent.

However, just as congressionalization is more or less advanced in various states, so too is the electoral activity of the legislative caucuses. A few states do not even have organized caucuses. They are mostly in the Deep South, where Democrats are still both the overwhelming majority of members and highly factionalized—to the point where leaders sometimes organize by getting votes from the minority Republicans and appointing them to committee chairmanships. There is also obviously no party caucus in the unicameral and nonpartisan Nebraska legislature.

Varieties of Congressionalization

The shape of legislative campaign politics in a given state is related to the sometimes overlapping factors of state political culture, the level of party competition, and the presence of particularly entrepreneurial leaders.

A state's political culture affects the extent of congressionalization and activity by legislative caucuses. They are almost always advanced in states with a history of strong traditional party organizations.[48] These old machine states stretch in a broad band across the northeast and the industrial midwest, precisely to the states—New York, New Jersey, Pennsylvania, Ohio, and Illinois—with strong and active legislative caucuses.

In the case of New York, as recent scandals involving the senate minority made clear, the legislature has become the repository of many of the patronage jobs once provided elsewhere. Many local party officials were paid staffers on the Albany legislative payroll but worked at least part of the time out of county party offices, in legislative district offices, or in campaign organizations.[49] In Illinois, every professional legislative staff position is partisan, and many staffers are deployed by the leadership to work in campaigns. One explains, "By the book partisan staff does campaign work on weekends and during leaves of absence—but everybody violates the rule. . . . There is a token effort made to prevent state resources from being turned into party resources."[50]

A second set of active legislative caucuses are found in the upper midwest, in states that also traditionally had strong party organizations, albeit based more on issues than patronage. Wisconsin and Minnesota's legislative caucuses and their fund raising coexist with partially public-financed elections and strict spending limits.

The Wisconsin caucuses are limited to raising approximately $150,000 per election cycle and donating a maximum of $3,000 per campaign. In 1986, total spending in individual Wisconsin assembly campaigns was limited to $17,000, and senate campaigns were limited to $34,000. Every dollar of PAC money a candidate chose to take reduced the public money stipend of $7,000 by an equivalent amount.[51] Because of the limits on accepting PAC contributions, and requirements that candidates raise a minimum on their own and have an opponent, the public money acceptance rate is lower in Wisconsin than it is in Minnesota, and the per capita expenditures in Minnesota are higher than they are in Wisconsin.[52] Yet within these limits, the

Wisconsin caucuses are as effective in using modern campaign technology to elect their people, especially challengers, as are the multimillion-dollar caucus efforts in neighboring Illinois and Ohio.

Finally, and in a class by itself, is California. There the caucus's electoral purposes were invented not to supplant or coexist with an old traditional party organization or issue-based party, but to substitute for the party organizations that never were. In the 1930s and 1940s, legislative fund raising was dominated by a legendary "super-lobbyist," Arthur Samish; now "legislative leaders fill this role." [53]

The large size of California's legislative districts and expensive media markets make California sui generis. In 1986, all California legislators spent about one-eighth as much as all U.S. congressional candidates. A dozen legislative races cost more than $1 million, and five spent more than $2 million. These figures help explain the extraordinary activities of its legislative caucus.[54]

In contrast, caucus activity is notably absent in small or heavily rural states with a tradition of localism and citizen legislatures. In a state such as New Hampshire, an expensive House campaign directed toward 2,500 constituents might cost $500, principally for lawn signs. Direct mail and radio advertising are unknown, and "the town dump is a good place to campaign." [55] The state Republican party and legislative caucus have for the past few years had a political action committee that raised about $10,000 to $15,000 for the 1986 campaign, but it is so low profile that some winning Republican candidates claim to have never heard of it. In Wyoming, it is rare to spend as much as two or three thousand dollars for a legislative job that occupies the sixty-three members for forty days in odd-numbered years and twenty days in even-numbered ones. In a 1982 race, an unprecedented $25,000 expenditure represented "by far the largest amount ever spent." [56]

In addition to political culture, the level of party competition is another factor affecting the extent of congressionalization and caucus activity. In states with a persistently low level of party competition, principally in the South, factionalism within the dominant party makes it difficult for an effective party caucus to emerge. Members of the minority party are likely to do better working with factions of the dominant party. In a number of southern states, the governor appoints legislative leaders, and there is a tradition of rotating them rapidly out of office, making the development of an independent power base impossible.

High or increasing levels of party competition have the opposite effect. Connecticut, for example, has truly strong state party organizations. State conventions, not primaries, chose all candidates for state office, including the governor.[57] Additionally, Connecticut was one of the few states in the nation that retained the party lever on their voting machines. When Republicans swept into legislative majorities for two years in the 1984 Reagan landslide, they managed to get rid of the lever beginning in 1988. Democrats then swung into action. A strong House leader and caucus operation emerged almost immediately; legislative salaries were raised somewhat; media campaigns dominated the 1986 governor's race for the first time; and plans were set into motion to build a new legislative complex and add large numbers of partisan staff and district offices.

Similarly, Colorado has had a sleepy state legislature, dominated by Republicans for decades despite repeated elections of Democratic governors. The professional legislative staff is small, and much work is still done by college interns. However, the advent of annual sessions and a successful "new-style" Democratic gubernatorial candidate in 1986, who brought some legislators in with him, has begun to change things. Some backbench Republicans frustrated by autocratic leadership defected to the Democrats. Although maintaining an almost 2-1 lead in the House, Republicans there who previously relied on state and local party organizations are beginning to develop a leadership PAC due to fear of Democratic competition.

In Wisconsin, both parties' legislative campaign committees were galvanized by the 1984 elections, which produced a seven-seat gain in the assembly for the Republicans, dangerously narrowing the Democrats' traditional margin. The Democrats faced the further disadvantage of an unpopular governor at the top of the ticket in 1986. In addition to compiling the voter lists that had been the committees' staple, competition brought the advent of several new activities. Targeting of resources became almost total; safe or hopeless candidates for the first time were completely shut out. Cash donations to individual campaigns were replaced by in-kind contributions. Money was spent on generic television advertising, individualized radio advertising, polls, and phone banks. The committees also provided issue papers, press releases, and speakers. Commenting on the suspicion and reluctance of candidates to adopt the new technology, an architect of the efforts concluded, "If there weren't the real threat of losing, it would not have happened. They would never have changed if they could always win." [58]

Finally, the entrepreneurial qualities and ambition of the leadership in a given state at a given time make a difference. In Connecticut, legislative Republicans were unable to capitalize on their 1984 takeover of both houses, perhaps because the Republican state chairman was regarded as "a joke," while the Democratic leadership was very strong. A year before the 1988 races, a capitol lobbyist reported that the house speaker, Irving Stolberg, was "holding seminars for people who are either going to run or are just thinking about it." She further observed of the speaker, "Stolberg's PAC gives money to campaigns to hire somebody, he actively recruits candidates. He does this not for the party but because it's the best way to stay speaker." [59] In New Jersey, fund raising by the Democratic senate leader and Republican assembly leader reached new heights in 1987; both became leading candidates for their parties' 1989 gubernatorial candidacies.

Summary

This review of state-level campaigns and elections indicates that they have taken on many of the attributes of executive and legislative contests at the federal level. Certainly, differences remain that seem immutable. Governors do not face the organizational challenges of presidential candidates, do not receive the same degree of national media attention, and are not expected to have the same grasp of foreign policy. But increasingly, like presidents, they run as individuals, succeed or fail because of their retrospective or prospective records as leaders and economic managers, communicate their messages through television, and find party labels and organizations increasingly less important to their endeavors. Also like presidents, their personal popularity is less transferable to their fellow partisans, although they may, if they so choose, be able to raise campaign money for them. That, however, is an individual decision.

Legislators generally represent smaller constituencies than their federal peers, are less well-known to their constituents, and cannot and need not raise the same sums to wage their campaigns. But like U.S. senators and representatives, they too rely increasingly less on party labels or executive coattails to bring them victory and more on their own efforts, incumbency, official resources, and candidate-centered campaigns. The costs of modern campaign technology have made legislative campaigns in some of the larger states almost identical in style and form to congressional campaigns, and as expensive as well-financed congressional contests were scarcely a decade ago. Even in capitals still populated with "amateur" citizen-legislators, candidates now raise much of whatever funds they need from political action committees, as do their federal counterparts. And like congressional candidates, that fund raising is much easier for incumbents and leaders.

In the most recent elections, legislative campaign committees in many of the larger states, organized by caucus leaders, have come to resemble the Washington-based congressional campaign committees. As in Washington, the targeting of resources to open seats, vulnerable incumbents, and strong challengers is growing. The campaign services the committees finance or provide are also similar—polling, direct mail production, targeting plans, and broadcast advertising.

As technology becomes more affordable and available—for example, personal computers, campaign software packages, and greater penetration of cable television—the similarities between contested legislative and congressional contests will grow even further. The major difference is that economies of scale, differences in the level of official resources, and fund raising capacity make most state legislative candidates, even incumbents, more dependent than federal officeholders on mutual rather than individual resources.

As state politics develops in the same directions as federal politics, the same concerns arise about the new circumstances. One common fear is related to campaign finance, particularly the role of special interest PACs and conversion of public funds. Newspapers and good government groups often inveigh against "the best legislatures that money can buy." Concerns are particularly strong in New York and California, where campaign costs and use of official resources for campaign purposes are highest. After a heated debate of several years, California voters in 1988 approved a ballot measure on legislative campaign financing that banned intercandidate transfers, restricted PAC contributions to $2,500 per candidate, and limited political parties and "broad-based committees" to contributions of $5,000 per candidate.[60] In the same year, the New York state senate minority leader, his chief of staff, and two former or current state senators went on trial for grand larceny and fraud, accused of using public money to pay full-time campaign employees who did no work for the legislature.[61]

Although California and New York are extreme examples, they point out some of the difficulties. Campaign spending can be regulated in only four ways: disclosure requirements, contribution limits, spending limits, and public financing. These are listed in the order of their current use and future feasibility.

Disclosure of contribution sources gives the public some information and requires some accountability on the part of candidates. Contribution limits place some checks on influence and encourage diversity of funding sources. Spending limits raise both legal and practical objections. In *Buckley v. Valeo*, the Supreme Court ruled that in elections, in the absence of public funding, expenditure limits constitute an abridgment of freedom of speech and are not permissible. Even when public funding is available, as is currently the case in presidential elections, candidates may opt not to take it, so long as they observe whatever contribution limits the law specifies. Many politicians argue that both spending limits and public funding discriminate against lesser-known challengers and serve as an "incumbents' protection act."

Finally, as a practical matter, in the states as in Washington, D.C., the political parties are so split on the issue of public funding—with the majority of Republicans opposing it and the majority of Democrats favoring it—that it is not likely to make much further headway.

A second frequently voiced concern relates to a number of apprehensions about the diminished role of the political parties. From a policy point of view, there are arguments that a collection of entrepreneurially minded officeholders who owe nothing to their parties makes for incoherent policy and lack of accountability. Further, the increasing number of long-term incumbents and seemingly "permanent partisan majorities" are said to inspire smugness and arrogance. But others see immobilism and incoherence as a reflection of public opinion and believe that politicians can and do move rapidly and decisively when the public will is clear. The "permanent majorities" are also a great deal less institutionally permanent than were the malapportioned and gerrymandered legislatures that preceded them, when an aroused majority of voters was often literally incapable of working its will.

Another concern about the political parties is related to the concern about PACs. Many believe that without the electoral protection that strong parties provide, special-interest influence peddling on the part of legislators will increase. Critics of this argument retort that so long as PAC contributions are limited (although in many states they are not), any single contribution is such a small part of a campaigner's war chest that its donor deserves nothing more than a hearing. There is indeed some evidence that PAC directors themselves increasingly feel they are getting the worst of the bargain.[62] Ironically, the sometimes maligned legislative campaign committees and legislative leaders that receive so much of the PAC money may in fact contribute to the diminution of PAC influence. In the words of Wisconsin house speaker Tom Loftus, "A utility gives a $500 PAC check to a committee consisting of me. I give it to someone who's for socializing electricity."[63]

However one feels about these issues, the inexorable trend is toward more, if not complete, presidentialization and congressionalization of state campaigns and elections. As the policy role of the states increases, governors have more stature and legislators have more resources and are more professional. There may never be multimillion-dollar media campaigns for the state legislature in New Hampshire or North Dakota. But there is plenty of room for expansion, particularly in a number of the larger southern states such as Florida or Texas that are likely to see more competitive partisan politics at the state level in the years ahead. If there are imperfections in this system and concern about it, one might remember the conclusion of a study of similar concerns about federal politics: "That all does not work to perfection reflects fundamental tensions of political life, and fundamental contradictions in political institutions, not just human failing. We can't always have everything we want." [64]

Notes

1. This argument is elaborated on in Stephen A. Salmore and Barbara G. Salmore, *Candidates, Parties, and Campaigns,* 2d ed. (Washington, D.C.: CQ Press, 1989).
2. Martin P. Wattenberg, *The Decline of American Political Parties, 1952-1984* (Cambridge, Mass.: Harvard, 1986); and Martin P. Wattenberg, "The Reagan Polarization Phenomenon and the Continued Downward Slide in Presidential Candidate Popularity," *American Politics Quarterly* 14 (1984): 219-246.
3. Much of the aggregate data in this section appears in Larry J. Sabato, *Goodbye to Good-Time Charlie: The American Governorship Transformed,* 2d ed. (Washington, D.C.: CQ Press, 1983); and Malcolm E. Jewell and David M. Olson, *American State Political Parties and Elections,* 3d ed. (Homewood, Ill.: Dorsey Press, 1988).
4. *Dallas Morning News,* November 7, 1986; exit poll conducted for the New Jersey Public Broadcasting Authority, November 6, 1986.
5. However, Republican presidential candidate Ronald Reagan carried both states in 1984. Maryland Republican senator Charles "Mac" Mathias also won reelection in 1980, and Dukakis himself had been defeated for reelection in 1978.
6. Martin Shefter, "Regional Receptivity to Reform: The Legacy of the Progressive Era," *Political Science Quarterly* 98 (1983): 459-483.
7. Malcolm E. Jewell, *Parties and Primaries: Nominating State Governors* (New York: Praeger, 1984); and Sarah M. Morehouse, "Money versus Party Effort: Nominations for Governor" (Paper delivered at the annual meeting of the American Political Science Association, Chicago, Ill., September 3-6, 1987).
8. Ruth Jones, "Arizona Gubernatorial Politics: 1982," in *Re-Electing the Governor,* ed. Thad L. Beyle (Lanham, Md.: University Press of America, 1986).
9. Mecham's behavior in office was so unacceptable to many Arizonans that he became the object of a successful recall movement. Many of the Republicans who had supported Barr were at the forefront of the recall movement. The recall election was canceled when the Arizona legislature voted to impeach Mecham.
10. *Miami Herald,* October 12, 1986.
11. *Columbus Post-Dispatch,* November 7, 1986.

12. J. Stephen Turett, "The Vulnerability of American Governors, 1900-1969," *Midwest Journal of Political Science* 15 (1971): 108-132; and Thad L. Beyle, "Gubernatorial Elections: 1977-86," *Comparative State Politics Newsletter* 8 (April 1987): 29.

13. Stephen A. Salmore and Barbara G. Salmore, *Candidates, Parties and Campaigns* (Washington: CQ Press, 1985), 67.

14. Salmore and Salmore, *Candidates, Parties, and Campaigns*, 66.

15. *Chicago Tribune*, October 27, 1986.

16. Jewell and Olson, *American State Political Parties and Elections*, 209.

17. John S. Bibby, "Statehouse Elections at Midterm," in *The American Elections of 1982*, ed. Thomas E. Mann and Norman J. Ornstein (Washington, D.C.: American Enterprise Institute for Public Policy Research, 1983), 115.

18. See for example, Bibby, "Statehouse Elections at Midterm"; and John E. Chubb, "Institutions, the Economy and the Dynamics of State Elections," *American Political Science Review* 82 (March 1988): 133-154.

19. Walter Dean Burnham, "The System of 1896: An Analysis," in *The Evolution of American Electoral Systems*, ed. Paul Kleppner (Westport, Conn.: Greenwood Press, 1981).

20. The data in this discussion are drawn from Herbert E. Alexander and Michael Eberts, *Public Financing of State Elections* (Los Angeles: Citizens Research Foundation, 1986).

21. New Jersey Election Law Enforcement Commission, *New Jersey Public Financing: 1985 Gubernatorial Elections* (Trenton: New Jersey Law Enforcement Commission, September 1986).

22. It was widely believed that incumbent Tom Kean intended to opt out of the public finance provisions in 1985 if the race showed any sign of becoming close. (He eventually won with a record-setting 70 percent of the vote.)

23. The original statement of the "surge and decline" argument is Angus Campbell, "Surge and Decline: A Study in Electoral Change," *Public Opinion Quarterly* 29 (1960): 397-418. An application to state elections is James E. Campbell, "Presidential Coattails and Midterm Losses in State Legislative Elections," *American Political Science Review* 80 (1986): 45-64.

24. See for example, Gary C. Jacobson, *The Politics of Congressional Elections*, 2d ed. (Boston: Little, Brown, 1987).

25. This explains the recent increase in negative advertising. If negative advertising were to disappear, even fewer challengers would be elected. Because research shows that persuasive negative advertising works (see *Congressional Quarterly Weekly Report*, December 7, 1985, 2559-2565), it is impossible to find cases to test this hypothesis empirically.

26. This argument, advanced by Thomas Mann, got strong empirical confirmation from Gary Jacobson, who demonstrated that incumbents in recent decades have had to increase their victory margins substantially to achieve the same probability of winning next time. See Mann, *Unsafe at Any Margin* (Washington, D.C.: American Enterprise Institute for

Public Policy Research, 1978); and Jacobson, *The Politics of Congressional Elections.*

27. Quoted in John F. Bibby, ed., *Congress off the Record* (Washington, D.C.: American Enterprise Institute for Public Policy Research, 1983), 43.

28. Among the most important of the many discussions of these developments are David Mayhew, *Congress: The Electoral Connection* (New Haven, Conn.: Yale University Press, 1974); and Bruce Cain, John Ferejohn, and Morris Fiorina, *The Personal Vote: Constituency Service and Electoral Independence* (Cambridge, Mass.: Harvard University Press, 1987).

29. A point made by David Adamany, "Political Parties in the 1980s," in *Money and Politics,* ed. Michael Malbin (Chatham, N.J.: Chatham House, 1984), 110.

30. Chubb, "Institutions, the Economy and the Dynamics of State Elections."

31. Alan Rosenthal, "And So They Leave: Legislative Turnover in the States," *State Government* 47 (1974): 148-152; and Richard Niemi and L. R. Winsky, "Membership Turnover in State Legislatures: Trends and Effects of Redistricting," *Legislative Studies Quarterly* 12 (1987): 115-124.

32. Jerry Calvert, "Revolving Doors: Volunteerism in State Legislatures," *State Government* 52 (1979): 174-181; Charles M. Tidmarch, Edward Lonergan, and John Sciortino, "Interparty Competition in the U.S. States: Legislative Elections, 1970-78," *Legislative Studies Quarterly* 11 (June 1986): 353-374; Lucinda Simon, "The Mighty Incumbent," *State Legislatures* 18 (July 1986): 31-34; and Keith E. Hamm and David E. Olson, "The Value of Incumbency in Legislative Elections: Evidence from the 1982-86 Elections in Five States," (Paper delivered at the annual meeting of the American Political Science Association, Chicago, Ill., September 3-6, 1987).

33. Some examples: In 1986, 75 percent of the candidates for the Massachusetts house, 73 percent of the candidates for the Tennessee senate, 72 percent of the candidates for the Georgia house, and 58 percent of the candidates for the New Hampshire senate ran unopposed. Tidmarch et al. found fourteen states in which at least a third of the House seats were uncontested in 1978; "Interparty Competition in the U.S. States," 366-369.

34. Jewell and Olson, *American State Political Parties and Elections,* 3d ed., 216.

35. See Bruce B. Mason, "Arizona: Interest Groups in a Changing State," *Interest Group Politics in the American West,* ed. Ronald J. Hrebenar and Clive S. Thomas (Salt Lake City: University of Utah Press, 1987), 28; Charles W. Wiggins and Keith E. Hamm, "Iowa: Interest Group Politics in an Undistinguished Place," (Paper delivered at the annual meeting of the Midwest Political Science Association, Chicago, Ill., April 9-11, 1987); Allan J. Cigler and Dwight Kiel, "Interest Groups in Kansas: Representation in Transition," (Paper delivered at the annual meeting of the Midwest Political Science Association, Chicago, Ill., April 9-11, 1987); and Greg Casey and James D. King, "Interest Groups in

Missouri: From Establishment Elite to Classic Pluralism," in *Interest Group Politics in the Midwestern States,* ed. Ronald E. Hrebenar and Clive S. Thomas, forthcoming.

36. See Campbell, "Presidential Coattails and Midterm Losses in State Legislative Elections"; Chubb, "Institutions, the Economy and the Dynamics of State Elections"; and Thomas M. Holbrook-Provow, "National Factors in Gubernatorial Elections," *American Politics Quarterly* 15 (1987): 471-484.

37. Stephen A. Salmore and Barbara G. Salmore, "Congressionalization of State Legislative Politics: The Case of New Jersey," (Paper delivered at the annual meeting of the American Political Science Association, Chicago, Ill., September 3-6, 1987).

38. Robert H. Salisbury and Kenneth A. Shepsle, "U.S. Congressman as Enterprise," *Legislative Studies Quarterly* 6 (1981): 559-576; and Burdett Loomis and Elizabeth H. Paddock, "The Congressional Enterprise as Campaign," (Paper delivered at the annual meeting of the Midwest Political Science Association, Chicago, Ill., April 9-11, 1987).

39. The most eminent members of the school arguing that the state parties are more consequential are Cornelius Cotter, John Bibby, Robert Huckshorn, and James Gibson, who have published numerous works on this subject. The fullest explication of their views is Cotter et al., *Party Organizations in American Politics* (New York: Praeger, 1984). The data presented here on party budgets come from this study, 39n, 88-89. The other major study of the role of state parties is considerably more restrained in its conclusions. See Advisory Commission on Intergovernmental Relations, *The Transformation of American Politics: Implications for Federalism* (Washington, D.C.: Advisory Commission on Intergovernmental Relations, 1986), Chapter 4.

40. Malcolm E. Jewell, "A Survey of Campaign Fundraising by Legislative Parties," *Comparative State Politics Newsletter* 7 (1986): 9-13.

41. David H. Everson and Samuel K. Gove, "Interest Groups in Illinois: The Political Microcosm of the Nation," in *Interest Group Politics in the Midwestern States.*

42. Tom Loftus, "The New 'Political Parties' in State Legislatures," *State Government* 58 (1985): 109-110.

43. Quoted in *State Legislatures* 13 (November-December 1981): 26.

44. Elizabeth Kolbert and Mark Uhlig, "Albany's Discreet Budget: A Tool for Political Ends," *New York Times,* July 14, 1987.

45. Kolbert and Uhlig, "Albany's Discreet Budget."

46. William H. Hedrick and L. Harmon Ziegler, "Oregon: The Politics of Power," *Interest Group Politics in the American West,* 106.

47. Loftus, "The New 'Political Parties' in State Legislatures," 108-109.

48. For a survey of this subject, see David Mayhew, *Placing Parties in American Politics* (Princeton, N.J.: Princeton University Press, 1987).

49. Kolbert and Uhlig, "Albany's Discreet Budget"; and Ronald Sullivan, "Judge Retains 400 Charges for the Trial of Ohrenstein, *New York Times,* June 16, 1988.

50. Private communication, fall 1987. In the fall of 1987, the student fellows of the Eagleton Institute conducted interviews with legislative officeholders, legislative partisan staff, lobbyists, and reporters in several states. This unattributed quote and others that follow come from interviews with persons who did not wish to be quoted with attribution.

51. However, in another example of the endless ingenuity of campaign fund raisers, this "PAC problem" can be bypassed. Company employees instead give donations of less than $20 to a person (the limit for unidentified contributions) designated as a "conduit," who then contributes the pooled money as an individual instead of as a PAC.

52. Frank J. Sorauf, *Money in American Politics* (Glenview, Ill.: Scott-Foresman, 1988), 264, 280.

53. John Syer, "California: Political Giants in a Megastate," in *Interest Group Politics in the American West*, 33-48.

54. Sorauf, *Money in American Politics*, 263-264; and *New York Times*, June 9, 1988.

55. Private communication, fall 1987.

56. Janet M. Clark and B. Oliver Walter, "Wyoming: Populists versus Lobbyists," in *Interest Group Politics in the American West*, 141.

57. The "challenge primary" law provides that a candidate who loses at the convention but gets at least 20 percent of the delegates' votes can call for a primary. Candidates rarely do. In 1986, the minority Republicans decided to switch to an open primary for governor in the hope of stimulating more public interest in their party.

58. Private communication, fall 1987.

59. Private communication, fall 1987.

60. They also approved a competing measure with campaign spending limits and partial public financing of legislative campaigns at the same time. However, because this more restrictive measure won by a narrower margin, state law apparently makes it subordinate to the more widely approved measure. See the *New York Times*, June 9, 1988. For the earlier discussions that led to the ballot proposals, see California Commission on Campaign Financing, "The New Gold Rush" (Sacramento: California Commission on Campaign Financing, 1985). A portion of this study is reprinted in *California Journal*, December 1985, 511-514.

61. However, a state supreme court justice threw out counts relating to legislative employees who did both legislative and campaign work. *New York Times*, June 16, 1988.

62. See the study by the Center for Responsive Politics, "PACs on PACs: The View from the Inside," (Washington, D.C.: Center for Responsive Politics, 1988). Results from this study are reported in the *New York Times*, February 14, 1988.

63. State of the States Symposium, Eagleton Institute of Politics, Rutgers University, New Brunswick, N.J., December 18, 1987.

64. Cain, Ferejohn, and Fiorina, *The Personal Vote*, 229.

9. THE ENTREPRENEURIAL STATES

Carl E. Van Horn

State government political institutions are infused with an entrepreneurial spirit. No longer passive partners in the federal system, the states are a driving force in American politics. They raise and spend vast sums of money; manage vexing public problems; and seek to conquer new policy frontiers. States aggressively set policy agendas for the nation and fashion innovative solutions for stimulating the growth of high technology firms, treating the medically indigent, curbing drunken driving, reforming the schools, and other important matters.

The foundation of the entrepreneurial states may be found in the changes in representation, governmental organization, and professionalization that appeared in the 1960s. Demands and expectations for a greater state government activism rose during the 1980s. A burgeoning federal budget deficit, cutbacks in domestic spending, and a popular president who sought a larger state role convinced citizens and interest groups to turn their attention away from Washington, D.C. Repeating a pattern that has occurred before in American history, the states were thrust forward as the federal government withdrew.[1]

Governmental activism has been stimulated and reinforced by institutional and individual entrepreneurship. Reforms ostensibly designed to strengthen the competence of state governments to perform their duties simultaneously made it possible for individualism to flourish. State government institutions are not only better equipped to assume leadership but also politically motivated to expand the scope of their endeavors. Governors, legislators, judges, and bureaucrats are moving boldly to assert power in the high stakes politics of state government.

Entrepreneurship creates a new set of problems for state government institutions, however. State politics are now more competitive and conflict-ridden. Power is fragmented. Policy makers generally agree that they want their government to tackle the state's tough problems, but they often have trouble endorsing a specific plan of action or budget request. As distrust deepens, governors, judges, legislators, and administrators jealously guard their personal and institutional prerogatives and plot to curb the power of each other. Frequently, conflicts have escalated into battles for control of the institutions and the policy agendas of state government.

Active, fragmented, and conflictual policy making decreases institutional accountability. Individuals have succeeded in gaining more power, but in the process clear lines of responsibility are blurred. Positive developments that created more democratic and responsive state governments also created some troubling problems.

Modernization

The states trailed the federal government in recognizing and responding to the challenges of the post-war era. But, contemporary state governments are capable and resourceful; they are strong participants in the design and implementation of public programs. Constitutions have been amended, political institutions have been restructured and strengthened, and professional expertise has been assembled.[2]

The first step in modernizing state government were changes that improved the representativeness of political institutions. The policy-making circles of state governments—in legislatures, courts, bureaucracies, and governors' mansions—have gradually expanded beyond the upper-middle class, white males that dominated politics throughout most of American political history. Stimulated by landmark reapportionment decisions, legislatures were transformed from unrepresentative, homogeneous institutions to modern, representative bodies.[3]

First, in *Baker v. Carr,* and then in *Reynolds v. Sims,* the U.S. Supreme Court removed barriers to direct representation of voters and reapportioned legislatures according to the principle of one person, one vote. The Voting Rights Act of 1965 provided for full participation by black Americans in the politics of their communities and states.[4] Black registration in the seven states of the deep South covered by the law increased by more than one million between 1964 and 1972, a jump from 29 percent to 57 percent of eligible voters. Paralleling legal mandates were remarkable improvements in the participation of minorities and women in all aspects of American society. Eventually, the new attitudes and behavior of millions of Americans were reflected in state government institutions.

Women and minorities still occupy far fewer seats than their numbers in the population would assume. However, today's legislatures and state government agencies have greatly increased their representativeness from twenty years ago. Women holding legislative office, for example, increased from 4 percent in 1969 to 16 percent in

1988. In some states—New Hampshire, Maine, Colorado, Vermont, and Washington—women hold more than 25 percent of the seats in the legislature. Women have been less successful in obtaining statewide offices. In 1988, three women were serving as governors. Only nine women have been elected governor and two women elected attorney general in American history. Women's participation in state government positions has risen, however, at the appointive policy-making levels.[5]

Minority participation in elected and appointed policy-making positions in state government has also increased significantly during the last twenty years. Blacks held 396 state legislative positions in 1988 versus 168 in 1970.[6] Hispanics have also increased their share of elected positions in states where they make up a significant part of the population—California, New Mexico, Arizona, and Colorado. Nationwide, there are now 120 state legislators of Hispanic origin.[7]

The election of individuals from heretofore unrepresented or underrepresented groups has ushered in new policy perspectives. Many of the newly empowered groups support government intervention as the preferred strategy for ameliorating social and economic problems and favor more benefits for disadvantaged groups or communities. These new state legislators reflect their life experiences and professional training. The substantial increase in teachers, working women, and others has injected new concerns about education and child care into the legislative process.[8]

The prevailing attitude about the responsibilities of a state representative also has changed. Late-1980s legislators are likely to act as delegates of their constituency's interests, rather than as free agents exercising their best judgment. Modern representatives aggressively pursue political self-interest, which usually translates into advancing the interests of their district and their political career.[9] Political leaders, such as county chairs, governors, and legislative leaders, no longer command those in their own party. With antennae tuned to the voters back home and campaign contributors, the legislators often ignore the appeals of their political leaders.[10]

Citizen participation in policy making has also grown enormously in the past two decades. State government agencies afford citizens an opportunity to voice their concerns through such devices as public boards and commissions, ombudsmen and public advocates, and public hearings about policy decisions. Environmentalists, consumer advocates, and senior citizen activists have increased in number and clout. They raise money and contribute to candidates, advertise in the mass media, and frequently exert considerable influence over governors and legislatures.[11]

Citizens and interest groups have also relied upon the initiative process, whereby public officials are petitioned to place issues on the ballot for approval or disapproval without waiting for the governor or state legislature to act. The number of ballot initiatives doubled between 1976 and 1986. Each election year more than fifty public propositions appear on state ballots. Voters are asked to establish regulations governing pornography, set limits on personal injury claims, and restructure state tax systems.[12] In 1988, for example, voters considered state policy on auto insurance rates in California, gun control registration rules in Maryland, and the right to an abortion in Michigan.

Along with the growth in democratic participation and representation, state governments have equipped themselves with the modern tools of governing—larger and more professional staffs, computer equipment, and consultant expertise. Like the changes that occurred in representation, the professionalization of state government came about gradually. But the cumulative effects were dramatic. State governments now plan and execute ambitious public policy initiatives. Decision-making authority was seized by the states or delegated to them by the federal officials; state governments acquired a new cadre of government professionals to do the job.

The size and competence of state government institutions have grown enormously.[13] Governors have increased their staff in nearly all the states. Legislators now meet regularly—in some cases year round. Many pay salaries that allow members to concentrate entirely on their legislative career. And legislatures have more and better trained staff. The number of full-time employees serving state legislatures has grown from approximately five thousand in the mid-1960s to fifteen thousand in the mid-1980s.[14]

In accord with entrepreneurship, institutions have often enlarged their staffs to remain competitive with the other players in state government. Governors expanded staffs overseeing the bureaucracy, monitoring developments in the nation's capital, and shepherding the flock of legislative proposals in the statehouse. Legislatures bolstered staffs to keep a watchful eye on the executive branch and to provide more effective service to the folks in their districts. Courts added judges, law clerks, and administrative officers to cope with rising demands for court review of policy and administrative cases.

The Entrepreneurial States

The politics of activism, growth, and innovation has become a central defining characteristic of state politics and public policy. State government political institutions and political professionals are delivering new programs, launching far-reaching initiatives, and building a record of accomplishment. The rise of the entrepreneurial states was made possible by changes in the economy and federalism. It was reinforced by greater democratization, representation, and professionalization in state government.

State governments are imperialistic, pragmatic, and nonideological. Governors and legislators clamor for new ideas that will permit them to expand government spending and regulation, but they are not excited by the topic of government management and coordination. States are leading the nation with ambitious efforts to improve public schools; reform public welfare programs; protect the environment; restructure the housing industry; and rebuild roads, bridges, and sewers. A trend, no matter how powerful, does not sweep all fifty states at once or always appear in the same form. But entrepreneurship has been under way for some time and is manifest throughout the nation in large and small states and in every region.

The strong desire to follow an entrepreneurial public policy course has blurred ideological and partisan distinctions. State political parties and elected leaders have undergone policy convergence. For instance, the policy differences that have traditionally distinguished Republican and Democratic governors are far fewer than they were twenty-five years ago. Republicans elected to statewide office are typically more centrist or even liberal than national-level Republicans. The policies of Republican governors Tom Kean of New Jersey, Jim Thompson of Illinois, and Lamar Alexander of Tennessee reflected pragmatic, progovernment positions long advocated by Democrats.[15]

State government policies and priorities have been nationalized in education, civil rights, economic development, and health care. State leaders are seldom ideologues for long. The pragmatic orientation of the states' principal policy-making institutions helps explain why the conservative policies of Ronald Reagan never took hold in state capitals. When states deal with AIDS, homelessness, uncompensated health care, or economic development, they usually adopt solutions that involve a heavy dose of government involvement and higher spending. For example, Democratic and Republican governors developed similar strategies for reforming public assistance and implemented them in their states. Federal welfare reform legislation incorporating principles advocated by a bipartisan group of governors was eventually adopted, but not without considerable partisan wrangling in Washington, D.C.[16]

The buzzwords of the 1970s—zero-based budgeting, executive reorganization, and cutback management—have been replaced by a new doctrine. State politicians have quickly moved away from the tax-cutting mood spurred by California's Proposition 13 and the fear of a taxpayer revolt. The love affair with the idea of curbing government growth turned out to be a brief flirtation.

Ironically, the spurt in government spending has its roots in the economic crisis of 1982-1983. Faced with the prospects of greater social welfare spending and reduced tax collections, twenty-eight states raised their income taxes, and thirty states raised sales taxes.[17] Even without additional tax increases these actions would have yielded a fiscal bonanza. Nineteen states boosted either their income or sales taxes again in 1984 and 1985. In addition, the 1986 federal tax reform law brought millions of additional dollars rolling into state treasuries.

Significant differences remain on fiscal policy. Republicans, as compared with Democrats, are less likely to raise taxes, usually opposing higher personal income or business taxes. Even so, traditional liberal/conservative distinctions are clouded because Republicans and Democrats alike have been raising taxes and expanding their budgets in the 1980s.

The engine of economic recovery—sustained, low-inflation growth—reduced government outlays for such costly entitlement programs as unemployment insurance and welfare, and pulled in more revenues. As state treasuries bulged, most state-level policy makers chose to spend the additional revenues rather than return them to taxpayers. Several states established so-called rainy day funds to cushion the shock of another recession, but typically new state revenues were quickly committed to new or expanded programs.[18]

In New Jersey, for example, both sales and income taxes went up in 1982 so that the state could balance its budget. Since then, the state budget has more than doubled, and the state enjoys a $500 million surplus. At no point during this period did any major political leader propose rolling back any major tax hikes.[19]

This rosy fiscal picture could turn sour when the economic growth ebbs, especially if the next recession is long lasting. The federal government is not going to prime the state government pump with substantial increases in expenditures because the federal government now suffers from a large budget deficit. Responsibility has shifted to the states. If the experience of the 1982-1983 recession is any guide, most states will respond to the next fiscal crisis by raising revenues rather than cutting state programs. Because states cannot borrow huge sums of money to satisfy their fiscal appetites, state officials may regard tax increases as the policy of first resort.

Activism by state legislatures and governors is matched by activism in the state courts. The courts have taken aggressive action on several public policy fronts. For example, the courts set forth strong liberal positions in the field of civil rights. They have expanded the rights of women, minorities, and criminal defendants, often relying upon state constitutions to establish rights that the U.S. Supreme Court has not found in the U.S. Constitution. They have also expanded the rights of individuals to recover for personal injuries and imposed strict liability rules for faulty products. Once regarded as the obstacles to civil liberties, the state courts have become the champions of change.[20]

Power Struggles

Power within state government institutions has been fragmented and decentralized. Reforms undertaken in the name of modernization carved up institutional power into bits and pieces and undermined the ability of any one institution or political leader to dominate. Power struggles are a common feature of state political life. Individualism was encouraged at the expense of institutional responsibility.

Competitive, conflict-ridden politics promotes entrepreneurship and policy convergence. Legislators, governors, and agency executives are eager to discover new policy approaches and distribute benefits to constituencies. This creates unrelenting pressure to boost government spending and an unceasing need to expand the pool of available resources. Because there is more to win and more to lose in the governance of states, everyone has a greater incentive to seek power and control.

Democratization within political institutions has engendered fierce battles for the control of policy agendas and outcomes. Greater competition and conflict are apparent in all phases of state political life from elections to state budget decisions. More legislators, judges, bureaucrats, and interest groups have sufficient clout to engage in the struggle, but few have enough power to rule for long.

The desire to hold onto power strongly shapes the political process within institutions, especially in legislatures where electoral considerations are paramount. The quest for power is hardly a new phenomenon in American politics, but entrepreneurial, careerist politics have made power struggles more intense.

Because legislators are obsessed with keeping their jobs, they must constantly deliver benefits, claim credit for accomplishments, and attack opponents in the executive branch or elsewhere.[21] They are also emboldened to seek out new territory for legislative involvement, through oversight of administrative rules and regulations, closer scrutiny of the state budget, and investigations into the performance of government agencies. Clearly, these strategies serve their intended purpose: incumbents rarely lose.[22]

Strategies mounted to protect incumbents are equaled by rigorous competition during elections. The costs of elections are rising because people are willing and able to spend huge sums of money to gain elective office. The staples of modern campaigns—media consultants, pollsters, and television advertising—are expensive.[23] The sudden jump in campaign costs has driven some people away from the arena and attracted others.[24] Statewide candidates must collect considerable amounts of money or have a large fortune to spend on getting elected. Even legislative candidates are now required to assemble substantial resources, except in the smaller states.

The practices of statewide interest groups buttress entrepreneurship. Educators, dentists, senior citizens, builders, and others are sophisticated and effective advocates for their interests. These groups often supply the campaign funds that keep incumbent politicians around to serve them another day. Groups and individuals who cannot afford to participate in this costly process are less likely to be heard and thus special interest politics usually triumphs.

State politics appears to be locked in a spiraling institutional arms race. Seeking more control over the direction of state government, governors, legislators, and bureaucrats are acquiring new techniques and strategies—new weapons and technology, larger troops—to carry out their mission. Governors have asserted greater control over the bureaucracy. Legislatures have stepped up efforts to challenge governors and oversee government agencies. Interest groups compete with elected officials by resorting to the initiative. State courts are adjudicating disputes between legislators and governors and making policy independently.

There is nothing wrong with conflict per se. Representative government and deliberation are often well served by sharp clashes of strongly held views. Few observers of American politics are nostalgic for a return to an era when only a handful of party bosses and top-ranking elected officials called the shots. But many of the conflicts in state government revolve around ambiguous authority, not disputed policy goals. And, in some cases, these conflicts between institutions have escalated so far that they have disrupted the policy process.

Governors and legislatures, the states' principal policy making entities, regularly engage in battles over the state budget, the interpretation of administrative rules, executive orders, political appointments, and the execution of policy. For example, it is now more common for governors to exercise the line item veto as a tool of institutional and partisan power rather than as a means to control expenditures.[25] Institutional conflicts are exacerbated by divided party control of the two branches—a trend that the electorate increasingly supports through a remarkable increase in split-ticket voting. Dual control of legislatures has also increased from four states in 1961 to twelve states in 1987.[26]

As battles for power multiply, others are drawn into the fray. When legislators and governors fail to reach clear decisions, they often delegate hard choices to the bureaucracy. Combative institutions may "resolve" their differences by creating new administrative entities. Thus, there has been a proliferation of commissions, "independent authorities," and other organizations made up of legislative and gubernatorial appointments, so that both institutions can influence outcomes.

State courts are frequently asked to mediate between the executive and legislative branches. In recent years they have ruled on such diverse subjects as the authority of governors to exercise their line-item veto power and their powers of appointment and removal. By entering into these disputes, the court "allocates and exerts political power." Such court interventions generate more controversy from those who regard themselves as the losers.[27]

Clashes over institutional authority have encouraged courts to become active policy makers. The courts' liberal activism in civil rights and other fields reflects the fragmentation of state politics and the rise of conservatism in the U.S. Supreme Court.[28] When courts extend government policy against the will of majoritarian institutions, legislators, governors, and voters may reassert control through initiatives, legislative decisions, or judicial elections. The courts become a battleground for both sides in an ideological struggle.

In recent years, interest groups, legislators, and governors have tried to overturn or amend court decisions. The courts have been able to fend off objections to their authority in the interpretation of constitutional law. But their power to interpret common law has been challenged. For example, state legislatures have narrowed the rights of injured parties, but they have been less successful in curbing the state courts' support for the civil liberties of criminal defendants and the rights of women in sex discrimination cases.[29]

Judicial confirmation elections have become the stage on which objections to the liberalism of judges and efforts to reign in the courts have been played out. Decisions on controversial issues, such as support for the death penalty, are frequently central issues in campaigns to oust judges. Spending on judicial elections and the number of direct challenges have risen substantially. Ballot initiatives have overturned liberal court decisions affecting criminal defendant rights. While the defeat of incumbent judges and anticourt initiatives are still rare, the fear of defeat may curb the courts' liberal leanings.[30]

As with the courts, bureaucracies are embroiled in disputes over their activities, purposes, and performance. Legislatures have increased their oversight of agency decisions through such mechanisms as sunset laws and reviews of administrative rules and regulations. Governors have exerted greater control through executive reorganizations—reducing the number of boards and commissions; centralizing budgeting techniques; and issuing executive orders that mandate direct accountability to the governor.[31]

The federal bureaucracy and federal courts have also asserted greater control over the states. For example, federal judges have ordered sweeping changes in state actions regarding the mentally ill and state prisoners.[32] The courts have argued that the federal constitution gives them the right to guarantee due process of law—asserting constitutional control over states. Governors and the federal government have gotten into battles over interpretations of federal statutes, such as environmental laws.

Governance

The rise of governmental, institutional, and individual entrepreneurship has important implications for the ability of state governments to cope with the problems they will face in the 1990s. The accountability of political institutions for their actions has been replaced by individual accountability. In many states, incumbent governors and legislators have successfully separated themselves from responsibility for the actions of their own government or institutions. They have inoculated themselves from corporate responsibility. Unfortunately, when everyone is responsible, no one is responsible.

Legislators have tried to insulate themselves from executive domination, party leaders, and legislative leaders. Governors increasingly portray themselves as the clarion of the people, not the head of state government. They play to the press and go over the heads of party and legislative leaders. Political parties have been nudged aside by candidate-centered politics, in which the actions of the incumbent, not the party, are open for judgment. Partisanship is on the rise, but responsible party governance may be on the decline. Even judges are now more wary of voter and interest group reaction to their decisions.

When political officials become independent contractors in the political system, leadership becomes problematic. Leaders serve at the pleasure of their members so they are more likely to wield influence by distributing campaign funds than by threats or the art of persuasion. Legislators and governors used to be primarily concerned with governing. They are now displacing local party organizations and taking over electoral functions through leadership caucuses and political action committees.[33]

The dramatic increase in the cost of elections and the desire to remain in office means that elected officials are more accountable to campaign contributors and special interest groups and less accountable to the public at large. The emphasis on fund raising diverts time from governing responsibilities and lowers ethical standards. It is, for example, quite common for legislators and governors to hold large fund-raising events while important policy issues are under consideration. Elected officials regularly solicit and receive campaign contributions from companies that either have contracts with the state or want to do business in the future. Partisan staff in the executive and legislative branches are routinely deployed to work on election activities.[34]

Institutional warfare between the legislature and governor have also increased the power of the bureaucracy and courts and thus reduced accountability to the public. Because it is more difficult to reach agreement and compromise, more decisions are delegated from democratic institutions to the bureaucracy. While administrative agencies appear to be more accountable than before, the custody battles between governors and legislatures and between courts and the bureaucracy may make it more difficult to establish who is in charge. Ultimately these conflicts may generate more contradictions, delay, rigidity, and uncertainty. As an increasing number of decisions are made by the courts, the "judicialization of state administration" may result.[35]

Of greatest concern are the possible effects of the new state politics on the shape of public policy. The entrepreneurial politics of the 1980s has boosted the power of narrow, special interests over the public interest. Policy makers favor policies that guarantee their political survival. This undermines their willingness to look ahead and to make difficult choices. It also encourages policy gridlock and delegation to the bureaucracy.

Governors and legislators are more reactive and responsive to their own short-run political needs, but less deliberative and responsible about the long-run interests of the state as a whole. If electoral expediency crowds out other values, state officials will practice the art of easy money, saying yes when they should say no. In the future it may be harder to exercise fiscal restraint. When everyone fights for a piece of the action, the compromise is to do a little of everything. Unlike the federal government, which has indulged in this practice for decades, the states cannot borrow their way out. State policy makers will have either to raise taxes or cut programs. In the current climate, government leaders will probably be able to slow the growth of spending, but not eliminate government programs.

The reliance on statewide initiatives to resolve public policy disputes represents a troubling development. In some of the nation's more populous states, such as California, state elected officials have ceded the responsibility for making many controversial decisions to political campaigns. These "issue elections" are seldom grass-roots citizen petitions of the government. Instead, they are dominated by interest groups that spend lavishly on television advertising, direct mail, and tracking polls. For example, the insurance industry spent $60 million attempting to defeat a proposal to cut insurance premiums in California. The consumer activists succeeded, in part, because they were able to raise $20 million. Not surprisingly, the issue is now so confused that it has landed in the lap of the California Supreme Court.

The decline of institutional responsibility raises serious implications for the ability of political institutions to cope with public policy problems. Expansion, distribution, and innovation are popular, but power struggles within and across institutions reduce the possibilities for reaching consensus on matters involving difficult trade-offs. State governments have vastly increased their capacity and power to help citizens and respond to the needs of their states. The entrepreneurial state politics of the 1980s have brought many positive changes in the performance of state government. Unfortunately, they have also unleashed forces that may undermine the practice of wise governance.

Notes

1. See Chapter 2.
2. Terry Sanford, *Storm over the States* (New York: McGraw-Hill, 1967); and Larry Sabato, *Goodbye to Goodtime Charlie: The American Governor Transformed*, 2d ed. (Washington, D.C.: CQ Press, 1983).
3. Timothy G. O'Rourke, *The Impact of Reapportionment* (New Brunswick, N.J.: Transaction Books, 1980).
4. Charles S. Bullock and Charles M. Lamb, eds., *Implementation of Civil Rights Policy* (Monterey, Calif.: Brooks/Cole, 1984), 20-54.
5. Center for the American Woman and Politics, National Information Bank on Women in Public Office, Eagleton Institute of Politics, Rutgers University, November 1988.
6. Joint Center for Political Studies, personal communication, Washington, D.C., December 8, 1988.
7. National Association of Latino Election Officials, personal communication, Washington, D.C., December 8, 1988.
8. See, for example, Alan Ehrenhalt, "In Alabama Politics, The Teachers Are Sitting at the Head of the Class," *Governing*, December 1988, 22-27.
9. See, for example, Malcolm Jewell, *Representation in State Legislatures* (Lexington: University of Kentucky Press, 1982).
10. See Chapter 4.

11. William T. Gormley, Jr., "The Representation Revolution: Reforming State Regulation through Representation," *Administration and Society* 18 (August 1986): 179-196.

12. Patrick B. McGuigan, *The Politics of Direct Democracy in the 1980s* (Washington, D.C.: Free Congress Research and Education Foundation, 1985); and Patrick B. McGuigan, ed., "Initiative and Referendum Report," December 1986/January 1987.

13. See, for example, Advisory Commission on Intergovernmental Relations, *The Question of State Government Capability* (Washington, D.C.: Advisory Commission on Intergovernmental Relations, 1985).

14. National Conference of State Legislatures, *Legislative Staff in the 50 States* (Denver, Colo.: National Conference of State Legislatures, 1986).

15. Tom Kean, *The Politics of Inclusion* (New York: The Free Press, 1988).

16. Julie Rovner, "Welfare Reform: The Issue That Bubbled Up from the States to Capitol Hill," *Governing*, December 1988, 17-21.

17. David Broder, "States Make Hard Decisions as Reagan Fantasies Wane," *Raleigh News and Observer*, August 5, 1987, 17a.

18. Steven D. Gold, ed., *Reforming State Tax Systems* (Denver, Colo.: National Conference of State Legislatures, 1986).

19. New Jersey State and Local Expenditure and Revenue Policy Commission, *Final Report*, July 1988.

10. Lawrence Baum, "The Courts as Policy Maker," (Paper delivered at the State of the States Symposium, Eagleton Institute of Politics, Rutgers University, New Brunswick, N.J., December 15-16, 1988).

21. See, for example, Joel A. Thompson, "Bringing Home the Bacon: The Politics of Pork Barrel in the North Carolina Legislature," *Legislative Studies Quarterly* (February 1986): 91-108.

22. Richard Niemi and L. R. Winsky, "Membership Turnover in State Legislatures: Trends and Effects of Redistricting," *Legislative Studies Quarterly* 12 (1987): 115-124.

23. See Chapter 8.

24. See Chapter 3.

25. See Chapter 3.

26. See Chapter 8.

27. Dave Frohnmayer, "The Courts as Referee," (Paper delivered at the State of the States Symposium, Eagleton Institute of Politics, Rutgers University, New Brunswick, N.J., December 15-16, 1988).

28. See Chapter 5.

29. See Chapter 5.

30. See Chapter 5.

31. See Chapter 6.

32. See Chapter 6; and Linda Harriman and Jeffrey Straussman, "Do Judges Determine Budget Decisions?" *Public Administration Review* 43, July/August 1983): 343-351.

33. See Chapter 8.

34. See Chapters 8 and 4.

35. See Chapter 6.

INDEX

WHITMAN COLLEGE LIBRARY